CATCHING

the

Wind

A GUIDE FOR INTERPRETING ECCLESIASTES

Dear Sharon,
May these words encourage you as
you have encouraged me through the
years to key the faith and continue the
battle!
Dale McIntire

DALE C. McINTIRE

ISBN 978-1-64468-073-5 (Paperback)
ISBN 978-1-64468-074-2 (Hardcover)
ISBN 978-1-64468-075-9 (Digital)

The text of Ecclesiastes is reprinted from the *Tanakh: The Holy Scriptures* by permission of the University of Nebraska Press. © 1985 by the Jewish Publication Society, Philadelphia.

Quotations marked (ESV) are from the Holy Bible, English Standard Version, © 2001 by Crossway, a publishing ministry of Good News Publishers. Used by permission. All rights reserved.

Quotations marked (NIV) are from the Holy Bible, New International Version, © 1973, 1978, 1984 by International Bible Society. Used by permission. All rights reserved worldwide.

Covenant Books, Inc.
11661 Hwy 707
Murrells Inlet, SC 29576
www.covenantbooks.com

CONTENTS

FOREWORD

"Depressing." "Cynical." "Fatalistic." "Futile."

These are frequent responses from common studies of Ecclesiastes. When was the last time you browsed a bookstore, googled available resources, or heard anyone promote a study of this book? When one of the wisest persons in the world describes life as "a vanity; a chasing of the wind", it certainly throws a cold, wet blanket on your passion for life to the fullest!

But wait!

What if the wise person intends something other than a depressing, cynical, fatalistic conclusion? What if he points us to a path of hope...an often overlooked path of fulfillment...a path that can be easily missed?

If we slow down, trust his map, and make the journey, the destination yields brilliant wisdom. But to arrive at the intended destination, it is critical to understand and follow the right signs. If I enter "St. Paul" into my GPS, it returns an unexpected number of hits. To end up at the correct "St. Paul," I must choose the correct map.

Like trying to enter a house with secure windows and locked doors, a key is needed. Dr. Dale McIntire offers us a key...not just any key but a key that fits the door and unlocks the beauty of this often misunderstood multilevel home. It is a key hiding in plain sight.

This is no "three-points-and-a-poem" sermonic treatment of this challenging book of the Bible. Using primarily internal evidence (yet interacting with secondary literature), McIntire deals critically with multiple major options. He begins with a view of the larger landscape, reflecting common questions, background/context and structure issues, and presuppositions. The journey turns quickly to a well-stated problem, hypothesis, and method to guide the traveler. These provide the signs to trek chronologically down the well-traveled highways of the wise man's map. With reflective and integrative study questions along each step of this journey, the faithful and alert traveler arrives at the unexpected but fulfilling "end of the matter." This is no adventure for the faint of heart. However, without disappointment, the studious person will discover hope, joy, and rescue in the midst of cynicism, futility, and hopelessness.

The style is easily readable. The organization and logic is clear and simple. The evidence is verifiable. The content is as much relevant for the twenty-first century AD as it was for the eleventh century BC.

So buckle up and take this journey. Enjoy a ride filled with pleasant surprises, personal anecdotes, confessions, humor, and even intriguing history. This is not a rehash or collection of others' conclusions. This is a fresh treatment of an overlooked and often misunderstood part of our sacred canon. The wise person will choose to read, study, and live out the truth of this pastor-scholar's challenge.

Chase the wind. You will not catch it…but maybe by the grace of God, the Wind will catch you, and along the way, lift you higher than you ever expected!

—Dennis Phelps, PhD
J.D. Grey Professor of Preaching
New Orleans Baptist Theological Seminary
New Orleans, Louisiana

PREFACE

M y wife spent twenty-seven years as a teacher, most of those years in third grade. Among the many endearing characteristics of developing children is that third graders are beginning to cultivate an intellectual sense of humor. They start to love jokes.

"Miss Fregeau?" a hand would go up as the plea for teacher's attention was uttered (usually after recess or lunch, after the little darlings had had an opportunity to gather in some corner of the playground and compare notes). "Miss Fregeau?"

"Yes, what is it?" she would answer, even though, year after year, she knew what was coming.

"Miss Fregeau, do you know where river fish keep all their money?"

Of course she knew. She knew fish didn't have or need money. She knew reality was not the point. She knew third graders were just encountering these experiences for the first time. She also knew the answer, for the umpteenth time in her career.

"Timothy, where do river fish keep all their money?"

"Why, in riverbanks, of course." Laughter, sometimes more than the joke deserved, but such joy at having contributed to the mirth now resounding in the classroom—the race was on.

Another hand shoots up. "Miss Fregeau! Miss Fregeau! Miss Fregeau!"

"One at a time, please. What is it, Katie?"

"Do you know where generals keep their armies?" Katie is so overwhelmed at the opportunity and potential in that moment, she doesn't wait for an answer, totally unable to contain herself and already laughing as she delivers the punch line in the same breath. "Up their sleevies!"

Now the crowd in the classroom goes wild as Miss Fregeau (who later married me and became Mrs. McIntire, which is much easier to pronounce) smiles broadly and casts a glance around the room. Learning takes many forms, and learning humor is as good a lesson as any.

"Okay, class, calm down. One more. Dylan?"

The mischief in Dylan's eyes betrays his confidence that he has the joke of the day. "Miss Fregeau, do you know how to eat an elephant?" he asks. This one has somehow missed the attention of the others. This is a new one.

"No, Dylan. I've never eaten elephant. Do you know how to eat an elephant?"

"Yes, ma'am. One bite at a time!"

As you're reading this, you are probably glad right this minute that you are not back in third grade and that you grew out of simple, silly third-grade jokes. But I'd like to warn you, you are about to eat an elephant. Ecclesiastes is a book like no other in the Bible and it, like eating an elephant, requires a strategy for consumption.

My Monday night study group raised the elephant issue on our fourth meeting. They were a bit frustrated with the course our study was taking. We had been meeting for a couple of years. We began together as a group committed to learning how to study the Bible for ourselves and actually get something out of it. We had completed that study and moved on to the Gospel of John. We finished Peter's first letter after that. In a moment of weakness, when we were pondering what to do next, they signed up for a Bible study on the book of Ecclesiastes but here it was, a month later, and we had still not started on the actual Bible text. We were still floundering (it seemed to them) in the vagaries and doldrums of introductory and background material. They wanted substance. They wanted truth. They wanted application. Determining the merits of authorship and various philosophical approaches to interpretation was just not stirring the spiritual juices for them. They were ready to eat the elephant.

But I asked them, and I ask you, to think about eating the metaphorical elephant. Would you sit down to a commitment to eating an entire elephant without knowing that you were eating an entire elephant? Would you commit to engaging and consuming without being aware of what it would take to eat the entire elephant? Sure, you eat an elephant one bite at a time, but how many bites are you prepared to take before you realize the immensity of the task you've committed to? Wouldn't knowing the entree was an entire elephant help you make a reasonable plan of action?

Too often Christians I know want to jump into study of the biblical text without knowing what they are getting into. They want to start taking one verse at a time, one bite at a time, without any conception of what their little bite connects to and what it will take to adequately consume (and thus gain benefit) from their spiritual meal. I am convinced that if you really want to understand, appreciate, and apply the message of Ecclesiastes, you have to step back and identify the elephant first.

I believe the message of Ecclesiastes is delivered by the book as a whole through a very specific format. I believe that, in this book in particular, the message is easily lost in the details. I believe that if you insist on examining the book verse by verse first, without considering the whole, you will very likely miss the meaning and message of the book, miss the reason it is included in the Scripture at all, and miss the opportunity to hear the voice of God through the words of the Preacher.

This guide for interpreting Ecclesiastes assigns the task of interpreting the Scripture to the readers of the Scripture. Any time we read for understanding, we engage in interpretation. Since we are interpreting, it makes sense that we bring as many tools as possible to the interpretive task, granting to ourselves the opportunity to interpret God's Word accurately and adequately for progress in spiritual maturity. Among the tools included here are surveys of background material, brief descriptions of common philosophical approaches to interpreting Ecclesiastes, and a focus on the role of personal presuppositions in Bible interpretation.

Most importantly, however, is included a detailed description of the communication strategy that conveys the message of Ecclesiastes. Ecclesiastes is more than the ramblings of an unhappy old man who failed to find meaning in the excesses of his life. This book is intentional, purposeful, meaningful, and, in my opinion, brilliant. Long before Sir Francis Bacon began to describe what we now recognize as the scientific method, the author of Ecclesiastes put it into practice and reported his findings!

The guide is intended to be academically credible and generally readable. There are footnotes and there are stories. There are instructions and there are exhortations. Some of it will require effort. Parts, I hope, make the effort easier. Directly and indirectly, I hope these words will assist you to dig deeply into the genius and glory of this Old Testament book of wisdom. So take the time to study through the introduction and overview chapters. Work the reading plan. Linger over the identity and function of the presenter. Embrace the communication scheme. Get a sense of the size of the elephant, and then take each bite with a much better idea of how many bites are left to take.

CHAPTER 1

ECCLESIASTES AS RESEARCH

Introduction

Grab a pen or pencil and a piece of paper. Find a nice, comfortable place to sit and write. Place a nice cup of tea or coffee nearby, within easy reach. Now you're ready. On your piece of paper, write down every impression or summary of the book of Ecclesiastes you can remember hearing. Whether the comment is overwhelmingly negative ("I never read that depressing book. I don't even know why it's in the Bible!") or subtly positive ("I just love that 'time for every season' bit!"), write it all down. Create a written background record for the study upon which you embark. You'll want to come back when you've completed the study and compare your own summary.

Next, write down the reason you are pursuing a study of Ecclesiastes. Add to that statement a declaration of expectation. What do you expect to find within Ecclesiastes? What do you expect to gain for yourself from a study of this book?

Finally, before you go one word further, pray. Jesus declared the Holy Spirit of God would assist the people of God as One who would "teach you all things."[1] Neither the presenter in Ecclesiastes nor the author of this study, though we bring insight for your consideration,

---

[1] John 14:26 (ESV).

can truly teach you the truth God reveals in this book. That task of revealing meaning and sealing it to the heart belongs to God, and we do well to ask Him to complete His work in us as we undertake the effort to know and love God through His Word!

Ecclesiastes may be an old, old book, written well over two millennia ago, but it is a thoroughly contemporary book that recounts our own personal story and the story of others in our human family. It's a story we've heard over and over again. Ecclesiastes examines our effort to find meaning in the lives we are given. Ecclesiastes strives to tell and make sense of the story of folks like Will and Bailee Byler.

Will Byler and Bailee Ackerman Byler were seniors at Sam Houston State University in Texas. They were married on Saturday, November 3, 2018, at the Byler family ranch in Uvalde, Texas. Two hours later, on their way to their honeymoon in San Antonio, the helicopter in which they were flying crashed on the side of a mountain. Will and Bailee Byler died in the crash. The pilot, Gerald Douglas Lawrence, Will's grandfather, also perished. All the dreams, hopes, aspirations, intentions, and potential that went into their wedding died with them just minutes after they vowed their undying love to each other.

Stories of doomed love and assertions like the one from humanist philosopher Daniel Meissler, who writes of the necessary "truth of intrinsic meaninglessness,"[2] illustrate the issue that Ecclesiastes begs us to consider—"What real value is there for a man in all the gains he makes beneath the sun?" The answer to this question beats in the heart of Ecclesiastes—"Where is the meaning in all this? When our best efforts still can't overcome erasure by something like death, does life have any meaning at all?"

---

[2] Daniel Meissler, "What is the Difference Between Existentialism, Nihilism, and Absurdism?" *Daniel Meissler*, December 11, 2014, https://danielmiessler.com/blog/difference-existentialism-nihilism-absurdism.

Overview of Ecclesiastes

Common questions

The debate rages over the enigmatic nature of this Old Testament treatise on the nature of human existence. Is the author King Solomon of ancient Israel or some other post-exilic author who wants us to think that Solomon is the author? If there is an author other than Solomon who posits Solomon as the author instead of himself, does it even matter? What did the author hope to accomplish?

Is the book an example of cynical wisdom or of "promise" wisdom?[3] Is the book intentionally negative and pessimistic or subtly positive pointing to genuine optimism? Does the book have unified form and structure, or is it a loose compilation of blocks of proverbs and laments with a lately contrived epilogue designed to provide a charade of unity? Is the message of Ecclesiastes descriptive and anticipatory or prescriptive and limiting?

"Ecclesiastes" and "Koheleth"

"Ecclesiastes" is not a Hebrew word. It is a Greek word. The English title of this book comes from the ancient Greek version of the Hebrew Bible known as the *Septuagint* (commonly abbreviated with the Roman numerals for seventy, LXX, for the traditional number of translators who worked on the project). When the translators chose a Greek word to translate the Hebrew name of the subject of this book, Koheleth, they chose the word *ekklesiastes*. When the Greek version of the Hebrew Bible was translated into Latin (the *Vulgate*), the title of the present book was given as *Liber Ecclesiastes*, "the Book of Ecclesiastes." Our English title comes from the Latin

---

[3] Gordon D. Fee and Douglas Stuart, *How to Read the Bible for All Its Worth* (Grand Rapids: Zondervan, 2003), Third edition, 243. Fee and Stuart make this distinction as they describe "polar opposite" approaches to the interpretation of Ecclesiastes. They cite one source as approaching Ecclesiastes "more positively, as an expression of how one should enjoy life under God in a world in which all die in the end." The label "promise wisdom" is mine.

title that comes from the Greek version of the Hebrew word central to the book.

"Ecclesiastes," or "Koheleth," is not a name as much as it is a title or a label for a function. Literally the word means "assembler" or "one who brings together." Some English traditions and translations translate Koheleth as "Preacher" or "Teacher" supposing that Solomon is the author of Ecclesiastes and has brought people together, in either a religious assembly or a classroom, to instruct them. That may or may not be the case. It is also possible, given the actual contents of the book, that the speaker in Ecclesiastes is called Koheleth because he has "brought together" sayings, teachings, observations, studies, experiences, and conclusions and has offered them for consideration.

Koheleth delivers a message wrapped in language unlike any other book of the Bible. For many, Ecclesiastes is depressing, subduing, even oppressive. Tremper Longman notes his reaction, "While the questions that Koheleth raised attracted me, his answers shocked me, coming as they do out from the midst of the sacred canon."[4] Koheleth's message in Ecclesiastes initially appears to be one that you would not expect to find in the Bible. It all seems so counterintuitive. Quite frankly, it is that visceral discomfort that drives the study approach we are embarking on now.

Ecclesiastes' basic format

Ecclesiastes lends itself to being read as a formal research report from the hand of a wise and careful social scientist considering the reality of the human experience. He reveals in this book his efforts to reach a conclusion about the meaning of life that is authentic, truthful, encompasses real life, *and* accounts for the existence and plan of the sovereign Creator God!

Like many research experiments described by the modern scientific method, Ecclesiastes comes complete with the identification and

---

[4] Tremper Longman III, "The Book of Ecclesiastes," in *The New International Commentary on the Old Testament*, ed. Robert L. Hubbard Jr. (Grand Rapids, MI: Wm. B. Eerdmans Publishing Co., 1998), xiii.

credentials of the experimenter, the hypothesis, a refined research question, and several series of experiments and observations as well as initial conclusions, all accompanied by a final conclusion relative to the entire body of work as recorded in the book. If Ecclesiastes were a sermon, it would follow an inductive rather than deductive pattern.[5] The book raises a series of questions but does not provide the answer to the initial dilemma until the end when other possibilities have been exhausted.

When we accept this book as the report of "scientific findings," a research report of a series of experiments designed to validate the hypothesis that life is meaningless, we can release the contents of this book from the bondage of despair. A man engages us in his research in order to lead us to the conclusion he himself has found in relation to the meaning of life. He is not presenting his own "autobiographical reflections." He is sharing the course of his research. He is bringing together his methods and his conclusions, his readers, and his efforts.

To better understand this "research report," it would be wise to set out protocols for our own study. First, we need to understand some things about the literary genre into which Ecclesiastes fits. We also need some background information about the author/subject. We have to make some decisions about the perspective from which we are going to conduct our experiment in order to develop a framework for drawing conclusions. Having a reading plan won't hurt either. (Diving right in and examining this book word by word without a preliminary reading or two [or three] can be counterproductive. It is possible, especially with this book, to lose sight of the forest for the trees.) We will also need to understand the basics of research procedure and reporting.

---

[5] We're going to find later that this format is typical of the methodology of current ethnographers who "proceed inductively rather than deductively; towards theory rather than from theory, often revisiting social environments, to narrow their observations or collect additional data raised by emerging questions" (Wilf Rieger, "Ecclesiastes as Research," *TEACH Journal of Christian Education*, 4:2, [2010]: 44).

Interpreting Ecclesiastes: The Reading Plan

The purpose of the reading plan: Preparation for interpretation

Jesus, in His prayer to the Father in the upper room on the night He was betrayed,[6] spoke of the authority God had given Him to "give eternal life to all" whom God had given Him. He went on to clarify that "this is eternal life, that they know you, the only true God, and Jesus Christ whom you have sent."[7] Eternal life is knowing God. Knowing God is both an objective and subjective experience. We know God subjectively through faith and the work of the Holy Spirit as we live in relationship with God. But we know God objectively through His self-revelation, the Bible. We encounter the objective self-revelation of God as we read the Bible.

"The Bible is meant to be read," wrote Irving L. Jensen.[8] No one sits down at a banquet just to admire the tablecloth! Jensen rightly separated the ideas of reading the Bible and studying the Bible to help us get to the important understanding of the necessity of reading. He quotes an earlier Bible scholar, Richard Moulton,

> We have done almost everything that is possible with these Greek and Hebrew writings. We have overlaid them, clause by clause, with exhaustive commentaries; we have translated them, revised the translations, and quarreled over the revisions; we have discussed authenticity and inspiration, and suggested the textual history with the aid of colored type; we have mechanically divided the whole into chapters and verses. And sought texts to memorize and quote; we have epitomized into handbooks and extracted

---

6 John 17:1–26 (ESV).
7 John 17:3 (ESV).
8 Irving L. Jensen, *Enjoy Your Bible: Making the Most of Your Time in God's Word* (Wheaton, IL: Harold Shaw Publishers, 1992), 31.

into school lessons. There is yet one thing left to
do with the Bible: simply to read it.[9]

If eternal life comes from knowing God and knowing God
comes, basically, from reading His Word, then we ought to read
the Bible and learn to read it well. Jensen suggests that good Bible
reading includes reading aloud, reading carefully, reading repeatedly, reading peripherally (paying attention to context), and read-
ing reflectively. Good Bible reading is assisted by recording what
has been read. Here Jensen suggests recording answers to four
questions:

- What is the main point of the passage?
- What do other portions of the Bible say that relate to some
  of these truths?
- What in the passage is difficult to understand, and what
  problems, if any, appear?
- How does this apply to my own life?

Finally, Jensen states the obvious, or at least what will be obvious for someone who is reading the Bible in the God-granted quest
for eternal life—respond to what you are reading. Respond with confession. Respond with faith. Respond with obedience.[10]

The reading plan itself

Since reading the Bible is the best way to begin Bible study, let's
start with a reading plan. I suggest you read through the book no less
than four times. Yes, four times. It's only twelve fascinating chapters,

---

[9] Richard G. Moulton, *A Short Introduction to the Literature of the Bible* (Boston: D. C. Heath and Co., 1901), iii–iv.

[10] Irving L. Jensen, *Enjoy Your Bible: Making the Most of Your Time in God's Word* (Wheaton, IL: Harold Shaw Publishers, 1992), 35–43.

and you only need to read the book through in one sitting three times. Here's the plan for you to follow:

- Read the entire book through in one sitting. On this reading, don't stop to ponder and don't get bogged down in content. Just read. Give yourself an opportunity to develop an attitudinal overview. You are not simply reading to determine the author's attitude toward his subject. You are reading to develop your own attitude toward the subject and you need the big picture to develop an accurate attitude. This will help guide the development of your interpretive outlook.

- Read the entire book through again. Once you've read the book completely through, first word to last word, read it through again a day later. This time, allow what you discovered in your first pass to inform your expectations and attitude. You've read all this before. Some of what you've read has stuck in your memory and made impressions. Note the flow of thought from the beginning to the end of the book. How does the author arrive at his final conclusion?

- Read it through again. "Third time's a charm," according to the conventional wisdom. Read the book through a third time, but this time, a bit more slowly. Here's where you might start taking notes, but not too many and not with great detail. (Many notes in greater details come next.) Examine the content of the book. Notice the literary devices employed. Make a list of repeated or potential key words. Label the various segments you recognize. Make outlines. Take note of changes. Write headings for the sections, if you like. You're still doing "survey" reading, building the big picture, but now you're adding color.

- Read it through again. Now you're ready to linger in this book. Read Ecclesiastes through a fourth time, but this time, take your time, linger. If you've created a mental map of the book, then start your journey. Think of it as driving from Chicago to Miami, but instead of driving straight through, take the opportunity to explore the small towns along the way. Make notes. Journal reactions. Make a list of questions. Jot down sayings that resonate with your own experience or current frame of mind. In fact, you might even want to argue with the author over the point of view he expresses. What arguments and/or proofs would you use in light of what the author uses to make his point? What insights intrigue you and why? What emotional or rational or spiritual reactions does this book raise for you? Make note of those reactions and evaluate why these ideas strike you as they do. This is the stage where you will make the message of this book personal.

Bible reading as interpretive preparation

The reading plan set out for you as we tackle Ecclesiastes intends to accomplish all that can be expected from good Bible reading, not the least of which is a discovery that reading the Bible with purpose can be a delightful, satisfying experience of the presence and glory of God Himself. It is also intended to prepare you, the reader, for the task ahead, the interpretation of the words of Ecclesiastes.[11]

Yes, readers, your task in reading the Bible and studying the Bible is ultimately to accurately interpret what you've read and to respond appropriately with confession, faith, and obedience. Reading the Bible is the first step. Interpreting the Bible is the undeniable result of understanding what we read.

Fee and Stuart identify two tasks related to reading and interpreting, exegesis and hermeneutics. These words don't need to frighten us. They simply mean determining what the text originally

---

[11] Michael V. Fox, "Ecclesiastes," *The JPS Bible Commentary* (New York: The Jewish Publication Society, 2004), xii. "To the degree that Ecclesiastes approaches philosophy [and therefore requires interpretation], it requires a special kind of analysis: an attention to precise meaning of its key terms, a description of its reasoning and arguments, and a synthesis of conclusions." This study guide, and the Reading Plan in particular, intend to assist the student in these interpretational requirements.

meant (*exegesis*) and understanding the original meaning in the "variety of new or different contexts in our own day" (*hermeneutics*).[12] Put another way, "you must try to understand what was said to them back *then and there* (exegesis)…you must learn to hear that same Word in the *here and now* (hermeneutics)."[13]

Exegesis, "the careful, systematic study of the Scripture to discover the original, intended meaning,"[14] and hermeneutics, "seeking the contemporary relevance of ancient texts,"[15] follow rules that enable accurate interpretation and appropriate responses. Not everyone agrees on all the rules, but there is general agreement that the rules for interpreting one type of literature in the Bible may not apply equally to another type, though still in the Bible. A person will not interpret the message of a biblical narrative the same as they might a biblical prophecy. That's why it is important to investigate what literary genre Ecclesiastes falls under, which is the next step in our overview of the book.

Interpreting Ecclesiastes: The Literary Genre of Ecclesiastes

Having read Ecclesiastes through four times and begun making your own notes, the next step is to access background material that is readily available but not necessarily included in Ecclesiastes itself. This material will help you better understand the function of this book. For instance, if you read Homer's *Odyssey*, it is helpful to know whether the work is a poem or a narrative or a biography or a myth or a political speech or a textbook on dating. Knowing what we call its "literary genre" helps us to know what to expect from the book and gives us some advance tools for interpreting the book correctly when we start taking a closer look at it.

---

[12] Gordon Fee and Douglas Stuart, *How to Read the Bible for All Its Worth* (Grand Rapids: Zondervan, 2003), 15.
[13] Ibid., 23.
[14] Ibid.
[15] Ibid., 29.

Ecclesiastes is included in the genre called biblical wisdom literature.[16] A. C. Myers, in *The Eerdmans Bible Dictionary*, under the entry on "wisdom literature," says this about the genre, "Strictly speaking, wisdom literature as a generic category encompasses only the books of Job, Proverbs, and Ecclesiastes in the Old Testament... and perhaps James in the New Testament."[17] After surveying some of the extant examples of wisdom literature from other ancient near-eastern cultures, Myers offers three "theological presuppositions" of wisdom literature:

- This world in which we live and move and have our being is an orderly world, ruled by Yahweh, its Creator. ("Yahweh" is the name God revealed to Moses at the burning bush as we think it might have been pronounced.)
- Knowledge of the aforementioned orderliness of the world is possible to the person who opens himself to wisdom.
- The wise person who thus aligns himself with God's order for the world will experience good things, while the fool will suffer for his folly.[18]

A quick Google search of the characteristics of biblical wisdom literature will bring you to www.crivoice.org and Dennis Bratcher's article, "The Character of Wisdom: An Introduction to Old Testament Wisdom Literature." Bratcher comments, "Wisdom is really an approach to life, a way of looking at the world and, for Israelites, a way of living out in very deliberate, rational ways their commitment to God." As the article progresses, Bratcher helpfully notes several characteristics of wisdom literature (it seems prudent to remind you here that what Bratcher has to say about "wisdom" refers

---

[16] Fox, x–xi. "Wisdom Literature. This is the body of writings that offer advice on how to succeed in life as well as reflections on its meanings and problems."

[17] A. C. Myers, "Wisdom Literature," in *The Eerdmans Bible Dictionary* (Grand Rapids, MI: Eerdmans, 1987), 3. Exported from Logos Bible Software, 10:20 a.m., May 10, 2018.

[18] Ibid.

to the literary genre and not to the divine or human attribute called wisdom):

- Wisdom is concerned with everyday life, how to live well.
- Wisdom does not appeal to revealed truth. (Bratcher's explanation of this point is important. He writes, "Wisdom does not address the human condition from the divine perspective, but rather from the perspective of human needs and concerns, and in terms of what human beings can and should do to address those concerns. Wisdom attempts to give expression to the way things are; it is descriptive and not prescriptive, describing and defining the world and the existing social order as a means to live within both in productive ways. Wisdom thinking grapples with understanding the world, especially the physical and social environment in which they must live; as such, it is both reflective, rational, and concerned with knowledge. It is concerned with learning enough to be able to choose the proper course of action for wellbeing in life, often expressed metaphorically as the 'two ways' or the 'two paths' (cf. Psa. 1).")
- Wisdom's claim to authority lies in tradition and observation.
- Israelite wisdom is rooted in reverence and commitment to God.[19]

Fee and Stuart, in the excellent book we've already referenced, *How to Read the Bible for All Its Worth*, add helpful notes for our understanding of biblical wisdom literature. They define wisdom as "the ability to make godly choices in life." They explain that a person achieves the goal of wisdom by "applying God's truth to your life, so that your choices will indeed be godly."[20] These authors remind us that though the definition of "wisdom" (as a literary genre) seems

---

[19] Dennis Bratcher, *The Character of Wisdom: An Introduction to Old Testament Wisdom Literature* (2016). www.crivoice.org, 5:16 p.m., October 11, 2018.
[20] Fee, 225.

pretty easy and straightforward, it is also easy to abuse "wisdom" literature by reading only bits and pieces and not taking in the overall message; by failing to adequately understand wisdom terms, categories, styles, and literary modes; and by failing to follow the line of argument presented by the biblical author in the whole book.[21] Because of the potential for error in interpretation, we are warned "in approaching Ecclesiastes to have an overall strategy for reading it."[22]

It is crucial to note the difference between biblical wisdom and the wisdom literature of other nations that flourished in the ancient Near East. Biblical wisdom put forth that the only good choices in life are godly choices.[23] This ties in with what Jesus said about eternal life being the result of knowing God. True wisdom is life lived out of the knowledge of God and His ways. So biblical wisdom literature, generally, "tends to focus on people and their behavior—how successful they are at making godly choices and whether or not they are learning how to apply God's truth to the experiences they have."[24]

It really is helpful to know what kind of literature Ecclesiastes is, especially as we move forward in identifying, understanding, and applying the message of the book in our own personal walk of faith. Imagine, now that you've read through Ecclesiastes several times, how you might have read the book differently, through a different lens, if you had already known to expect Ecclesiastes to be an exploration of life as it is, from our perspective as human beings rather than from God's perspective! Think of what a difference it makes now to know that the power of this book comes from the observations that are made by the author rather than from the infinitely more insightful self-revelation of God. (This does not mean that Ecclesiastes or the other books are less inspired. This means that Ecclesiastes and the other wisdom books are inspired by God as a different approach than narrative, for example, where the point is in the story, or didactic, where the instruction carries the point.)

---

21 Ibid., 226–227.
22 Ibid., 243.
23 Ibid., 228.
24 Ibid.

In biblical wisdom literature, God makes His point through the eyes and experience of the author as the author surveys the life experience that surrounds him. In Ecclesiastes, it is probably true that the author is "not so much trying to provide answers as to remind readers of the hard questions—ones that ultimately point us to Christ's death and resurrection for the answer."[25] We'll say more about this when we lay out our own interpretive presuppositions for studying Ecclesiastes.

Interpreting Ecclesiastes: The Issue of Authorship

Who wrote Ecclesiastes and why does it matter?

There is another question related to the background material for Ecclesiastes that we would do well to address. It will, however, probably be impossible to arrive at a definitive answer. (Are you intrigued?) The question is this, who wrote Ecclesiastes? A second, more answerable question is this, what difference does it make?

Meaning and authorial intent. The question regarding the identity of the author matters, but not perhaps in the same way that the identity of the criminal matters to a court, or the way the identity of a candidate matters to voters, or even the way the identity of a parent matters to a child. The significance of the author's identity in Ecclesiastes is much less direct than any of these.

The meaning of a text derives from the intent of the author who wrote the text. An author intends to communicate their own thoughts so that others may know and act on them with an appropriate response. Successful communication, however, involves more than just a series of select words on a page. Consider for a moment the number of conflicts and misunderstandings, heartaches, and hurt feelings that plague social media today because we get texts and tweets, words alone, without really knowing the intent of the author. How many messages would be better taken and better understood,

---

[25] Ibid., 244.

more effectively transferred, through an accompanying smile or frown than just the words themselves, unassisted by contextual support. Knowledge of the person or character of the author is essential for the best communication efforts.

Expectations, assumptions, abnormal behavior, etc., all require familiarity with the author's person for accurate interpretation. My mother-in-law suffered from dementia in the years just before she died. She would sometimes behave caustically toward her family or caregivers, speaking to them or of them in ways that were harsh and unkind. Knowing her prior to the onset of the disease, knowing her as a woman of grace, love, and spiritual depth of concern for others, allowed us to understand her irrational outbursts for what they were—uncharacteristic expressions of a terrible disease process and not the expressions of a terrible person. There were times, in fact, when, because we knew her to be more than the words she uttered, we were able to interpret some of her words and actions as a new form of communication for feelings and experiences she could no longer convey in the old way. Knowing her helped us interpret her authorial intent and therefore correctly interpret her communication efforts.

Author identification and intent in Ecclesiastes. Knowing the author of Ecclesiastes helps us know what to expect of his thinking, his outlook, his history, and his worldview. However, with Ecclesiastes, we have a problem. We don't know who the author is. The early church considered Solomon, King David's son, to be the author. Most recent scholarship rejects or debates this assumption. Linguistic evidence within the Hebrew text suggests that the book is written much, much later than Solomon's time. Michael V. Fox summarizes the evidence as (1) the book's language and background assumptions indicate a post-exilic dating, (2) the epilogue does not speak of Koheleth as king, and (3) Koheleth blames the royal administrative apparatus for social injustice (which presumably Solomon, as the founder of the royal administrative apparatus, would not have done).[26]

---

[26] Fox, x.

So it seems there may be valid reasons to conclude that Solomon is not *the* author of Ecclesiastes, but there is an equally, if not more, valid reason to think of Solomon as the author even if he is not. Whoever the author is, that person clearly wanted to associate the book with Solomon even to the point of having readers regard Solomon as the author. Armed with "authorial intent" held tightly in our hands, we are led to ask, "Why?" Why does the author of Ecclesiastes want us to think Solomon wrote this book? What does the inspired author hope to achieve by attributing the book, even fictitiously, to Solomon?

The most obvious answer to these questions would be credibility. I like reading Clive Cussler novels, particularly the early ones featuring Dirk Pitt as the adventurer/hero character. More recently, Mr. Cussler has expanded his primary character list with new series and a new group of coauthors. On the cover of the paperback novels, Cussler's name appears much larger than the coauthor's name. A person may pick up one of those novels based on a reading history with Cussler, but the personality of the coauthor is not absent in the writing of the new novels. Clive Cussler's name on the cover gives the coauthor credibility and increases sales.

The author of Ecclesiastes could simply be seeking credibility the way a lesser known author might like to have the name of a famous author on the cover of his first novel, or not. More likely, the author of Ecclesiastes, by attributing the work to Solomon, is handing us a brilliant interpretive key. Ecclesiastes, if not from the hand of Solomon, will, at the very least, bear the image of its proposed maker.

Author identification and divine integrity in Ecclesiastes. A further frequently asked question relative to authorship deserves attention. An unnamed author presenting Solomon as the source of his work rather than himself seems deceitful and therefore morally and intellectually unacceptable, to some readers. According to this reasonable rejection of deceit in the biblical canon, Solomon must be the author.

The question is whether the practice described is actually "deceitful." It certainly could be. There could be occasions when an author means to hide his identity from an audience for malicious reasons, which would be the definition of "deceit." The Scripture is rife with examples of the Adversary appearing as a wise serpent[27] or an angel of light[28] or a powerful leader in order to deceive human audiences,[29] but his intent is always vile and malicious. His intent is always to deceive, to lead the human heart away from God's redeeming truth. So misrepresenting oneself certainly could be a strategy of deceit when the intent is to mislead.

But is the intent of Ecclesiastes to mislead or deceive? Has this book been inspired and included by God in His Word in order to lead human hearts away from the redeeming truth He everywhere else presents as vital to our eternal salvation and joy? No. Nothing about Ecclesiastes stinks of deceit. In fact, the major complaint Ecclesiastes faces is its stark, unrelenting honesty about the human condition.

It is also helpful to acknowledge a finding of Tremper Longman III in ancient Akkadian literature.[30] Three texts, of fifteen Akkadian texts Longman studied, closely parallel Ecclesiastes in form and function. They are clearly written by an author who presents the content under a different persona than his own identity. The implication is that this "authorial substitution" was likely a known, understood, and acceptable practice at the time Ecclesiastes was written. It was a culturally effective means for communicating authorial intent with target audiences. It is not a question of deceit, but of effective communication strategy.

Every biblical author, inspired by the Holy Spirit, whether decisively identified in their work or not, writes in the style and standard of the time period in which they live to the sensibilities of the audience to which they are writing. So it may be with Ecclesiastes. If there is an unnamed author using a fictional persona to convey inspired truth, then we may consider it consistent with God's demonstrated strategy for self-revelation. He simply uses a communication tool recognized and effective in the time period in which the work is written. And if, as the earliest commentaries on Ecclesiastes assume, Solomon is both the subject and the author, God's goal is still accomplished.

---

[27] Genesis 3:1–15 (ESV).
[28] 2 Corinthians 11:14 (ESV).
[29] Revelation 13:5–9 (ESV).
[30] Longman, 8, 18–20.

Given these ideas, let me make two clarifying personal statements about this issue.

First, it is the message of Ecclesiastes, the inspired truth, that is more important than the identity of the inspired author, so the question we are pursuing presents no obstacle in the task of finding God in His Word. Divine inspiration of the Scripture is the underlying foundation for interpretation. Moses wrote Genesis. He wrote truthfully and accurately of events that occurred millennia before he was born. I trust the inspiration of the Holy Spirit to have worked adequately and accurately in Moses' mind and heart to produce a work that reflects exactly God's truth and fulfills completely God's purpose, even though Moses is writing about events and lives he never personally witnessed. That is the nature of inspiration, and it applies to Ecclesiastes in both process and product. God oversaw the writing of the book as well as determined the content and message of the book.

Second, there is no agenda in this study to persuade anyone to believe that Solomon is the author of Ecclesiastes or that he is not. All students are free to accept the implications of the question and act on them as they will. Some will find traditional arguments for Solomonic authorship convincing and necessary. Others will not. The agenda of this study, however, is to persuade you that the message of Ecclesiastes can be known and loved and lived and that it is worth every effort to discover the treasures in Ecclesiastes.

The way forward, whether we are convinced of Solomonic authorship or not, is to acknowledge that regardless of who the author is, we are to understand Solomon as the "life context" for what we read. It is Solomon, the real live person, whose life will help us understand the content and intent of Ecclesiastes.

Solomon as intended author

About Solomon in general. What are some basic facts you know about Solomon? He was the son of David by Bathsheba. He was king after David over Israel, expanding the nation's borders and influence to the greatest they would ever be, and he had seven hundred wives and three hundred concubines. (Okay, that is a fact, but what is important about that fact is that 1 Kings 11:3 notes that all these intimate relationships "turned his heart away from the *LORD*." Such an apostasy might have bearing on Solomon's life outlook, might it not?) Also, Solomon, having been interviewed by God and given the opportunity to ask for anything he wanted, was granted by God the wisdom to make him the wisest man that ever lived.

Solomon had a relationship with God and Solomon was wiser than any other sage. That fact alone has great implications for interpreting and understanding Ecclesiastes. Remember what Fee and Stuart said about wisdom? "Wisdom is the ability to make godly choices in life."[31] Since people make godly choices, wisdom is decidedly personal. Accordingly, "wisdom is...something that exists only when a *person* thinks and acts according to truth when making the many choices that life demands."[32] That means that as a "wise" man, and the wisest of all at that, he is a man devoted to "being able to formulate the sorts of plans—that is, make the sorts of choices—that would help produce the desired results in life."[33]

Solomon is no dummy. Read the description of Solomon in 1 Kings 4:29–34 (ESV).

> [29]And God gave Solomon wisdom and understanding beyond measure, and breadth of mind like the sand on the seashore, [30]so that Solomon's wisdom surpassed the wisdom of all the people of the east and all the wisdom of Egypt. [31]For he was wiser than all other men, wiser than Ethan the Ezrahite, and Heman, Calcol, and Darda, the sons of Mahol, and his fame was in all the surrounding nations. [32]He also spoke 3,000 proverbs, and his songs were 1,005. [33]He spoke of trees, from the cedar that is in Lebanon to the hyssop that grows out of the wall. He spoke also

---

[31] Fee, 227.
[32] Ibid.
[33] Ibid.

of beasts, and of birds, and of reptiles, and of fish. [34]And people of all nations came to hear the wisdom of Solomon, and from all the kings of the earth, who had heard of his wisdom.

Having been granted immense wisdom by the divine hand, it is not likely that he finally becomes an abject fool who can't see past his most recent pleasure. Solomon's personal history informs our understanding of the content and message of Ecclesiastes. It must, for that is the author's intent in connecting the book with the king. Who Solomon was is an important guide for interpreting the meaning of Ecclesiastes. That's why the author, whether Solomon or someone else, attaches Solomon's name to the book. Solomon's personal life experience provides the contextual framework for understanding authorial intent in Ecclesiastes. That being the case, rather than spending more time trying to decide whether Solomon is the actual author, we need to spend time learning all we can about Solomon, the "intentional" author.

About Solomon in Ecclesiastes. What are some things that we know about Solomon from within Ecclesiastes that might help us understand Ecclesiastes? Solomon is probably the subject of 1:1, 12, and 12:9–12. In the first of these verses, we find that Solomon is both koheleth and king. We discover that his kingship is related to kinship with King David. We observe that Jerusalem is the geographical (and therefore the cultural) context in which the koheleth lives and in which both his activities and his analysis develops. Given the use of the first-person singular pronoun, "I," Koheleth/Solomon is certainly the understood speaker of the rest of the first-person narrative.

In the second passage, the narrator speaks to the larger character of Koheleth, telling us Solomon was a sage, a wise man, whose function in the community included instructing the people, "listening to and testing the soundness of many maxims, discovering useful sayings, and recording genuinely truthful sayings."[34] These functions well describe the activities and conduct of a social science researcher

---

[34] Ecclesiastes 12:9–10 (ESV).

and give support to our claim that it is this very function that characterizes both Koheleth the man and the book.

What overall impression about Solomon do we gain from Ecclesiastes? Certainly this—Koheleth (Solomon) is no pessimist. If he had been, he would have abandoned this treatise after the first utterance. Instead he pushes on, taking each observation in hand, turning it over and about, comparing it, learning it before returning it to the shelf of ideas he is considering. Each idea leads him closer to the ultimate truth he seeks, and he is unrelenting in his pursuit. These are the mental activities of a studious and wise man.

About Solomon in the Scripture. Here's a helpful exercise. Ask yourself, What do we know about Solomon from the Scripture that reinforces the idea that he was an optimistic realist? What about 1 Kings 4:29–34? What about Proverbs 1:1? What about 1 Kings 3:1–28 (especially his conversation with God and his ruling between the two prostitutes)? Reading Solomon's history in the Scripture and using other sources to access his biographical data, consider this question, How does Solomon's biography illumine or provide credibility to the driving questions and the methodology described in this research report entitled "Ecclesiastes"? Deciding whether Koheleth is a pessimist or optimist is a major interpretive decision. How would you label the Teacher?

About Solomon in critical analysis. The *Lexham Bible Dictionary* includes an entry, "Solomon, King of Israel, Critical Issues," that presents "a brief exploration of the figure of Solomon in 1 Kings, 2 Chronicles, the Second Temple period, and the New Testament." What is most helpful about the article are the summary statements of how Solomon is presented in each of these textual contexts. In other words, when you read the passages about Solomon in each of these books, this is the perception of the man you might come away with after your study.

Essentially, according to the author of the article, "rather than presenting a monolithic picture of Solomon, the biblical witnesses present a portrait of Israel's wise king that is 'shot through with ambivalence.'"[35] The literary picture is not one of a great man with a single redeeming characteristic, but of a great man, a complex man, who is presented as a tarnished hero who built the temple but sinned in his excesses, including the multiplication of wives, which are "seen as the cause of the problems of succeeding generations."[36]

As a student of Solomon moves forward in the biblical history and the extrabiblical history regarding Solomon as well, the historians focus more on Solomon's temple-building legacy and less on his personal foibles. Solomon's wisdom and Solomon's efforts to enable the worship of Yahweh and Solomon's seasons of personal spiritual success at the hand of God take center stage in the narrative of his significance. By the New Testament time, Solomon is primarily noted as the great king of Israel responsible for building the temple. Jesus refers to Solomon's wealth when comparing his grandeur to that of lilies (Matthew 6:29) and again to Solomon's wealth, wisdom, and character when he teaches that "one greater than Solomon" is here (Matthew 12:42).

About Solomon and interpretive expectations in Ecclesiastes. When considering Solomon as a person and as the intended author of Ecclesiastes, one whose life and outlook give structure to the work described here and the conclusions drawn, three biographical points and three expectations impress:

- It is important that Solomon had a relationship with Yahweh, the God of Israel, and that the relationship was personal.
- It is important that Solomon's life experiences provide both the laboratory and the substance for the social/philosophical experiment described in Ecclesiastes.[37]

---

[35] Mark E. Gordley, "*Solomon, King of Israel, Critical Issues*," in *The Lexham Bible Dictionary*, eds. J. D. Barry, D. Bomar, D. R. Brown, et al. (Bellingham, WA: Lexham Press, 2016). The author attributes the phrase "shot through with ambivalence" to Walter Breuggemann.

[36] Ibid.

[37] Wilf Rieger, "Ecclesiastes as Research: Autoethnography Through a Rear-vision Mirror," in *TEACH Journal of Christian Education* Vol. 4, Issue 2, Article 11, 44. "More specifically, in autoethnography the researcher is simultaneously the study's observer and actor; discrete roles that call for an approach of conscious

- It is important that Solomon's career achievements, most notably the collection of proverbs and the writing of songs, demonstrate his ability to accurately observe and analyze life from a human standpoint.

Given these biographical points, these expectations emerge:

- The expectation that written wisdom from the wisest man who ever lived, who had a personal relationship with God (and who apparently abandoned that relationship only to return to it in later life), and who had the means and opportunity to conduct a philosophical experiment of the scale described in Ecclesiastes will reflect a life that is not approached or understood without any awareness of Israel's or his own covenant relationship with God.
- The expectation that Solomon's musings will reflect a mind capable of sifting through the full range of human experiences recorded in Ecclesiastes without getting lost or mired in confusion.
- The expectation that the author (or the subject of the book identified by the author to be Solomon) will have the personal capacity to identify and reflect wisely on wisdom and folly in the life experiences and processes encountered and subjected to analysis and commentary. A comment Koheleth makes in chapter 2 verse 3 is telling here. He writes, "I ventured to test my flesh with wine, and to grasp folly, *while letting my mind direct with wisdom*, to the end that I might learn which of the two was better for men to practice in their few days of life under heaven."[38] His conduct, which was admittedly excessive, was intentional, guided by wisdom in pursuit of genuine truth. He demonstrates the capacity to engage his own life experience

---

detachment." The comment on Ecclesiastes 2:3 evidences this very detachment in Koheleth.

[38] Ecclesiastes 2:3 (JPS) (emphasis added).

as both the laboratory and the experiment without being intellectually compromised by either one.

Interpreting Ecclesiastes: Structure, Strategies, and Presuppositions

Having set out a reading plan, conducted a cursory examination of the literary genre of Ecclesiastes, and begun to consider some of the issues related to authorship, we have a fourth consideration to make as we begin our study. We have to make some decisions about the perspective from which we are going to conduct our experiment in order to develop a framework for drawing conclusions. Those decisions relate first to the structure and organization of Ecclesiastes, then to reviewing other interpretive approaches, and then to identifying our own assumptions that will affect the manner in which we approach our analysis of the book. We also need to outline the purpose of our study, the method we will use, the duration of the study, and the expected outcomes of our study.

The structure of Ecclesiastes and the scientific method

The structure of Ecclesiastes seems to perplex many commentators. Michael Fox, commenting in the *JPS Bible Commentary on Ecclesiastes*, writes, "The question of an overarching structure and cohesiveness is one of the most vexing issues in the study of Ecclesiastes."[39] He goes on to comment, "The test of any inferred structure or design is whether it matches the reader's experience— that is, whether it emerges from your own reading, and whether awareness of it helps you organize the book's thoughts and deepens your understanding of its message."[40] Fox recognizes a "deep cohesiveness" in Ecclesiastes. He also judges it to lack an "organized literary structure."[41] I don't agree, as you'll soon discover in more detail.

---

[39] Fox, 15.
[40] Ibid., 16.
[41] Ibid.

Tremper Longman III, commenting on Ecclesiastes in his volume from the *New International Commentary on the New Testament* series, writes,

> The book of Ecclesiastes is divided into three parts. It begins with a short prologue, introducing some of the themes of Qohelet's thought (1:1–11), continues with a long monologue by Qohelet (1:12–12:7), and concludes with a brief epilogue (12:8–14). The prologue and epilogue are differentiated from the body of the book by their third-person references to Qohelet. Together they frame Qohelet's speech. The bulk of the book is Qohelet's speech that is made up primarily of autobiographical reflections on the meaning of life.[42]

While Longman's outline is simple and to the point, it seems too simple. Furthermore, labeling the bulk of Ecclesiastes "autobiographical reflections on the meaning of life" makes the entire book too narcissistic to actually be helpful. The label "autobiographical reflections," while not untrue, may misdirect from the point of what is actually happening in the book.

Longman goes on to further describe the bulk of the Ecclesiastes narrative as rambling, repetitive thoughts that occasionally contradict themselves.[43] He concludes by admitting, "Within the broad tripartite structure of the book and the fivefold outline of Qohelet's autobiographical speech, I do not find a clear and obvious structure."[44]

But consider this—commentators frequently note that Koheleth "reports" his actions and findings and conclusions. The word "reports" seems a clue to understanding the structure of Ecclesiastes. This is a report, not merely of casual musings about life, but of an intentional exploration of desirable human activity against the backdrop of the

---

[42] Longman, p. 21.
[43] Ibid.
[44] Ibid.

flow of history. In other words, Koheleth (Solomon) is investigating not a life, but all of life, and he is presenting a summary report of his findings based on extensive research.

Ask yourself, What kind of report makes an observation, proposes a hypothesis, constructs a plan to explore the hypothesis, implements the plan, records results, draws conclusions, and reports the findings? A science research project report utilizing the scientific method looks almost exactly like the report we've just described. "The scientific method is a process for experimentation that is used to explore observations and answer questions."[45] Here is a chart illustrating the flow of procedure in the scientific method (see figure 1).

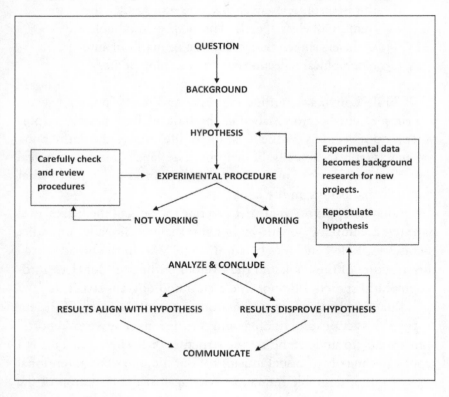

45 www.sciencebuddies.org/science-fair-projects/steps-of-the-scientific-method.

It is always a good idea to define new and unfamiliar terms to make sure we understand them as we attempt to make sense of the message their use intends. Take a look at the terms used for the phases in a scientific inquiry that would include a detailed report of methodology and results.

- Question (Observation): Taking note of a phenomenon that piques your interest and urges investigation for greater understanding
- Hypothesis: An educated guess about how things work[46]
- Experiment: A carefully thought-out procedure designed to test whether or not a hypothesis is valid or accurate
- Data: The results each stage of the experiment yields
- Analysis: Thoughtful consideration of the evidence provided by the experiment in relation to the hypothesis
- Conclusion: Reasonable assertion that accounts for data evidence relative to the hypothesis

Understanding the structure of Ecclesiastes as a detailed science report, similar in structure and function to a report organized like that based on the scientific method, is a reasonable approach. I am not suggesting that the author of Ecclesiastes knew the format of the modern scientific method or that he intentionally used such a format. I am saying the book falls into the pattern of a formal science report because it is a detailed report of one man's test of a basic life assumption; it is the report of an experiment.

Wilf Rieger would, I think, agree. Rieger is an Honorary Senior Research Fellow at Avondale College in New South Wales, Australia. He is also the author of an article "Ecclesiastes as Research: Autoethnography through a rear-vision mirror," in *TEACH Journal*

---

[46] Kendra Cherry, *Forming a Good Hypothesis for Scientific Research*, https://www.verywellmind.com/what-is-a-hypothesis-2795239. Accessed December 2, 2018. Cherry would argue that this definition is too simplistic since a good hypothesis is not a guess at all but a prediction of what a researcher expects to be the relationship between two variables after some background investigation has been done.

of Christian Education.[47] Rieger cites four distinct occurrences of research recorded in the Bible: Gideon's fleeces (Judges 6), Daniel's diet request (Daniel 1), Luke's historical narrative of Jesus, and Ecclesiastes. Of these four inquiries, Rieger writes, "It is evident from the cited instances, that research was conducted in situ to inform decision-making and as a vehicle to strengthen personal faith; also to validate the veracity of historical accounts for listeners and readers, rather than for academic purposes."[48] He goes on to generally describe Ecclesiastes as the reported results of intentional data collection and analysis that closes with "a clear succinct answer to its central research question, based on the findings."[49]

I was pleased to find Rieger's article nearly a year into my own research. I had wondered that no one else seemed to see the potential for Ecclesiastes to be ordered and understood as a formal research report, but here it is. A scholar in Australia saw it long before I did, sitting there at my in-laws' dining room table in rural Alabama. We are on solid ground in this pursuit, perhaps more solid than some other popular approaches.

The potential of other philosophical approaches to Ecclesiastes

Other philosophical approaches have been offered as frameworks for understanding the message of Ecclesiastes. They are suggested as avenues for understanding the mind and intent of the author and thereby interpreting the message of the book. They each have the benefit, I think, of approaching the book from the same plane of consideration from which the book is written, human observation of human experience. However, each of these philosophical approaches is a type of humanist philosophy, and because each is a human-based philosophical approach, each fails to provide an adequate interpretation of Ecclesiastes. The focus of each is too narrow and too earthbound.

---

[47] Rieger, 43–50.
[48] Ibid., 44.
[49] Ibid., 49.

There are at least six named philosophical approaches you might encounter as you study Ecclesiastes. They are fatalism, pessimism, nihilism, absurdism, existentialism, and empiricism. We could also include hedonism, materialism, and deism, since examples that coincide with these philosophies abound in Ecclesiastes as well.

Fatalism. Fatalism is the belief that all events are predetermined and therefore inevitable. The Stanford Encyclopedia of Philosophy notes more specifically that "though the word 'fatalism' is commonly used to refer to an attitude of resignation in the face of some future event or events which are thought to be inevitable, philosophers usually use the word to refer to the view that we are powerless to do anything other than what we actually do."[50]

With the ideas of inevitability and powerlessness in mind, it is no wonder some students characterize Koheleth's perspective as fatalistic. Just take a look at those famous words in Ecclesiastes 3:1–8. They are not the only example of fatalism in the book, but they are certainly the clearest.

> A season is set for everything, a time for every experience under heaven:
> A time for being born and a time for dying,
> A time for planting and a time for uprooting the planted;
> A time for slaying and a time for healing,
> A time for tearing down and a time for building up;
> A time for weeping and a time for laughing,
> A time for wailing and a time for dancing;
> A time for throwing stones and a time for gathering stones,
> A time for embracing and a time for shunning embraces;
> A time for seeking and a time for losing,

---

[50] *Stanford Encyclopedia of Philosophy*, https://plato.stanford.edu/entries/fatalism. Accessed November 21, 2018.

A time for keeping and a time for discarding;
A time for ripping and a time for sewing,
A time for silence and a time for speaking;
A time for loving and a time for hating;
A time for war and a time for peace.[51]

Everything, every activity of life, from A to Z and everything in between, is ordered and ordained and set in place. There is little, if anything, any one human being, or the sum of us, over the course of history, can do about it. This perspective of these verses represents fatalism as an understanding of Koheleth's message in Ecclesiastes. The question we will have to determine is whether fatalism is the answer to the question, "What real value is there for a man in all the gains he makes beneath the sun?" or is this merely an example, an illustration of a potential answer, to be rebuffed in the final analysis.

Pessimism. Fatalists consider life a series of inevitable events over which we are powerless. Pessimists are quite depressed about it. Pessimism, also called "cynicism" and "negative thinking," is the "glass is half empty and the rest is leaking out the hole in the bottom" approach to life.

Pessimists incline toward negativity and tend to expect the worst in every situation. (Though pessimism can contribute to mental and physical health issues, it may not be all bad. *Psychology Today* suggests that "pessimists sometimes make better leaders, particularly where there is a need to ignite social change, and their skepticism may make them more resistant to propaganda and false advertising.")[52]

Koheleth reveals a measure of pessimism as he reviews his appraisal of wisdom, madness, and folly in Ecclesiastes 2:12–16.

My thoughts also turned to appraising wisdom and madness and folly. I found that
Wisdom is superior to folly

---

[51] Ecclesiastes 3:1–8 (JPS).
[52] https://www.psychologytoday.com/us/basics/pessimism. Accessed on November 21, 2018.

As light is superior to darkness;
A wise man has his eyes in his head, Whereas
a fool walks in darkness.

But I also realized that the same fate awaits
them both. So I reflected: "The fate of the fool
is also destined for me; to what advantage, then,
have I been wise?" And I came to the conclusion
that that too was futile, because the wise man,
just like the fool, is not remembered forever; for,
as the succeeding days roll by, both are forgotten.
Alas, the wise man dies, just like the fool![53]

Search for wisdom, spend your life becoming the wisest man
in the land, or pitch it all and live like a fool, unaware of God and
unconcerned—either way, you reach the same goal, dead. Is pessimism the best way to understand the message of this book? Is it best
to simply realize that nothing has real value, no effort to advance in
life has any substantial meaning since in the end, no matter what,
you're still dead? Or are these pessimistic sentiments yet again an
example of a potential answer to the refined research question but
not the answer at all?

Nihilism. Nihilism, rather than fatalism or pessimism, seems to
come the closest of the humanistic philosophies to grasp the outlook
of Ecclesiastes. Nihilists believe that nothing can be known for certain,
so there is no basis for "absolute truth." Ethical nihilism rejects the
possibility of moral or ethical values. Existential nihilism is "the notion
that life has no intrinsic meaning or value."[54] This last represents the
way nihilistic philosophy is most generally understood today.

Under existential nihilism, given that the basic assumption is
that the world lacks any inherent meaning or purpose, "existence
itself—all action, suffering, and feeling—is useless and empty."[55]
Does that sound familiar, those of you who have now read through

---

[53] Ecclesiastes 2:12–16 (JPS).
[54] https://www.iep.utm.edu/nihilism.
[55] Ibid.

Ecclesiastes at least four times? Having catalogued all the excesses of his youth in the pursuit of wisdom, pleasure, happiness, and satisfaction, Koheleth reports,

> Then my thoughts turned to all the fortune my hands had built up, to the wealth I had acquired and won—and oh, it was all futile and pursuit of wind; there was no real value under the sun![56]

Reminds a person of Shakespeare, doesn't it? Remember these words from Macbeth when he learns of his wife's death (from Act 5, scene 5, lines 16–27)?

> Out, out brief candle!
> Life's but a walking shadow, a poor player
> That struts and frets his hour upon the stage
> And then is heard no more; it is a tale
> Told by an idiot, full of sound and fury,
> Signifying nothing.[57]

Is this really all there is, the end of the matter? Death and nothing. Death counting up the deeds and days of life and summing them all up as zero? Is there nothing more? No, there is nothing more, if one merely surveys life "beneath the sun." But life doesn't exist only in the realm "beneath the sun," does it? Koheleth is no nihilist. He is not offering futility as "an absolute proposition negating all possible activities and values."[58] As we will discover throughout his report,

---

[56] Ecclesiastes 2:11 (JPS).

[57] https://www.sparknotes.com/shakespeare/macbeth/quotes/page/5. The commentator here observes that this is "a speech of such pessimism and despair—one of the most famous speeches in all of Shakespeare—that the audience realizes how completely his wife's passing and the ruin of his power have undone Macbeth. His speech insists that there is no meaning or purpose in life.

[58] Fox, xxx.

Koheleth does find some things worthwhile in life and worthy of embracing wholeheartedly as our "portion" from the Lord.

Absurdism. Fatalism, pessimism, existential nihilism, enough already, eh? No! More. Absurdity is the sister of existentialism and nihilism. Absurdist thinking "is a philosophical perspective which holds that the efforts of humanity to find meaning or rational explanation in the universe ultimately fail (and, hence, are absurd) because no such meaning exists, at least to human beings."[59] Albert Camus, the French philosopher, argued that the search for meaning in life must always be a conflict between the necessity of the search and the impossibility of success. You can't help but reach for it, but you'll never attain it.

Some students of Ecclesiastes explain the closing verses of the book as an expression of absurdist philosophy,

> The sum of the matter, when all is said and done: Revere God and observe His commandments! For this applies to all mankind: that God will call every creature to account for everything unknown, be it good or bad.[60]

Life certainly can seem absurd, can't it? The example in the introduction of the couple who spent months planning their dream wedding and their helicopter escape to their honeymoon only to crash minutes from takeoff is as definitively absurd as it gets, a massive effort at happiness that ends in futility. But were their efforts truly meaningless since they died without realizing the full joy of their efforts, or did their efforts represent the value they placed on their lives and their future in that moment? That is the difference between absurdism and existentialism.

Existentialism. "Existentialism is a philosophy concerned with finding self and the meaning of life through free will, choice, and per-

---

[59] http://www.newworldencyclopedia.org/entry/Absurdism. Accessed November 21, 2018.

[60] Ecclesiastes 12:13–14 (JPS).

sonal responsibility."[61] Essentially, meaning is derived from human effort at life. Viktor Frankl, author of *Man's Search for Meaning*, wrote this of his observations of labor camp prisoners in World War II,

> The way in which a man accepts fate and all the suffering it entails, the way in which he takes up his cross, gives him ample opportunity—even under the most difficult circumstances—to add deeper meaning in his life.[62]

The idea here is that meaning in life is what we each make of it through the choices we make for which we are personally and individually responsible. Frankl observed that men who refused to give up, refused to give in to cruelty, hate, and the vain repetitions of pointless effort in the labor camps, fared better than those who clung to the past, living in a life long gone and assigning no value to their current circumstances. Frankl notes that "psychological observations of prisoners have shown that only the men who allowed their inner hold on their moral and spiritual selves to subside eventually fell victim to the camp's degenerating influences."[63] For those who did not maintain their hold on their selves, "Life for such people became meaningless."[64]

Koheleth's existentialist song can be seen in the closing verses of chapter 11,

> O youth, enjoy yourself while you are young! Let your heart lead you to enjoyment in the days of your youth. Follow the desires of your heart and the glances of your eyes—but know well that God will call you to account for all such things—and banish care from your mind, and

---

[61] https://www.allaboutphilosophy.org/existentialism.htm. Accessed November 21, 2018.

[62] Viktor E. Frankl, *Man's Search for Meaning* (London: Rider, 2004), 54.

[63] Ibid., 56.

[64] Ibid., 58.

pluck sorrow out of your flesh! For youth and
black hair are fleeting.[65]

Make choices while you can and make the most of the choices
you can make because old age and failing strength are inevitably
cruising the horizons of your future. Sounds reasonable, doesn't it?
Be the master of your own fate! If it feels good, you might as well do
it! Be the person you want to be! And yet where is the Creator in all
that? That's the real question, isn't it?

Empiricism. Let's take a brief look at one final philosophical
approach to understanding the subject and substance of Ecclesiastes.
Empiricism is the view that what is true comes only from what is
experienced. Where Ecclesiastes is concerned, empiricism understands life to mean nothing more than what can be explained by
experience, so any concept of meaning or hope is derived from the
good or sorrow experienced in life. Empiricism in Ecclesiastes looks
like this in chapter 5 verses 17 and 18,

> Only this, I have found, is a real good: that
> one should eat and drink and get pleasure with
> all the gains he makes under the sun, during the
> numbered days of life that God has given him;
> for that is his portion. Also, whenever a man is
> given riches and property by God, and is also
> permitted by Him to enjoy them and to take his
> portion and get pleasure for his gains—that is a
> gift of God.[66]

If you experience food and drink and pleasure, that is what you
get in life, so find your joy in it. If you experience riches and property
and you get to enjoy them while you live, be glad. That is all you get,
and you might as well let your experience define your responses. Still,
we have to ask, are these things, good though they are, all we have to

---

[65] Ecclesiastes 11:9–10 (JPS).
[66] Ecclesiastes 5:17–18 (JPS).

experience? And what if we don't get any of these things? Is life only meaningful if we get stuff?

Each of the approaches summarized above, as examples of humanist philosophies, fails to provide a fully adequate explanation and interpretation of Ecclesiastes because each fails to account for the relationship between God's sovereign purpose in creation and human experience as an integral component of God's creation. Their weakness is not that they fail to offer an explanation for human experience. Their weakness is that they leave God and His activity out of their social equation. We will see as we study Ecclesiastes that Koheleth does not abandon God nor leave God's presence utterly out of his experiment to understand human experience and the meaning of life. Any interpretive effort that does not account for God fails be to an adequate tool for interpreting Ecclesiastes.

The role of personal presuppositions when interpreting Ecclesiastes

Another necessary constituent in our preparation to delve into both the meaning of Ecclesiastes and with it the "meaning of life" is our list of preliminary assumptions, presuppositions, that we will take with us into the study. These are ideas, outlooks, assumptions, and even worldviews that are a normal part of our thinking. They are the personal filters through which we evaluate all our experiences. For example, as part of our normative worldview, most people take for granted that the earth under our feet is stable, reliable, and dependable and does not move with unexpected, destructive force. Interestingly, people in California and earthquake-prone areas of the globe do not share this normative worldview to the degree that people from nonearthquake zones do.

All of us have built in assumptions about the world, about life experience, about how things are, about right and wrong, and about what is valid in communication and what is not. We have developed these assumptions over the years of our lives. They have been molded by our studies and by our own personal experience. They provide our internal tool kit for understanding our world, our place in the world, and the place the world has in our own lives. It is helpful for two reasons to identify some relevant assumptions as we head into our study. First, these are some of the factors that will assist our efforts at understanding the message from the author of Ecclesiastes. Second, these are some of the factors that will sabotage our efforts at understanding the message from the author of Ecclesiastes.

Presuppositions and assumptions work both for us and against us in the learning process, so it is helpful to spotlight them in the beginning, enabling us to watch for their effect, particularly when one of our assumptions about the reality of things is challenged by something we read in God's Word. Our assumptions will likely guide our process of resolving the challenge and adopting or rejecting whatever meaning the text presents. Being aware of our assumptions up front may help us make informed and perhaps nontraditional (for us) choices about handling what we encounter in Ecclesiastes.

Let me give you a list of preliminary assumptions of my own that I identified as I've worked through this study. They involve the purpose of the Scripture, the role of the author, the nature of "biblical understanding," and my place in history relative to Ecclesiastes.

Presupposition #1: Ecclesiastes in the biblical canon. First of all, the presence of the book of Ecclesiastes in the Bible means that this book must serve the purpose all of the Scriptures serve—to reveal the person of God and the plan of God to fill the earth with the knowledge of His glory (cf. Habakkuk 2:14). I believe the inclusion of Ecclesiastes in the canon of the Scripture is providential and inspired, not accidental and imaginary. The book is there because God wants it there, for His purpose. I believe that God's Word, as a whole, is God's self-revelation, His autobiographical exposition of His person and His purposes. Therefore, since Ecclesiastes is part and parcel of the whole of God's Word, it too must serve the purpose, in part and as a whole, to reveal accurately the truth of God's person and purposes.

In addition, as I mentioned previously, since Ecclesiastes is divine revelation, humanist philosophy is probably not an adequate tool for interpreting, understanding, internalizing, and applying the message of this book for two reasons. First, humanist philosophy often assumes an inherently meaningless universe. Second, it does not account for assignment of meaning to creation by its Creator.

Furthermore, since the function of the Scripture is to give a true and accurate account of God from His perspective for our consumption and personal spiritual transformation, then it is not unthinkable God would include in His Word an examination of life where He is marginalized or absent in order to demonstrate the "meaninglessness" of such a life.

Presupposition #2: Ecclesiastes as Solomon's work. My next presupposition relates to the role of the author. From my vantage point, whether or not Solomon actually wrote this book is mostly irrelevant in terms of interpreting the book. Clearly the author of the book intends readers to identify the book with Solomon. As I've already set out for you, what we know of the man, Solomon, son of David, informs how the author wants us to understand the content and message of Ecclesiastes. Therefore, I perceive that Ecclesiastes is not the venting of a wasted old man who regrets an unsatisfying and unsatisfied life. It is instead the brilliant reflection of a wise man intentionally examining the functional worldview prevalent in his day with an eye to drawing a better, more praiseworthy and satisfying conclusion. Solomon's personal credentials as king, as son of David, and as wise man whose wisdom came from the hand of God Himself lend credibility to both the experimental procedures and the analytical conclusions included in Ecclesiastes.

Related to this notion of the role of the author is the idea of interpretive approaches, how we go about discerning the message for us that God presents in His Word. For simplicity, let me suggest the following three generalized interpretive approaches, all of which can be helpful, but only one of which comes with the guarantee of right understanding:

- Internal approach: The Scripture is interpreted through the lens of human intellectual and emotional experience. This approach begins its efforts to know and understand God through human experience, typically one's own life experience. I call this the "internal" approach because it tends to be the product of considering God through the internal lens of "I/Me/Mine." This is the interpretive approach of humanist philosophy.

Catching the Wind:
A Guide for Interpreting Ecclesiastes

BY DALE C MCINTIRE

www.CovenantBooks.com/books/?book=Catching-the-Wind

COVENANT
BOOKS

(843) 507-8373

CATCHING
the
Wind

A GUIDE FOR INTERPRETING
ECCLESIASTES

DALE C. McINTIRE

- Eternal approach: The Scripture is interpreted through the lens of divine self-revelation to which humans may or may not subscribe in faith. This approach accepts the Scripture as God's personal self-revelation, which includes His understanding of Himself, His creation in general, and human experience in particular. This approach not only accounts for God and His influence upon the author and the author's understanding of reality but also reaches to see the perspective of God Himself in what is recorded relative to the topic at hand. This is the best approach for fruitful Bible study.
- Infernal approach: The word and works of God interpreted through the perspective of the identified enemies of God. Portions of Job, Isaiah, the Gospels, and most of the book of the Revelation report this perspective. These are the passages where either the Adversary speaks or is otherwise described in person or activity by the biblical author, and we are to understand something of God through the description of that which vehemently opposes God.

Presupposition #3: Ecclesiastes as discipleship. The third assumption I identified for myself involves the nature of "biblical understanding." Not everyone who reads the Bible understands it, and not everyone who thinks they understand it actually does, and sometimes, even the best of us don't understand all there is to understand. I affirm this for myself based on this—the evidence that divinely revealed truth has been genuinely and accurately understood is not only transformed thinking but also transformed living. Where new "understanding" does not yield new behaving, real understanding, the understanding of Himself God seeks of us, has likely not yet occurred. We will understand the message of Ecclesiastes not when it changes the way we think about God, but when it affects the way we love and serve God with the lives and love we have.

Presupposition #4: Ecclesiastes as personal encounter. There is a final assumption I realized one day as my wife and I were driving from our home in northeast Minnesota to visit a friend who lives in central Minnesota. We were talking about some passage of the Scripture or another, and we kept saying to each other, "Yeah, but try and put yourself in their shoes." Then we would spend several more miles trying to figure out what the instruction in the Scripture would mean to a person living at the time the instruction was given and how their life experience would provide a different context for understanding than ours does. What I came away with from that discussion is the commitment to understand that I am not Solomon, or Solomon's son, or a sage living in post-exilic Israel. I am a theologically Reformed-leaning Christian pastor living in twenty-first-century America, and no matter how hard I try, I cannot be other than I am when it comes to encountering the reality of God in His Word.

When I come to God's Word, I am going to look for Him. I am going to look for the gospel of Jesus Christ. I am going to look for the hand of the Holy Spirit. I am going to ask, "What is the message of this book for my church, for my family, for my community, for my soul?" For example, I have, at times, reminded the people of my congregation in the days before our annual celebration of the death and resurrection of Jesus that no matter how hard we work at it in our worship practices, we cannot go back to the days before Jesus died and before he rose from the dead. To do so is to engage in a pretend reality, and because it is pretend, it has limited benefit to offer. So I encourage people to approach Good Friday for what it is, the day the Creator of the universe took on Himself the punishment for sin that every human being since the dawn of days deserves in order to offer to us eternal days we do not deserve. This is what makes that Friday "Good."

By the same token, I encourage you to study and experience in the present Ecclesiastes and the revelation of God and His plan for you that it offers. If you are Reformed in your theological thinking, search out the sovereignty of God and His effort to fill all of creation with the knowledge of His glory. If you are Wesleyan-Arminian, look for the relationship between the free will of man and the sanctifying work of the Spirit. If you are among the charismatic/Pentecostal brothers and sisters, find the weaknesses of a powerless life described in Ecclesiastes and let Koheleth lead you to reaffirm the filling of the Spirit as the empowerment for fruitful spiritual life in the world. Come as you are to Ecclesiastes and allow God to make of you as He will through His Word. I like what Michael Eaton notes when commenting on the canonicity of Ecclesiastes,

A certain circularity is inevitable, whatever one's position. The person who is hostile to claims for authority in any religious document will bring his presuppositions to Ecclesiastes and find his doubts confirmed. Another person who comes to the Bible, perhaps to Ecclesiastes, with openness is ready to hear and find that the Preacher speaks to him as never before.[67]

Come to Ecclesiastes and find what God has for you.

We will visit many of these background ideas, philosophies, and assumptions throughout the study. One assumption underlies all the others—as a teacher/preacher, the subject of this book intends to communicate a message of truth to those who read this book. As the divine author, God intends Ecclesiastes to communicate a message of truth as He knows it to those who need to know His truth. This book, like all the others in the Bible, intends to communicate the mind and heart of God to those caught in the human experience of a spiritually dead, morally corrupt, sin-enslaved world. Whether it serves as a warning, a judgment, or an invitation depends greatly on the work of the Holy Spirit in the reader's life and on the reader's willingness to receive the intended message.

Ecclesiastes requires and deserves prayerful consideration and Spirit-led, Spirit-directed attention. Don't jump to conclusions. Follow the line of thinking presented and ask hard questions, just as the Teacher does. Take the parts and hold them up to the light of God's glory and God's mission to fill the earth with the knowledge of His glory. You will find Ecclesiastes radiates with glory as you find God's truth laid bare in this book.

---

[67] Michael A. Eaton, "Ecclesiastes: An introduction and commentary," *Tyndale Commentary on the Old Testament*, vol. 18 (Downers Grove, IL: InterVarsity Press, 1983), 32.

Interpreting Ecclesiastes: A Few Final Considerations

Finally, as we bring this overview to a close and prepare to initiate our core study of the text of Ecclesiastes, for the sake of clarity, let us set forth our own research parameters. The purpose of this study can be summarized as follows:

> To demonstrate that real meaning in life is assigned by our Creator, not derived by human effort, and is experienced most joyfully in relationship with Him

Our method will be *to interpret the message of Ecclesiastes as a research report made by an informed social scientist reviewing conventional wisdom regarding the meaning of life.* Study questions are provided at the end of each chapter covering each section of the proposed outline. As for expected outcomes (objectives), I'll offer these four:

1. To develop a greater appreciation for the impact of divine sovereignty on personal experience
2. To commit life activities more completely as the pursuit of joy in the knowledge of the glory of the Lord
3. To actively seek rather than merely passively assume God's purpose in all of life and in each of life's moments
4. To embrace "fear God and keep his commandments" as the most precious means for experiencing personally the true meaning of life

The text copied below for study is taken from the 1988 Edition of the *Tanakh: The Holy Scriptures: The New JPS Translation According to the Traditional Hebrew Text*.[68] While most English translations are perfectly adequate for studying Ecclesiastes, we have chosen the JPS edition for the sake of getting an intrinsically Hebrew filter through

---

[68] *Tanakh: The Holy Scriptures: The New JPS Translation According to the Traditional Hebrew Text* (Philadelphia: Jewish Publication Society, 1988), 1441–1456.

which to view the various translation challenges inherent in bringing an ancient Hebrew text to the world of modern American English. It provides a rich linguistic soil from which our understanding of God and His purpose in the book of Ecclesiastes can grow and flourish and produce within us that harvest of grace and faith for which God sent forth His Word in the first place.

Study Questions

The questions included at the end of each chapter are intended to help you engage with the biblical text and the message of Ecclesiastes as a whole. There are also questions that will take you beyond the immediate text to themes and ideas presented by the text. Most questions will not be the "write down what you just read on the page" type questions. Enjoy!

Introduction

1. To begin, make a list of impressions you've encountered regarding Ecclesiastes.
2. Make note of your own reasons for studying Ecclesiastes.
3. There is a common cultural philosophy that assumes life, regardless of how good or poor the quality, lacks real meaning in any ultimate sense. What do you think about that idea?

Overview

1. "Koheleth" is the Hebrew term commonly translated "Teacher" or "Preacher" in English Bible versions. You will study more about this specific term in the next chapter. What is the relationship between the word "Koheleth" and the word "Ecclesiastes" as explained in this chapter?
2. What basic logical format does the book of Ecclesiastes follow? What experience do you have with this format?

Interpreting Ecclesiastes

1. Into what literary genre does Ecclesiastes fall? How does knowing the literary genre of a book assist in interpreting that book?
2. What is the primary goal of biblical wisdom literature?
3. How does knowing Ecclesiastes is "biblical wisdom literature" inform your interpretive outlook?
4. What effect does knowing the identity of an author have on interpreting their work?
5. What are some facts you've discovered about Solomon that are new to you? How does knowing more about the life of Solomon prepare you for interpreting Ecclesiastes?
6. Make your own chart showing the general flow of the scientific method. You may want to leave room on the chart for assigning the various passages of Ecclesiastes to their appropriate function on the chart.
7. List the six philosophical approaches mentioned in this study and provide a description of each in your own words.
8. Why do humanist philosophies fail to provide an adequate interpretive approach for understanding the message of Ecclesiastes?
9. How has exposure to this chapter in the study changed your expectations regarding studying Ecclesiastes?

CHAPTER 2

THE RESEARCHER AND THE
RESEARCH PROBLEM (1:1–2)

Introducing the Researcher and His Credentials (1:1)

¹ *The words of Koheleth son of David, king in Jerusalem.*

Presenting the presenter

You have perhaps heard the proposition that "experience is the best teacher?" The proverb has been around for a very, very long time. The phrase suggests that most people learn best by doing something rather than by reading about it. Apparently, it was the Romans who first found the idea worth writing about. Julius Caesar recorded the earliest known version of the proverb around 52 BC, "Experience is the teacher of all things." Pliny the Elder wrote in *Naturalis Historia* (c. AD 77), "Experience is the most efficient teacher of all things." The Roman historian Tacitus (c. AD 209) observed, "Experience teaches."[69] I bring this idea about experience and teaching to your attention because we are about to learn some things from a teacher

---

[69] Information excerpted from www.phrases.org.uk, from a response dated June 29, 2003. The site notes *Wise Words and Wives' Tales: The Origins, Meanings and Time Honored Wisdom of Proverbs and Folk Sayings Olde and New,* Stuart Flexner and Doris Flexner (Avon Books, New York, 1993) as the source for the article.

who has both the wisdom and the experience to back up what he presents.

I was a biology major in college. The final class I took before I graduated was Comparative Anatomy. The class was devoted to studying the similarities and differences between anatomical structure and development in the bodies of various species of animals, birds, and fish. The professor focused his research efforts on comparing the embryonic development between the inner ear of humans and reptiles (snakes, in particular) in an effort to demonstrate an evolutionary connection between the two. Much of his time back in those days was spent preparing cross sections of snake embryos at various stages of development for study under the microscope. When it came to comparative anatomy, this man knew what he was talking about! I learned a great deal from him as a result of his expertise and his competence in sharing what he knew. Although I was not then (nor am I now) a fan of evolutionary theory, I came to understand the ideas of evolution from someone who held those ideas closely and operated his entire life work in the context of that theoretical perspective. Teachers who know from experience what they are teaching make the best teachers.

A narrator opens Ecclesiastes by presenting the presenter and his credentials. The narrator seems to want us to be comfortable that we have embarked on learning with a competent teacher. The identification and credentials regarding Koheleth are clues in the introduction as to what we might expect to follow.

Whether or not the narrator and Koheleth are the same person is unclear. It would not be the first time a person introduced himself/herself to an audience using the third person, but for casual audiences, it does seem a bit awkward. When I was writing my doctoral thesis for Bethel Seminary, one of the "rules" that stumped me for months was that the introduction could not be written in the first person. In my mind, however, I needed to tell a first-person account that provided the background for the entire study. There was an academic standard for third-person perspective when inaugurating the report. I finally got permission from my advisor to use the first-person story but maybe Koheleth didn't?

More likely, Koheleth is presenting a formal report and uses the third person to introduce himself. Or, perhaps, the author, whoever he is, uses a narrator to introduce Koheleth in order to retain some control over what Koheleth says and does, as a novelist would for characters they are developing in their story so that Koheleth presents what appears to be his own thoughts but are actually the thoughts and intents of the behind-the-scenes author. In either case, the result is to identify the content of the report with Koheleth, who, by description, appears to be identified with Solomon, son of David, king in Jerusalem.

Who, or what, is Koheleth?

Let's assume that by fact or intent, Solomon and Koheleth are one and the same and that a narrator has been used to introduce Koheleth to his audience as the primary communicator. If Solomon is the author/presenter, why call him Koheleth? Why not just call him Solomon and be done with all the mystery? The answer lies in the probability that Koheleth is not a name but a title, a label for a position or function within the community.

Koheleth is used seven times within Ecclesiastes (1:1, 2, 12; 7:27; 12:8, 9, 10). In two instances (1:1, 12), Koheleth is identified as the son of David, king in Jerusalem. In two instances (1:2; 12:8), he is the presenter of the research problem. In one instance (7:27), Koheleth is presented as the meticulous researcher of "the reason of things." In the last two instances (12:9, 10), further characteristics of Koheleth's function in the community are listed. Kaiser notes that in 12:8, in the Hebrew, "koheleth" appears with the definite article ("the koheleth") providing further evidence that "Koheleth" should be understood as a title rather than a proper name.[70]

I had a name once. My mother gave me a short four-letter name that was unlikely to be reduced to a nickname. She named me "Dale." And that turned out to be a very fine name, a reasonably adequate

---

[70] Walter C. Kaiser Jr., "Ecclesiastes: Total Life," *Everyman's Bible Commentary* (Chicago: Moody Press, 1979), 24.

name right up until I became the undershepherd of a small Baptist congregation in rural northeast Minnesota. I got a new name when I embarked on that adventure. I became "Pastor."

Sometimes, I am "Pastor Dale." Most times I am simply "Pastor." Once, in front of the whole congregation and quite accidentally, my wife called me "Pastor Honey." When she recovered from her misstatement and everyone else stopped laughing, she immediately claimed exclusive rights to that moniker and no one else has dared use it since!

Koheleth treats his title much like I treat the word pastor. Yes, it is a title, a label, that describes my function within the community, but after twenty-five years, "Pastor" is so much my identity that it has become my name (though, from time to time, it gets shortened to "Rev" or "Preach"). So it is for Solomon who is Koheleth both in practice and in person.

That leads us to ask, if Koheleth is a title, what does the title mean? The use of "Preacher" and "Teacher" as translations for Koheleth in various English versions reveals an attempt to get at the heart of this word. Functionally, the word means either "one who collects or assembles" or "one who does something in the assembly."[71] Given the expanded description in 12:9–10 of Koheleth's role in the community as "instructor of the people" and as a gatherer of useful and truthful sayings for public education and given the example of 1 Kings 8:1[72] where Solomon "assembled" the people, it seems best to understand the Koheleth as one who gathers wisdom for the purpose of public dissemination. Since the subject presented is "wisdom" in the biblical sense, we can understand that the purpose of the assembling, of both people and subject, is for spiritual edification in the pursuit of a covenant relationship with God.

---

[71] Fox, 3.

[72] "Then Solomon assembled the elders of Israel and all the heads of the tribes, the leaders of the fathers' houses of the people of Israel, before King Solomon in Jerusalem, to bring up the ark of the covenant of the *Lord* out of the city of David, which is Zion" (1 Kings 8:1 ESV).

What about the "words"?

The book we are beginning to study is a book of words. We are told definitively that these are "the words of Koheleth." Knowing now what we know of Solomon the person and Solomon the Koheleth, what might we expect of these words? We ought to expect that what follows is a collection of wisdom presented to the public for their consideration and edification in their pursuit of covenant relationship with God. If our expectation aligns with the evidence provided, we ought to expect to be instructed in life about life for the sake of life in relation to God, the giver and sustainer of life.

With the opening words of this book, we are denied the opportunity to dismiss this teaching as depressing or irrelevant to our lives as followers of Jesus. This gathered wisdom has a single purpose, to lead us on a personal journey to discover for ourselves some truth about God and our relationship with Him.

I'm reminded of the evangelism strategy Ray Comfort uses on the streets of southern California. Rather than try to convince the average person of the goodness and relevance of Christ to their daily lives, Ray takes people right to the heart of the issue of salvation. He takes them to God's statement of divine standards for righteousness, the Ten Commandments. Ray will ask someone if they have ever lusted or taken something that didn't belong to them or cursed using the Lord's name. Invariably, the answer is yes. Ray then points out to them the logical conclusion that they have broken God's Law, are lawbreakers, and are therefore guilty and subject to punishment under God's Law. He points out that the name for lawbreaking is "sin" and that the penalty for sin is death.[73]

In the next step, for those who willingly follow the logic, Ray poses the question, "Are you, as a lawbreaker, subject to the penalty of guilt?" When the answer is yes, Ray explains the grace of God outlined in the scripture, how God sent His Son Jesus to live the life we cannot live (sinless) and to die on our behalf the death we deserve.

---

[73] "For the wages of sin is death, but the free gift of God is eternal life in Christ Jesus our Lord" (Romans 6:23 ESV).

He lays out for them why we need a Savior and how God meets that need with Christ. Then he asks the closing question, "Will you accept by faith that God sent Christ to die for you so that you could live with God forever?"

Ray Comfort gathers the "sayings" of God that we call the gospel and he gathers the people of southern California. He brings them together to lead them on a personal journey to discover for themselves the truth about God and their relationship to Him. Ray Comfort, in his day, simply follows the function of Koheleth in that day. Often, the people to whom Ray Comfort reaches out refuse the logic of grace and gospel and walk away unchanged. They are not looking for Christ in the words of the preacher, and subsequently, they do not find Him. It need not be so with us, as we study Ecclesiastes. God is here, in these words, so let us allow Koheleth and his words to bring us together with God for His glory and for our good!

Identifying the Research Problem: The Experimental Hypothesis (1:2)

[2] *Utter futility!—said Koheleth—Utter futility! All is futile!*

Real-life conditions for the hypothesis

Futility. Meaninglessness. Emptiness. Vanity. Each of these English words is used to translate the Hebrew word used emphatically by Koheleth in this verse.[74] The assertion is bold. Intense. Unexpected. Poignantly familiar. Not everyone reflects on their lives as a balance of successes and failures, good deeds and bad, joys and sorrows, advances and setbacks, that when taken all together add up to a big, fat zero. But some people do. And if we're being honest here,

---

[74] Fox, 3. "The key term is *hevel. Havel havalim* is literally "vapor of vapors," which is to be understood as a superlative, "utter vanity, utter futility" (NJPS), or (as I prefer) "utterly senseless" or "utterly absurd." Here the superlative is heightened by fluid, alliterative, repetition: Havel havalim, 'amar ha-kohelet, havel havalim, ha-kol havel. The reiteration of hevel emphasizes the universality of this truth and also the pervasiveness of this quality."

there may be a moment for all of us when we wonder deep within ourselves, "Is this all there is? Why am I here? Has anything I've done really amounted to anything? What is the meaning of this? What is this really all about?"

Various life events stand out like markers and beg these kinds of questions. A marriage, a death, a sudden realization of how much gray has overtaken that once youthful head of hair in the mirror. Any of these can lead to one of those moments of clarity that trap us temporarily between mortality and meaning with questions too big for pat answers.

A wise man knows these questions exist and that they will catch up with each of us at some time or another. A wise woman remains nonplused in such a moment, realizing the opportunity at hand, choosing to mine the moment for the treasures hidden just beyond the obvious. I believe this is Koheleth's position at the beginning of his report. He is not just lamenting the course of his life. He takes the opportunity presented by the course of his life to evaluate and analyze in light of a single hypothesis the true meaning of life, and he does so for the public benefit.

The nature of a scientific hypothesis

A hypothesis is a proposition based on observation that has been chosen for testing through extensive experimentation. Hypotheses, by definition, cannot be proven "right" because it is impossible to guarantee that somewhere in the universe, there is not some experiment that will prove it wrong. Ellie Simpson quotes Einstein as saying, "A thousand scientists can't prove me right, but one can prove me wrong."[75] Her explanation helps,

> Absolutely proving an hypothesis is impossible. As to prove something implies it can never be wrong. However, well designed scientific

---

[75] Ellie Simpson, https://ellies1mpson.wordpress.com/2011/12/08/is-it-possible-to-prove-a-research-hypothesis. Accessed December 3, 2018.

experiments can allow researchers to strongly
infer from empirical evidence that their hypothesis is correct.[76]

Significantly, no number of experiments can absolutely prove a
hypothesis, but it only takes one observation to refute the hypothesis
and prove it wrong. Koheleth offers us futility as a problem to be
rebutted by calculated trial. Rieger, writing to help us understand
Ecclesiastes as research, provides a contemporary parallel for us when
he explains that current "ethnographic research is open-ended, context specific, and interpretive in nature, aiming to develop understanding rather than establish statistical relationships."[77]

Koheleth's intent is to examine his own efforts at finding meaning in life in order to develop understanding both for himself and for
his audience. He measures his efforts against a commonly accepted
maxim, "Life is meaningless." Rieger points out (by quoting Chase)
the commonality of using one's own life as a resource for teaching
lessons to others. He notes contemporary autoethnographers "turn
the analytic lens on themselves...and write, interpret, and/or per-
form their own narratives about culturally significant experiences."[78]
Based on self-experience and self-observation, and for our own spiritual benefit, Koheleth offers us a hypothesis for analysis.

Examining Koheleth's hypothesis

A few questions of our own will guide our perspective regarding
Koheleth's proposition. First, we ought to understand for ourselves

---

[76] Ibid.

[77] Rieger, 44. Ethnographic researchers "seek to understand people's view of
the world; how they create and understand their daily lives and what meaning people construct around life events, assuming there are always multiple
perspectives."

[78] Ibid. Original footnote by Rieger. E. Chase, "Narrative inquiry: Multiple
lenses approaches and voices," in *Qualitative Educational Research: Readings in
Reflexive Methodology and Transformative Practice*, ed. W. Luttrell (New York,
NY: Routledge, 2010).

what Koheleth means by the word "futility." Next, we have to examine whether there is reasonable cause to call the cry of "futility" a proposition, a proposal, and a question for examination rather than an assertion representing Koheleth's views. If it is a proposal, then there is no inherent need to understand Ecclesiastes as Koheleth's personal polemic against the course of his life. If "utter futility" is a hypothesis and not an assertion, then we have room to explore whether Koheleth embraces this view or simply offers it for guided exploration. If this is an assertion, then we have no such room for possibility. Finally, it would seem wise to ask whether there is evidence within the body of the report to understand that Koheleth sets limits on the inclusivity of the word "all." Any such limits may have bearing on the interpretation of the message of the book as a whole and on the understanding of "utter futility" as an assertion or a proposition.

"Futility" and other key words in Ecclesiastes. If a picture paints a thousand words, then some words paint better pictures than others. Want to know what Koheleth means by "futility"? He tells us (repeatedly) that "futility" is "chasing after wind." Futility is energy expended in pointless effort. "Futility" is Sisyphus doomed in Hades to forever roll the boulder uphill only to lose it to gravity at the crest of the hill and have to start all over again, perpetually. "Futility" is the German shepherd dog, face into the wind, snapping his jaws to catch the movement across his face, but still going hungry. "Futility" is sadder, harder things, like five hours of hard labor to deliver a stillborn child or years of hard work and scrimping and saving only to lose the uninsured diamond from your anniversary band on the third loop of the roller coaster at Adventure Land.

Futility, vanity, emptiness, and meaningless—these all translate the Hebrew word *hevel.* The JPS version of the Hebrew Bible also uses the words "senseless, absurd, fleeting, illusory, and frustration" to translate *hevel.* The idea here is of a world that is trite and worthless, a world that is all too brief to accomplish anything of lasting value, a world that, no matter how great the intellectual prowess, simply cannot be understood. It is a world where life rarely goes as it should, falling into the senseless and absurd.[79]

Craig G. Bartholomew notes that *hevel* literally means breath or vapor, and he cites an occurrence in Isaiah 57:13 where *hevel* parallels the Hebrew word for "wind" (*ruach*),[80] which adds no little interest to Koheleth's use of "futility" and "wind" in the same sentence often in Ecclesiastes.

What we find in Ecclesiastes is that *hevel* fills both a physical and metaphorical role and our interpretation will by necessity have to account for both functions. It is the drive to decide the meaning of *hevel* based on the evidence at hand that I believe drives the research reported in Ecclesiastes. What does it mean that "all is futility"?

We've noted that "futility" is a key word in Ecclesiastes. It is used thirty-eight times in twelve chapters. Before we move on to other key words used by the author, take a moment or two and think about this—the apostle Paul notes in what may be the only allusion to Ecclesiastes in the New Testament that futility is characteristic of all creation.[81] The word translated "futility" in the ESV rendering is the same Greek word that the Septuagint uses for "futility" in Ecclesiastes.[82] Thinking in an "ultimate cause" sense, what is the ultimate reason for "futility" in all creation and human experience, according to the scripture? In other words, what really lies at the root and makes life meaningless for any of us?

The answer, of course, to the question of root cause, is sin. The wages of sin is death, but the fruit of sin is futility. Sin rejects God. Sin denies the reality of God's sovereign claim upon all He has cre-

---

[79] Fox, xix. This is the view propounded by Fox from whose commentary much of this paragraph is paraphrased.

[80] Craig C. Bartholomew, "Ecclesiastes," *Baker Commentary on the Old Testament Wisdom and Psalms*, ed. Tremper Longman III (Grand Rapids, MI: Baker Academic, 2009), 105.

[81] "For the creation waits with eager longing for the revealing of the sons of God. For the creation was subjected to futility, not willingly, but because of him who subjected it, in hope that the creation itself will be set free from its bondage to corruption and obtain the freedom of the glory of the children of God" (Romans 8:19–21, ESV).

[82] Longman, 39.

ated, including the human will, the human life, the human destiny, and the human purpose. Futility is the result of sin, leaving God out of the very lives He created for His glory.

Futility denies Him, through faithlessness, the right to use lives He created for His purpose to fill the earth with the knowledge of His glory.[83] Though sin does not stymie God, it stymies fruitfulness and meaning in us. The entire motivation of Koheleth's research is to prove that all the activities of life, when God is omitted, amount to sin (in this case a lifelong effort to find satisfaction without God) and gain nothing more than the fruit of sin—emptiness, vanity, and futility. To find meaning in life, one must find the rightful place of God in life.

As long as we are focusing on "futility" as a key word in Ecclesiastes, we will profit from making note of other words the author uses with impact. I appreciate the list from Michael V. Fox that includes toil (*'amal*), work (*'asah*), portion (*chelek*), futile (*hevel*), wisdom (*hokhmah*), pursuit of wind (*re'ut ruach*), pleasure (*simchah*), good (*tov*), and profit/value (*yitron*).[84] Douglas Sean O'Donnell has a list of his own, "vanity (thirty-eight times), wise/wisdom (fifty-three times), God (forty times), toil (thirty-three times), give/gives/given (sixteen times), death (mentioned or alluded to twenty-one times), sun as in 'under the sun' (thirty-three times), and joy and derivatives such as rejoice, enjoy, enjoys, enjoyed, and enjoyment (seventeen times)—as well as key themes such as God and man, futility and fleetingness, time and chance, gain and portion, work and toil, wealth and poverty, power and domination, wisdom and folly, justice and judgment, eating, drinking, and pleasure."[85]

---

[83] "For the earth will be filled with the knowledge of the glory of the LORD as the waters cover the sea" (Habakkuk 2:14, ESV). This is God's "mission statement" for all His work within the realm of creation. All that God does in creation, He does so that ultimately all that is other than He is will be filled with the experiential knowledge of Him in all His perfections.

[84] Fox, xviii–xxi.

[85] D. S. O'Donnell, "Ecclesiastes," in *Reformed Expository Commentary*, eds. R. D. Phillips, P. G. Ryken, and I. M. Duguid (Phillipsburg, NJ: P&R Publishing, 2014), 10.

Assertion of perspective or proposal for study? Warren Berger wrote an article for the *New York Times* in July of 2016. The editors gave the article the title "The Power of 'Why?' and 'What If?'" Midway into that short essay about the trend in large companies to encourage curiosity among executives, the author writes,

> Companies in many industries today must contend with rapid change and rising uncertainty. In such conditions, even a well-established company cannot rest on its expertise; there is pressure to keep learning what's new and anticipating what's next. It's hard to do any of that without asking questions.[86]

Apparently, asking "what if" opens the door to innovative thinking, new discoveries, improved products and delivery systems, and a host of other personal and market benefits.

This study in Ecclesiastes is built on the shoulders of a single "what if" question. It occurred to me while reading Ecclesiastes at my father-in-law's dining room table in Arab, Alabama. I was reading in a copy of the *Tanakh* I just happened to spy and buy in a Half-Price Books store with my niece and nephew a few days earlier in Indianapolis. I was overwhelmed with the social negativity I experienced on Facebook at the time, was concerned about the effectiveness of my own personal pastoral ministry at the time, and was discouraged by some developments in my family of origin that appeared unresolvable. I turned to Ecclesiastes mostly because misery loves company, and I was miserable and looking for company.

As I began to read through Ecclesiastes with blue pen in hand, I started drawing lines on the pages where I thought there should be logical section divisions. Halfway through the book, I stopped, shook my head, and thought, *This doesn't make sense. Why does the author do*

---

[86] Warren Berger, *New York Times* (July 2, 2016), https://www.nytimes.com/2016/07/03/jobs/the-power-of-why-and-what-if.html. Accessed October 22, 2018.

this here and not over there? It was that jog in the flow of the logic, that often commented upon enigma for which Ecclesiastes is famous, that led me to ask, *What if I'm reading this all wrong? What if this is not a personal complaint for me to identify with, but a professional challenge for me rise up to? What if this is a teacher presenting the evidence of my life as I currently feel it and challenging me to arrive at the conclusion that none of the evidence can provide? What if "utter futility" is not a resigned assertion, but a calculated proposition?* A whole new world of meaning and application opened for me with one small "what if."

Koheleth offers "utter futility" not as an assertion to be embraced, like a man accepting the inevitable retreat of his hairline from his forehead, but as a proposition to be explored and proven or disproved and discarded for a more tenable truth. Many commentators assert the Koheleth is providing personal opinion, or answers, and that it is the narrator who saves the day by rejecting Koheleth's cynicism in favor of divine grace. That certainly could be, but what if? What if Koheleth is posing a question disguised as an assertion? What if the implied question goes something like this, "You all say life is 'utterly futile,' but is it? Is it true that life is utterly futile or is there another truth that is the source of meaning for our lives?" What if this is the grand research question the eminently wisest social scientist of the day has pursued and is now reporting to us with the hope that the survey report will persuade us to adopt an entirely different conclusion?

I wasn't sure where to go with the idea, so I turned back to Ecclesiastes and started to read the book again from the beginning. In the course of the second read through, I began to expand the idea of "utter futility" as a proposition to Ecclesiastes as a research report that followed the general outline of the modern scientific method. The outline took shape, and now we will follow it to examine and learn from one man's report of an intentional investigation into an observable "truth" that naturally follows the same general flow a science report does.

How inclusive is "all"? "Utter futility," said Koheleth. "All is futile!" Longman reads these words and determines that "the book of Ecclesiastes leaves no doubt about Qohelet's ultimate conclusion—

everything is completely meaningless."[87] That seems pretty straight-forward, but what if "all" or "everything" doesn't mean "all all"? What if there is, within the pages of this book, a quantifier that qualifies how much "all" Koheleth intends us to understand as context for this experiment? What if the author doesn't mean for us to think he is talking about all that exists, but all of a portion of what exists? What if "all" is defined by the parameters he sets as the limits of the subjects of his observation/study?

There is no doubt the author wants the reader to think inclusively, but by leaving something important out of consideration until the very end, does not that strategic absence make the point that "everything" is not futile, that there is something that is not futile though everything else is? Does proclaiming "all is futile" not make me want to shout, "Wait! 'Everything?' Isn't there something that isn't futile?" That question sets me up for the experiment where "everything" is surveyed only to discover that of all that exists only one thing is not futile. And does not the repetition of the proposition (more than thirty-five times in the book) serve both to increase the credibility that all is futile and my relief when I discover at the end of the experiment that there is, after all, something that is not futile at all? The very structure of the content of the book suggests that "utter futility" may be more proposition than declaration.

And then there is the qualifier he introduces in verse 3 and repeats thirty-two times as either "under the sun" or "under heaven." Koheleth deliberately limits "all" to all that exists in the physical realm of creation and not the heavenly or spiritual realm. It is "the fallen world that both the secular and nonsecular share as sinners under God's curse."[88] "All" is defined by the researcher setting the limits on his experiment to the realm within which human beings exist from conception to death. He purposely excludes God and anything genuinely related to God, like the Law and the covenant relationship that stems from faithful observance of the Law, from consideration

---

[87] Longman, 61.
[88] O'Donnell, 17.

as "futility." Every human effort, every condition of human existence that is derived from human effort, is identified as futile, but that which comes from God or relates to God is "gift."[89]

Koheleth's definition of "all" is clearly earthbound! The reason for that is supplied by taking verse 2 as a proposition and not as an assertion. Koheleth intentionally sets up the limits of the experiment to point us to the only real conclusion, the only meaningful conclusion, which he gives in the final sentence of the book (12:13–14, JPS):

> The sum of the matter, when all is said and done: Revere God and observe His commandments! For this applies to all mankind: that God will call every creature to account for everything unknown, be it good or bad.

We could skip from 1:3 to 12:13 and find the entire book in two sentences. Everything in between amounts to reducing the journey before us to the divine rather than mundane option. All is futile, except this—knowing and loving God as He has revealed Himself to be and doing so as the reason for your existence.

We will delve more completely into the nature and function of the epilogue when we get to that point in the study. It is not a last-minute feeble attempt to make sense of the book. It is the point the author intended for Koheleth to make all along. This experiment, from hypothesis to conclusion, has the single purpose to disprove the proposition that real meaning is absent from human existence. The entire experiment supports the assertion that real meaning in life is assigned (or derived) from the Creator and not from anything in creation. That is the "big picture" that must be in place to appreciate Ecclesiastes as a detailed report of one very wise man's extensive intellectual investigation into the meaning of life.

---

[89] For example, "That whenever a man does eat or drink and get enjoyment out of all his wealth, it is a gift of God" (Ecclesiastes 3:13, JPS).

Study Questions

Presenting the presenter

1. Go back to the section on Solomon in the introduction and review what you know about this man, Solomon, son of David, king in Jerusalem.
   a. Given what you know, what would you expect to be true of what he writes?
   b. What would you expect to be true of any methodology he proposes or describes?
   c. What would you expect to be true of any conclusions he draws regarding his observations?
2. Using a Bible dictionary (or other source), define "Koheleth." How does this word help us understand the purpose and content of Ecclesiastes?

Identifying the research problem

1. Choose a key word from the two lists that are referenced in this section. Using a concordance or a Bible software program, make a list of the occurrences of each word as it appears in Ecclesiastes.
   a. What does their location and usage in the text tell you about the meaning of these words relative to understanding the message of Ecclesiastes?
   b. How do they contribute to the message?
   c. How do these words connect the message of Ecclesiastes to your life and experience?
2. The word "futile" occurs thirty-eight times in Ecclesiastes. The word "God" or a reference to God is made forty times in the book. Speculate on any interpretive significance for the frequency difference. Give reasons why you think your speculation might be valid?

3. How do Koheleth and the Apostle Paul demonstrate that they share a common view of the current condition of the world?
4. How is futility related to sin? Give examples of how the relationship works.
5. How does identifying the root cause of futility give direction to your approach to Ecclesiastes?
6. What is the significance of interpreting "futility" as a proposition (hypothesis to be researched) rather than an assertion (truth to be embraced)?
7. Trace the use of "under the sun" or "under heaven" in Ecclesiastes. What do the occurrences of the phrase in each case suggest about the context for experimentation?

CHAPTER 3

THE REFINED RESEARCH QUESTION (1:3)

Refining the Research Question

3 "What real value is there for a man in all the gains he makes beneath the sun?"

Every good experiment needs a focused research question that limits the scope of the investigation. Such limits protect the experiment from becoming bogged down in secondary pursuits that may be worthwhile but offer little assistance in advancing understanding of the actual hypothesis in question. According to guidelines offered undergraduate students at George Mason University,

> Research questions help writers focus their research by providing a path through the research and writing process. The specificity of a well-developed research question helps writers avoid the "all-about" paper and work toward supporting a specific, arguable thesis.[90]

---

[90] "How to Write a Research Question," George Mason University Writing Center, https://writingcenter.gmu.edu/guides/how-to-write-a-research-ques-

Limiting the focus of an experiment (and its subsequent report) to a single question helps define the appropriate methodology for the experiment and the appropriate subjects for study. If one wants to study any evolutionary connection between human beings and slithering reptiles, one does not ask, "Do American bison have inner ear bones?" Instead a researcher will ask a more open-ended topic-specific question like, "What similarities exist between the embryonic development of the inner ear bones of snakes and human beings that might suggest an evolutionary connection?" Of all the possible facets and avenues of consideration that the proposition "all is futile" offers, Koheleth chooses this particular path, "What real value is there for a man in all the gains he makes beneath the sun?"

A good research question offers other benefits to both researcher and report reader. A good research question is a critical question that "leads to more questions, provokes discussion, concerns itself with audience and authorial intent, derives from a critical or careful reading of the text or understanding of a topic, addresses or ties in wider issues, or moves you out of your own frame of reference to your author's frame of reference."[91] The question Koheleth asks of his hypothesis clearly touches each of these criteria.

Embracing Personal Assumptions
Revealed by the Research Question

Defining a focused research question has the added benefit of enabling us to further identify presuppositions and assumptions we bring to the investigative effort. Look at the question as it's translated here. You've already read Ecclesiastes several times. You have had basic exposure to the message and method of the book already. Try rewriting the research question in your own words. What does your understanding of Koheleth's question reveal about your interpretive assumptions at this point?

---

tion. Downloaded October 27, 2018.

[91] "Refine Research Questions," University Libraries, University of Toledo, https://libguides.utoledo.edu/c.php?g=284276&p=1893702. Accessed October 27, 2018.

Consider Mark 8:36, "For what does it profit a man to gain the whole world and forfeit his soul?"[92] Here is a passage with which you are likely already familiar, a saying of Jesus regarding human effort "under the sun." What does the question Jesus asked have in common with the question Koheleth asked? Your answer is a potential presupposition to be aware of as you advance through this book.

Now consider Genesis 3:17–18,

> And to Adam he said, "Because you have
> listened to the voice of your wife and have eaten
> of the tree of which I commanded you, 'You shall
> not eat of it,' cursed is the ground because of you;
> in pain you shall eat of it all the days of your life;
> [18]thorns and thistles it shall bring forth for you;
> and you shall eat the plants of the field."[93]

How is the curse God administered to Adam in Eden after the Fall reflected in the words of Koheleth? When will man's labor under the sun once again have real value? Under what conditions is the curse lifted from human beings? The rest of creation? When will humanity realize the full measure of a curseless existence? Again, the answers you bring to these questions identify potential presuppositions that will guide your understanding of this book.

What of Jesus Himself and all you know about Him? We know something as fact that Koheleth knew only as promise. How does the life and death of Jesus Christ recontextualize the reality of which the Koheleth writes?

You can't help it. There is no reason you shouldn't bring your assumptions to Bible study. The key is to know them and know how they function as filters for you so that you don't sift out some detail that might give you a deeper insight into the text you are studying. Many people assume Koheleth is the ultimate pessimist, and they interpret this book based on that assumption and the evidence that

---

[92] Mark 8:36 (ESV).
[93] Genesis 3:17–18 (ESV).

appears to support that assumption. But what if he is no pessimist at all, but an open-minded scientist doing careful, intentional research on the human experience and meaning of life?

Examining Directive Clues in the Research Question

Koheleth asks, "What real value is there for a man in all the gains he makes under the sun?" There are three clues in this research question that help direct the focus, the scope, the method, and the subjects of the ensuing study.

The use of Hebrew yitron as an interpretive clue

The first clue is given to us in the phrase "real value," which other versions translate as "gain" (ESV), "advantage" (NASB), and "profit" (KJV). These words translate the Hebrew word *yitron* that occurs nine times in Ecclesiastes and nowhere else in the Old Testament. Some commentators find the English word "gain" too simple, since, within the scope of a single human life, a working person usually does gain something from their labor, more in adulthood than in infancy. The research question here is larger in scope and makes a bigger, lasting, eternal comparison; therefore, the *Tanakh* uses not only the word "value" but intensifies and specifies the value by using the phrase "real value" in its translation. "Real value" is value that both lasts and satisfies.

Yitron comes from a Hebrew root word *ytr* that means "to be left over" or "to remain." It is that which remains when everything else has been swept away. Koheleth's use of the word *yitron* may send us in an interesting direction in terms of understanding the methodology and intent of this book. Rephrasing the question with this expanded definition suggests a question that reads, "What is left for a man in all the gains he makes under the sun, when everything else is swept away?" A question like that would cause us to expect the experimental procedure to include a close examination of human effort with an intent to "sweep away" anything not permanent in order to see what remains after we have subjected it to such neutralizing scrutiny. We would also expect any conclusions to account for what legitimately remains after the exclusionary activity of our experiment. It would not surprise us to find in this research report a detailed review of efforts to sweep away the impermanent or unprofitable or disadvantageous in order to reveal in the conclusion that which has "real value."[94]

It is here, under the consideration of *yitron*, "real value," that we ought to clarify something for ourselves. What do we mean by "meaning"? I asked an adult Sunday school class that question and got words like "purpose," "significance," and "value." I went on to ask them whether it is possible for a person to have value, but not have value. The question was meant to force us to focus on the difference between our own self-perception and the perception others have of us, and which one leads to genuine, personal satisfaction and contentment. It is possible for a person to be valued by others yet sense no real value for themselves. Too many instances of self-harm can be traced back to this all-too-human dilemma.

"Meaning" and/or "real value" requires the affirmation of someone whose opinion matters to us. For most people, that someone is ultimately themselves. But what happens when no one greater than ourselves affirms our significance? Then we tend to reduce life to "meaninglessness." This is the heart of Koheleth's inquiry. Is there anyone or anything of greater authority than ourselves who can speak of our purpose in life in such a way that our soul is satisfied with the response?

The boundary of human effort as an interpretive clue

The second interpretive clue this refined research question offers is found in the phrase "gains he makes." Here again a comparison of the various English versions helps us find some depth of understand-

---

[94] Matthew 7:24–27. Jesus's use of the parable of the wise man who built his house on the rock and the foolish man who built his house on the sand illustrates the nature of *yitron*. Wisdom, which Jesus defines as hearing and doing His words, is not swept away when the floods come. Foolishness, the antithesis of wisdom, those who hear but do not put his words into practice are swept away when the floods of life come. Wisdom, faith, and obedience to Jesus are the essence of *yitron*.

ing of this phrase. The ESV gives us "all the toil at which he toils." The NASB offers "all his work which he does." The NIV renders "all his labor at which he toils." The research question limits the object of experimental scrutiny to human effort and its effect on the human experience of meaning in the world and in life ("meaning" being suggested by *yitron*).[95] Koheleth is asking what difference our personal efforts makes on our experience of meaning and purpose in life. We therefore expect his methodology to include an examination of stated gains from work and to include an inquiry into whether all that toil and the gains received from it, truly, ultimately provide the anticipated outcome.

Human beings seek real value even though we engage in myriad insufficient life practices to disguise or displace our search. We amass wealth. We multiply degrees. We move from one marriage to the next, one relationship to the next, always hoping the next one will be better, that we'll avoid tomorrow the mistakes of yesterday and today. It takes real courage to do more than ask the question but to hold the activities of life up to the divine purpose and pursue an answer that is at once selfless and sovereign. What real value does my life as a pastor, a Christian, a husband, a son, a man, a friend, a resource have? Beyond the misty moment soon to vanish like so much fog on a summer day, what real difference does my existence make?

If I use only the framework of world and time, the answer I find robs me of hope, "Utter futility. All is futile." But if I raise the framework of the search to the reality of the creation purpose of the almighty, sovereign God, my search and the results take on a whole new dimension since, in that framework, "meaning" is not derived from my efforts, but assigned through my relationship to the Creator and His will. That is the message of Ecclesiastes.

---

[95] Fox, xviii. In the list where Fox defines key terms, he says of the Hebrew word *'amal* "the noun basically means arduous, wearisome labor." However, he acknowledges that the scope of "the word is so broad that life's experiences in general can be called 'toil.'"

The limits of physical creation as an interpretive clue

Finally, we should mention again, as the third clue, that this carefully stated research question limits the type and scope of human efforts under consideration. This is work done "under the sun." It is normal everyday effort as one might find anywhere, especially in one's own life.

Heavenly work, spiritual work, is not under consideration here, but every other effort made to find purpose for human existence is observed and evaluated. In effect, the entire work of man from birth to death is held up to the light of examination except for that work that is defined for him by God. Any effort that derives from self-interest, self-indulgence, self-exaltation, or self-expectation is evaluated. "Under the sun" provides a refined and limited scope within the whole of potential human experience for experimental consideration.

A good, well-focused, critical research question "leads to more questions, provokes discussion, concerns itself with audience and authorial intent, derives from a critical or careful reading of the text or understanding of a topic, addresses or ties in wider issues, or moves you out of your own frame of reference to your author's frame of reference." What other questions does Koheleth's research question lead you to ask? What discussion points come to mind? What does it suggest to you that Koheleth already knows about the topic at hand? What wider issues does the question beg to consider? How does knowing more about the vocabulary of the question move you from your own impressions of this question into the author's framework for the question?

Longman labels the question in verse 3 a rhetorical question that is asked "merely for effect."[96] What of the evidence presented so far convinces you to take a different approach to the question? What evidence might you still need, or what objections remain that you hope to see addressed? Make note of them and either pose them for group discussion or reference them throughout the study to see if other considerations along the way support skepticism or supply answers.

---

[96] Longman, p. 65.

Study Questions

Examining directive clues in the research question

1. Look up the nine verses where the word *yitron* is used in Ecclesiastes (1:3; 2:11, 13; 3:9; 5:8, 15 [9 and 16 in English versions], 7:12; 10:10–11).
   a. Considering what you now know about the word and considering the contexts in which you find it, what does the use of this term contribute to the message of Ecclesiastes?
   b. How does the repeated use guide and direct the flow of the experiment and the clarity of conclusions?
2. How would you define "meaning" in the Ecclesiastes context?
3. What examples can you think of in pop culture that point to the human search for "real value"?
4. What examples come to mind from your own search for significance?

CHAPTER 4

PRELIMINARY OBSERVATIONS (1:4–11)

> [4]*One generation goes, another comes,*
> *But the earth remains the same forever.*
> [5]*The sun rises, and the sun sets—*
> *And glides back to where it rises.*
> [6]*Southward blowing, Turning northward,*
> *Ever turning blows the wind;*
> *On its rounds the wind returns.*
> [7]*All streams flow into the sea,*
> *Yet the sea is never full;*
> *To the place [from] which they flow*
> *The streams flow back again.*
> [8]*All such things are wearisome:*
> *No man can ever state them;*
> *The eye never has enough of seeing,*
> *Nor the ear enough of hearing.*
> [9]*Only that shall happen*
> *Which has happened,*
> *Only that occur Which has occurred;*
> *There is nothing new Beneath the sun!*

[10]*Sometimes there is a phenomenon of which they say, "Look, this one is new!"—it occurred long since, in ages that went by before us.* [11]*The*

earlier ones are not remembered; so too those that will occur later will no more be remembered than those that will occur at the very end.

In northeast Minnesota where I live, winter can be quite fierce and spring desperately welcome. January freezes under subzero temperatures in the double digits. Snow that falls in December may still resist the sun's transforming grace into late April and even May, but once the winter reservoir of frozen water begins to melt, the runoff can be magnificent. Barren rock face cut along Minnesota Highway 61 surges with seasonal waterfalls returning winter's hostages to Lake Superior. There is one stretch of road west of Grand Marais, between Fall River and Cut Face Creek, that flows with a half dozen mini-Niagaras each year. You can count them as you stand east and look west down the road, each waterfall surging like a horizontal fountain from the sheer volume of water flowing over the stacked basalt ledge rock.

I sat there one day, my car parked in the emergency parking lane on the north side of the highway, just to take in the beauty of that moment. As I sat there silently marveling at the power of the water and the wonder of that shore-bound snow melting under the influence of the sun and returning with such fervor to its origin in the largest inland lake in the world, my reverie was shattered by a thought that betrayed my southern upbringing and general disease over the long, unrelenting northeast Minnesota winters. *Sure,* I thought, *it's beautiful now, but in just a few short months, you'll be shoveling it out of your driveway again.*

That's the interminable water cycle. Water in Lake Superior vaporizes and is carried by wind and cloud over land where, given the season, it condenses into rain or snow, falls to the earth, and returns to Lake Superior to start the journey all over again, year after year, season after season, blizzard after blizzard. Lake Superior neither dries up nor overflows. It gives and receives as it always has and always will until heaven and earth pass away and there are no more seas. It was just such a set of natural observations that Koheleth offers as the substrate from which his hypothesis and research question developed. Bartholomew paraphrases Koheleth's question as: "If [natural] history simply repeats itself and has no telos [goal], then of what value is labor?"[97]

Koheleth's Seven Observations

Michael V. Fox opens his commentary on Ecclesiastes with this thought about Koheleth, "The man speaking in Ecclesiastes, 'Koheleth,' sees things that are distressing to observe: the distortions and inequities that pervade the world; the ineffectuality of human deeds; the frailty and limitations of human wisdom and righteousness."[98]

Koheleth takes a long hard look around him, and what he sees drives him to ask the question, "What meaning is there in all this? What does a man gain for all the toil with which he toils under the sun?"

Koheleth marks seven observations relevant to his pursuit. He sees in the natural world these seven unrelenting cycles and conditions that seem to neutralize the significance of human effort—unchanging earth, rising sun, blowing wind, flowing water, seeing eyes, hearing ears, and recurring events. These are observable natural processes that continue perpetually without regard for any single human existence. Generation after generation of human beings are born and live and die, each striving in some way to make a difference upon the world in which they live. Still, no matter the magnitude of the monument building, the earth is neither larger nor smaller, nor does it pass through the heavens with greater or lesser speed, nor is a single day lengthened or shortened as a result of human effort. Despite the efforts of our existence, the earth remains the same forever.

The sun rises and makes its way across the heavens, but the appearance of progress is exactly that—an appearance—for on the next day, the sun will take up its course and return by the same path once again. The wind blows, advancing fiercely in one direction only to turn and waft gently in another, persistent whether in furor or

---

[97] Bartholomew, 112.
[98] Fox, ix.

respite, but never finished. The waters flow into the seas but the seas are never full. The eye never has enough of seeing nor the ear of hearing. There is nothing new under the sun. How do they say it? "Same old, same old."

The Role of Observations in the Pursuit of Truth

Observations, like these seven, drive scientific inquiry. Because of their important role in creating intellectual tension and raising questions, casual observations require the gathering of facts and analysis before they will fit accurately and with integrity into truthful conclusions. This conscientious data gathering and analysis is what makes thoughtful research of observations different from many opinions posted on Facebook and from the bulk of so much fake news that assaults our sensibilities on an almost daily basis. Research is the careful, thoughtful investigation of the realities suggested by observations. Ecclesiastes is one inspired man's report of his research into a question raised by consideration of specific observations.

If an observation is found through careful research to be factually true or accurate, then a new question arises, What do these observations mean and what impact do they have on my life, including ways in which I perceive my life, my place in the world, and the appropriate responses to reality? Consider these seven observations Koheleth has made about the world in which we live and the personal questions they raise. How might his observations affect your life and perceptions? How might these observations have affected your outlook prior to coming to faith in Jesus? How do they affect you now as a person devoted to following Jesus Christ as a faithful disciple? What do those two different responses suggest about God's purpose in including Ecclesiastes in the canon of the Scripture?

Science as the pursuit of empirical fact is often touted in our culture as a more certain explanation for the way things are than faith or divine revelation. Yet, here in Ecclesiastes, we have a book in the Scripture where "science," or at least scientific exploration, examines real-life observations, draws conclusions, and reports them to us for our consideration and adoption, which would be an act of faith. There is no opposition here, but a real opportunity for us to ask questions ourselves. For instance, given the general interpretation of Ecclesiastes, what happens when observations can be recorded in detail, and even mechanisms for existence can be described and explained, but the "why" remains unanswered?

Some Specific Observations of the Observations

We've made some general references to the seven observations as a unit, now let's take a look at the specifics relative to a few of them.

Cascading generations

Koheleth notes in verse four that "one generation goes, another comes, but the earth remains the same forever." Commentators continue to wrestle with the exact meaning of the word "generations" in light of the word order ("goes" then "comes"), but it appears that the underlying idea is that of cyclic motion where one thing replaces another repeatedly and continually.[99] I think the contrast between the cycle of going and coming and the permanence of the earth is the point. The cycle has no effect on the earth. This observation raises questions like these: "Doesn't each generation make its mark in some way?" and "Is there a difference, then, between making a difference and changing the earth?"

Uncatchable wind

Then, there's the "wind" in verse 6, blowing first one direction and then another, ceaselessly, coming and going without apparent source or goal. The wind provides a powerful metaphor throughout this book. Scan Ecclesiastes for each mention of "wind." The word is used thirteen times, usually in the phrase "pursuit of wind" or "chasing the wind" or "striving after wind." Have you ever tried to chase the wind in order to hold it in your hand? It cannot be held, so why

---

[99] Fox, 5.

chase it, the absurdist might ask. Koheleth implies from observing the wind the same question, If this metaphor should hold true, then what truly warrants the vast amount of energy, resources, and angst we so regularly invest in our lives?

Perpetual sunrise

Sometimes Koheleth uses single words to paint pictures that extend his larger point. Take the description of the daily travels of the sun through the sky in verse 5. In English, the sentence looks fairly ordinary. The sun rises, the sun sets, the sun rises from the same place the next day. But where JPS uses "glides" in the second half of the verse and where ESV uses "hastens," Koheleth uses a Hebrew word that means "to gasp, pant, pant after." It is a word that poses extreme effort used in a sentence that speaks of repetition without ultimate achievement. And what is extreme repetitive effort that achieves little or nothing, according to Koheleth? *Hevel.* Vanity. Futility. Meaningless. Empty.

Physical senses

There is another example here in Koheleth's brief survey of natural phenomena that contributes to his interest in the futility of all human effort under the sun.

> All such things are wearisome: No man can ever state them; The eye never has enough of seeing, nor the ear enough of hearing.[100]

The JPS translation makes an interpretive judgment here and includes the English word "such" in the opening sentence where no such word exists in the text. They do it, probably, to make sense of the fact that the entire poem (1:4–9) is talking about specific "things" but not "all things." They also, along with the ESV, translate the

---

[100] Ecclesiastes 1:8 (JPS).

word that is present in the text as "things." The word is *debarim*. It is the plural form of the Hebrew word for "word." (You've heard of the Ten Commandments? In Hebrew, each commandment is stated as a single word, *debar*. Taken all together, they are called the Ten Debarim, the Ten Words.)

The sentence could be translated as "All words are wearisome; man is unable to speak."[101] Koheleth means us to understand that no matter how many words we use, or how much effort we make to understand and express the realities that exist in the world around us, we will never explain it all sufficiently to put every question to rest for all time. We can wear ourselves out with the effort, but there will always be one more thing to see and one more word to describe and one more effort to understand.

Historical social amnesia

We also should be careful not to overlook the significance of verses 10 and 11 and the observation Koheleth makes there. Koheleth describes a phenomenon we can call historical social amnesia. This means that things are new to us only because what has come before us has been forgotten. One morning, an eight-year-old in our Sunday school brought in an amazing discovery he had made at a local recycle/thrift store. He set it on the table and opened it up. The other children were enthralled.

"What is it?" they asked.

"Can I do it?"

"How does it work?"

Elijah inserted a sheet of paper and began to hit keys and type nonsense on the old typewriter, a device the children had not seen and did not recognize even though they were very well familiar with computer keyboards and printers. Not long ago, I used carbon paper as part of a sermon illustration related to Paul's challenge to the Corinthians, "imitate me as I imitate Christ." I couldn't find carbon paper to bring as an example and no one in the congregation younger than twelve even knew what I was talking about.

---

[101] Fox, 6.

Historical social amnesia is the tendency as a culture to forget what has come before us. This tendency to forget has implications for our own personal devotional development as well as implications for the ministry of the church and the gospel in the world. Have you noticed how there seems to be barely an echo of Bible literacy in the culture where once at least the general contents of the Bible were widely recognized even if not believed or accepted?

A woman I know told me the story of entering a bookstore to find a Christmas book for her grandchildren. *Frosty the Snowman*, *Santa Claus*, and the *Grinch* filled the shelves but she did not find what she was looking for. She approached the young man standing at the cash register and asked whether they had any books about the birth of Jesus in their Christmas inventory. With total innocence and a straight face decorated with a puzzled look, he responded and asked, "What does the birth of Jesus have to do with Christmas?"

Today the majority of people in our country (and perhaps our churches) cannot name all ten of the commandments and, perhaps more significantly, have little idea why they are even important. What was once considered common knowledge is now cultural mystery. The echo of biblical literacy has grown silent. We have forgotten what came before, what we once knew, what we once held as universally true. I have heard of a movement to relegate the Nazi genocide of Jews in World War II to fiction. We are overcome with historical social amnesia.

Koheleth and Natural Equilibrium

In the end, Koheleth's primary concern with this poem is not the repetitive nature of natural phenomena, but with the futility of human effort. His observations of the natural world seem to have raised a question for him that demands investigation. All that we do on the face of the earth during our lifetime fails "to achieve anything new and can thus attain no true 'profit' [real value]."[102] If even the natural, global processes set in place by the creative hand of God

---

[102] Fox, 6.

make no lasting change upon the earth through the endless ages of their existence, how can humanity with all our limitations of strength and reason and time expect more than futility?

The first law of thermodynamics, a significant explanation of realities related to energy in the physical universe, states that energy can neither be created nor destroyed, energy can only be transferred or changed from one form to another.[103] The amount of energy present in the universe is static. As the first law of thermodynamics describes the static state of energy in the universe, Koheleth describes the static state of human effort in the universe of "meaning." Koheleth surmises from his observations that the incessant natural cycle that proceeds perpetually without net gain suggests that "feeble human exertions cannot be expected to affect the course of events"[104] in any ultimate (and therefore meaningful) sense.

If that which is created by God and sustained by God does not gain through its effort, then what hope of gain does man have in his efforts, asks Koheleth. It is this tension marked by the fruitlessness inherent in the world and the firm belief in the sovereign God of creation that drives the pursuit of truth by experiment in Ecclesiastes. This is the same tension all people who live by faith in God must experience in this world. It is a tension that cries out for resolution but will only find that resolution where the Koheleth finally concludes it is to be found, in faith and obedience to God.

Bartholomew closes his comments on this section with this conclusion,

> Theologically, the poem therefore raises the issue of how we view history and of where we locate our identity or meaning in life. Scripture and the Christian tradition rightly recognize, with this poem, that a cyclical view of history is hopeless, and also alert us to the fact that we can-

---

[103] https://courses.lumenlearning.com/introchem/chapter/the-three-laws-of-thermodynamics. Accessed October 30, 2018.
[104] Fox, 4

not root our identity in others and their remembrance of us.[105]

So let's turn the question around that Koheleth asks, relative to these observations. If, scanning the horizon of natural history, Koheleth poses as his hypothesis "utterly futile, all is futile" and then offers the question, "What real value is there for a man in all the gains he makes beneath the sun?" as a direction for inquiry, I say we reverse it and ask, "If all is meaningless, then what is meaningful?" And Koheleth will answer that question for us once he has worked through all the meaningless possibilities.

Study Questions

1. How would you restate these seven observations if you were writing from your own experience and observations about the world in which you live?
2. What parallels between you and Koheleth can you identify?
3. What are some areas of personal and cultural development in your observation that show signs of historical social amnesia?
4. What personal choices arise when the effects of historical social amnesia are identified?

---

[105] Bartholomew, 117.

CHAPTER 5

METHODOLOGY AND INITIAL CONCLUSIONS (SERIES 1) (1:12–2:26)

Koheleth Describes His Experimental Methodology (1:12–2:12)

¹²*I, Koheleth, was king in Jerusalem over Israel.* ¹³*I set my mind to study and to probe with wisdom all that happens under the sun.—An unhappy business, that, which God gave men to be concerned with!* ¹⁴*I observed all the happenings beneath the sun, and I found that all is futile and pursuit of wind:*

¹⁵*A twisted thing that cannot be made straight,*
A lack that cannot be made good.

¹⁶*I said to myself: "Here I have grown richer and wiser than any that ruled before me over Jerusalem, and my mind has zealously absorbed wisdom and learning." * ¹⁷*And so I set my mind to appraise wisdom and to appraise madness and folly. And I learned—that this too was pursuit of wind:*

¹⁸*For as wisdom grows, vexation grows;*
To increase learning is to increase heartache.

I said to myself, "Come, I will treat you to mer-
riment. Taste mirth!" That too, I found, was futile.

²*Of revelry I said, "It's mad!"*
Of merriment, "What good is that?"

³*I ventured to tempt my flesh with wine, and*
to grasp folly, while letting my mind direct with wis-
dom, to the end that I might learn which of the two
was better for men to practice in their few days of life
under heaven. ⁴*I multiplied my possessions. I built*
myself houses and I planted vineyards. ⁵*I laid out*
gardens and groves, in which I planted every kind
of fruit tree. ⁶*I constructed pools of water, enough*
to irrigate a forest shooting up with trees. ⁷*I bought*
male and female slaves, and I acquired stewards.
I also acquired more cattle, both herds and flocks,
than all who were before me in Jerusalem. ⁸*I further*
amassed silver and gold and treasures of kings and
provinces; and I got myself male and female singers,
as well as the luxuries of commoners—coffers and
coffers of them. ⁹*Thus, I gained more wealth than*
anyone before me in Jerusalem. In addition, my wis-
dom remained with me: ¹⁰*I withheld from my eyes*
nothing they asked for, and denied myself no enjoy-
ment; rather, I got enjoyment out of all my wealth.
And that was all I got out of my wealth.

¹¹*Then my thoughts turned to all the fortune*
my hands had built up, to the wealth I had acquired
and won—and oh, it was all futile and pursuit of
wind; there was no real value under the sun! ¹²*For*
what will the man be like who will succeed the one
who is ruling over what was built up long ago?

Flour, water, and yeast. These three are enough to make bread. Maybe not the greatest-tasting bread, but bread nonetheless. But there is something missing. What is missing here are instructions. How much flour? How much water? How much yeast? In what ratios? At what temperatures should the ingredients be combined? Baked? How do they need to be mixed? For how long? How should they be treated once they are mixed?

The answers to these types of questions, in a cookbook, are called recipes. In a lab report, they are called experimental methodologies, the strategies and activities used to conduct the experiment, produce data, protect data, and draw conclusions. Having stated his hypothesis and his research question and noted some of the observations that spurred the research, Koheleth now describes his methodology for this first in a series of three experiments with which he will put his hypothesis to the test. He offers his method in four statements:

1. I set my mind to study and probe with all wisdom all that happens under the sun (1:13).
2. I set my mind to appraise wisdom and to appraise madness and folly (1:17).
3. I said to myself, "Come, I will treat you to merriment. Taste mirth!" (2:1).
4. I ventured to tempt my flesh with wine, and to grasp folly, while letting my mind direct with wisdom, to the end that I might learn which of the two was better for men to practice in their few days of life under heaven (2:3).

The first methodology statement acknowledges the scope of the experiment, the general nature of the experiment, and the tools involved in the experiment. The scope he defines as all the activities of human life, all that happens under the sun. The general nature of the experiment he describes as "study" and "probe," and the tools are two, his "mind" and "all wisdom."

The scope of the experiment

We've already seen something of what Koheleth wants us to understand about the scope of his inquiry when we considered both the phrase "under the sun" and the word "all." It is important to remind ourselves that this experiment is intentionally horizontal in scope and perspective. As the people of Israel, led by their priests, would ascend the hill of the Lord, the temple mount, to the temple itself to worship, they would stop periodically along the way and sing psalms specific to the occasion. Psalm 121 is one of those songs, called songs of ascent. The opening verse of Psalm 121:1 reads, "I lift up my eyes to the hills. From where does my help come? My help comes from the *LORD* who made heaven and earth." There are those moments in life that the very best direction we can look for help is upward to God.

But Koheleth does not look there. Not yet. Not here. Here he examines the plight of man not from God's perspective, but from that of one who shares in the same plight, from the perspective of a human being not looking up, but looking around. He limits the scope of his inquiry to human wisdom applied to the human condition. He is focusing on human life lived "under the sun" as one as sunburned as the rest of us.

Experimental variables. Any well-designed research experiment contains a dependent variable, independent variables, and often a control. The dependent variable is that one in which the researcher expects change to occur or the variable against which the action of the experiment is measured. It is the variable that is observed and likely changes in response to the independent variable.[106] In Ecclesiastes, "futility" is the dependent variable.

The independent or manipulated variable is the variable the researcher intentionally changes over the course of the experiment. The pursuit of pleasure described in 2:3–10 provides an example of

---

[106] https://www.mansfieldct.org/Schools/MMS/staff/hand/Variables.htm. Accessed December 3, 2018.

independent variables, various experiences engaged in for the purpose of discerning what change they might make on the reality of "futility."

A control is a variable that is not included or acted on in the implementation of experimentation. It is the variable that is intentionally not included for observation. You may notice the absence of God's perspective on Koheleth's activities in Ecclesiastes. God serves as the control in this experiment. In this experiment, Koheleth pursues the question, "What real value is there for a man in all the gains he makes beneath the sun?" by intentionally leaving God, and any effect He might have on the outcome, out of the experiment.

That does not mean God is entirely absent from the book. Koheleth himself gives evidence that he personally recognizes the right involvement of God in an accurate understanding of human experience. Within Ecclesiastes, God gives, endues, causes, dooms, judges, expresses anger and favor, and a host of other activities suggesting His sovereignty over all He has created. However, here he is intentionally sidelining that consideration in order to establish a control, to make the point of what life disconnected from God really is—meaningless, futile, empty, vanity.

Christopher Cone notes that the phrase "under the sun" "emphasizes an earth-centered perspective, and provides the scope for [Koheleth's] blistering critique of all things considered apart from a proper perspective of and relationship to God: 'Vanity of vanities! All is vanity.'"[107]

Experimental limits. "Under the sun" is an important qualifier. The Bible begins with God ("In the beginning, God…") and ends with God ("The grace of the Lord Jesus be with you all") and is full of God in between. I make this point because people need to realize that if they really want to understand themselves and the world in which they live and God's relation to it all, they do best to start with God and stay with God. Here in Ecclesiastes, other than noting

---

[107] Christopher Cone, *Life Beyond the Sun: An Introduction to Worldview & Philosophy through the Lens of Ecclesiastes* (Ft. Worth, TX: Tyndale Seminary Press, 2009), 18.

some activities of His, God's perspective, his rationale for action is intentionally left out of consideration. That strategic decision should not be abused. In other words, as this man asks questions of human experience from a purely human perspective, it is unwise and notably unfair to apply the conclusions derived to God. The conclusions apply as the questions do, to everything "under the sun," to earth and the realm of human life activity, and not to anything "beyond" or "above" the sun where God is and dwells.

What might happen if we apply Koheleth's hypothesis to life "beyond the sun" rather than to life "under the sun"? We would wind up suggesting that God Himself and all that involves Him are meaningless, empty, futile, vanity. That creates a fundamental problem, you can see. Limiting the scope of the inquiry to "all that happens under the sun" keeps us from drawing conclusions we already know are false. The Old Testament book of Numbers declares that "God is not a man, that he should lie, or a son of man, that he should change his mind."[108] Job recognizes the same truth, "For he [God] is not a man, as I am, that I might answer him, that we should come to trial together."[109] We will get ourselves into trouble and confusion if we attempt to understand and know God through the lens of human wisdom rather than divine revelation. For this reason, Koheleth limits the scope of his experiment to a consideration of human life through the lens of human wisdom, not because he doesn't know any better, but because he does and is out to prove the very point we've just encountered.

The general nature of the methodology

Using wisdom (which Solomon gained from the heart of God at the hand of God),[110] Koheleth evaluates the activities of daily life against the research question, "What real value is there for a man in all the gains he makes beneath the sun?" Koheleth does not deny there

---

[108] Numbers 23:19 (ESV).
[109] Job 9:32 (ESV).
[110] 2 Chronicles 1:7–12 (ESV).

are apparent gains, but his question compares the effort expended with the permanence or eternal significance of the outcomes, especially in light of the value we give our work in doing the work.

Three phrases are worth investigating for ourselves, "set my mind," "study," and "probe." The Hebrew of Ecclesiastes 1:13 literally reads, "I applied my heart to seek and to search out by wisdom all that is done under heaven." The *Enhanced Strong's Lexicon* provides the range of meaning for the Hebrew word *leb* (here translated as "mind"): (1) inner man, mind, will, heart, understanding [(1A) inner part, midst; (1A1) midst (of things); (1A2) heart (of man); (1A3) soul, heart (of man); (1A4) mind, knowledge, thinking, reflection, memory; (1A5) inclination, resolution, determination (of will); (1A6) conscience; (1A7) heart (of moral character); (1A8) as seat of appetites; (1A9) as seat of emotions and passions; (1A10) as seat of courage.[111]

Set my mind. Translators have to decide which of these potential definitions is intended with each use of the word. Some use the English word "heart," while others use the word "mind." When we take into consideration the varied uses of the word and the fact that the author of Ecclesiastes would have known fluently the full range of uses, it seems he intends for us to understand that this was an inquiry that engaged the deepest essence of who he was. This is no casual pursuit of a minor curiosity. There is purpose, intent, heart and soul and mind investment in this search for truth. He is bringing his whole personhood, his A game, to the task.

I find a real challenge in this. Studying is hard for me. I like to stick with what comes easy. But aren't there some questions so valuable, so worthwhile, they deserve our wholehearted investment in the search for answers? What to have for lunch is not one of these questions, but what will happen to me when I die certainly is! And yet, I fear, most people put more effort into answering the former question than the latter.

Jesus said, "And this is eternal life, that they know you, the only true God, and Jesus Christ whom you have sent" (John 17:3, ESV).

---

[111] J. Strong, *Enhanced Strong's Lexicon*, Woodside Bible Fellowship (1995).

If knowing God is the means to eternal life, then isn't knowing God as He reveals Himself worth the effort of your whole self? And if the way to know God as He reveals Himself is through the study of His Word, the Bible, then doesn't that study deserve more than just a casual glance from time to time? Or more than a few minutes of devotional search for some phrase or idea that plucks the heart strings? Isn't eternal life worth the effort to engage your whole self? Eternal life for us was worth God sending His only begotten Son to die on the cross on our behalf so that through Him we might find our way back to God. If eternal life for us was that valuable to God, I suggest it is no less valuable to us, and we ought to set our minds and hearts, our whole selves, and get on with our studies with the same determination and joy to know Him as He reveals Himself to be in His Word and in His Son.

Study. The second word that Koheleth uses to describe the methodology that will follow in his report is the word the JPS translates as "study." The word is used 164 times in the Hebrew Bible. "Study" is one translation. "Seek" is another. "Search" is another. "Inquire" is another word often used for this Hebrew word.

A short survey of the occurrences of this word yields an interesting picture of what Koheleth might intend for us to understand by his use of this word. The word in Deuteronomy 4:29 promises restoration by God after Israel's rebellion provided they search for Him with all their heart and all their soul. Later in Deuteronomy, Moses uses the word to describe the intense investment of favor God makes in the land to which He is leading His people, "a land that the Lord your God cares for. The eyes of the Lord your God are always upon it, from the beginning of the year to the end of the year."[112] The word "cares" is the same word here as our word "study" in Ecclesiastes 1:13.

Interestingly, 1 Chronicles records David's charge to his son, Solomon. It is a charge that might have had a significant impact on the study Solomon pursues that is recorded in Ecclesiastes. David said to his son,

---

[112] Deuteronomy 11:12 (ESV).

And you, Solomon my son, know the God
of your father and serve him with a whole heart
and with a willing mind, for the *Lord* searches all
hearts and understands every plan and thought.
If you seek him, he will be found by you, but if
you forsake him, he will cast you off forever.[113]

David tells Solomon that the *Lord* "studies" all hearts and understands every plan and thought and then proceeds to tell him that if Solomon "studies" the *Lord* who "studies" his heart, then Solomon will find the *Lord*!

Both studying/seeking/searching/inquiring and not doing so have an impact according to God's Word. Solomon's son, Rehoboam, is called evil because he did not set his heart to "study" the *Lord*.[114] According to Psalm 10:4, it is pride that keeps the wicked from "studying" God, preferring to believe "there is no God." But others encounter prosperity and other blessing from God as a result of "studying" Him. Uzziah, king of Judah, "set himself to seek God in the days of Zechariah, who instructed him in the fear of God, and as long as he sought the *Lord*, God made him prosper."[115] The Psalmist exults in the grace of God that comes when someone "studies" God with their whole heart, "Blessed are those who keep his testimonies, who seek him with their whole heart."[116]

Three other references in the Psalms complete our survey of this important Hebrew word that Koheleth uses to describe his investigative method. Psalms 14:2 and 53:2 both reference God's desire for His people to seek/study Him. The two verses use almost the exact same wording, except that Psalm 14 refers to God as "the LORD" and Psalm 53 refers to God as "God." Psalm 14:2 (ESV) reveals, "The LORD looks down from heaven on the children of man, to see if there are any who understand, who seek after God."

---

[113] 1 Chronicles 28:9 (ESV).
[114] 2 Chronicles 12:14 (ESV).
[115] 2 Chronicles 26:5 (ESV).
[116] Psalm 119:2 (ESV).

These words make me think of Ezekiel where God says, "I sought for a man among them who should build up the wall and stand in the breach before me for the land, that I should not destroy it, but I found none."[117] There must be nothing sadder than God searching among His people for someone who would take His side and save His people and Him not finding anyone. Psalms 14 and 53 express a similar idea that God looks for those who will devote themselves to seeking Him, to studying Him, to knowing Him. Will He find someone in you, someone who will apply his or her heart to study?

Perhaps Paul had these ideas in mind when he wrote to Timothy and urged him, "Do your best to present yourself to God as one approved, a worker who has no need to be ashamed, rightly handling the word of truth" (2 Timothy 2:15, ESV). The KJV translates this verse as "study to show yourself approved." Too much of what Christians today pass off as "study" is really light devotional reading where it is not the knowledge of God that is the goal, but some "warm, fuzzy feeling of God's presence" for the sake of personal encouragement that we're after. Study takes time, effort, energy, determination, and a heart empowered by the Spirit for endurance.

Study is what disciples are made for, for only a disciple who studies the Master with his life can master life and become a disciple-maker.

The final occurrence of the word "study" to bring to your attention is Psalm 111:2. It is not the last occurrence of the word in the Old Testament by any means, but it is the use I want to leave you to think about as you ponder Koheleth's intent. People do not have to use the same word in the same way, and they often don't, but think about this, "Great are the works of the Lord, studied by all who delight in them."

Those who delight in the great works of the *Lord* study them. Could it be possible that one reason Koheleth studies human life and notes the handiwork of God in the lives of human beings is because he delights in the great works of the *Lord* and desires to pursue and

---

[117] Ezekiel 22:30 (ESV).

ponder them with vigor and interest and with his whole heart? Could it be possible that one reason Christians today often do not invest in real study of God and His Word is because we take little or no delight in Him and the works of His hand?

Much of Pastor John Piper's ministry has been dedicated to leading the followers of Jesus into God's delight in being God, with the benefit that as they see God's joy in His own perfections (His glory) for themselves, their own delight in God will multiply, and they will increasingly enter into God's delight in God's glory. In responding to the question, "What does 'delight yourself in the Lord' mean, practically?" on his *Ask Pastor John* podcast, Piper provides a three-part answer. He says, "Delight in God as most admirable. Delight in God as your intimate Savior and friend. Delight in God through his gifts."[118] He explains his first point as "seeing and savoring the diverse excellencies of God, especially as they are manifest in Christ, especially as he brings them to fulfillment at the cross."[119]

We find meager enjoyment in so many things, so why not the greatest joy in the best of things? God has manifested the incredible worthiness of His glory in His Son so that we might see and know and love that which is most loveable for our own delight! And the way in which we will access the greatest understanding and appreciation of what God has done for us in Christ, how God has worked in the world and in His Son and has "shone in our hearts to give the light of the knowledge of the glory of God in the face of Jesus Christ,"[120] is through the study of God's Word.

Probe. The last of the three words Koheleth uses to describe his methods is "probe." This word is like the word "study" but has this nuance—where "study" carries a measure of intensity, "probe" carries a measure of expansiveness. It means to explore. It takes into account possibilities and potential that need to be identified and accounted for. I find it to be a very science-lab-related word. Working in com-

---

[118] John Piper, https://www.desiringgod.org/interviews/how-do-i-delight-myself-in-the-lord. Accessed November 5, 2018.

[119] Ibid.

[120] Philippians 4:6 (ESV).

parative anatomy lab, we found probes very useful for exploring. They helped us reach where our fingers wouldn't go, moving internal structures and obstacles aside so we could get a clear view of that tissue or organ or structure for which we were searching. (I'll spare you the specific details!) Probes allowed clarity and refinement, exploration, and discovery.

What Koheleth means is that he is going to painstakingly dissect the comings and goings of human life in his search for understanding. He is taking nothing at face value. He is digging and moving, rooting around in the everyday adventures of life, and refusing to come up empty. He is on a treasure hunt and will leave no clue unconsidered, no stone unturned, no evidence untouched.

What about you? Are you ready to be as intent and intense as Koheleth regarding the truth about your life and God's role in it? Or, to be a bit more precise, God's world and your role in it?

Here's an exercise you can practice. There are approximately nineteen verbs in Ecclesiastes that Koheleth uses to describe his actions in pursuit of wisdom, for example, "I set my mind" or "I learned." How many can you find? Make a column list of the words you find and provide a definition for each English word. Once you've identified and defined your words, take two different colored pens or pencils, and with one color, circle all the words that apply (honestly) to your practice of Bible study. After you've done that, circle with the other colored pen or pencil all the words Koheleth uses for his study methods that do not apply to your practice. What opportunity is revealed to you by this exercise? What will be your next step in making the most of that opportunity?

I found these words that indicate Koheleth's personal investment in the studied probe of this hypothesis that "all is futile."

1. Learned
2. Said to myself
3. Ventured
4. Appraised
5. Realized
6. Reflected

7. Concluded
8. Noted
9. Observed
10. Mused
11. Accounted
12. Found
13. Tested
14. Sought
15. Ascertained

These words describe a well-rounded, well-focused, intentional, extensive investment of self-effort in the pursuit of wisdom and of God who uses wisdom for His glory in our lives.

The tool kit for the experiment

Every good lab report records the equipment necessary to conduct the experiment. This information is provided primarily to enable others to duplicate the experiment. Call it a quality control issue. An experiment that cannot be duplicated means results cannot be independently verified and that means the results lack a measure of credibility. In fact, results that cannot be verified are often shelved, rejected, or dismissed.

We identified two tools Koheleth proposes to use in this experiment. We've already talked about his "mind." The other tool he mentions is "wisdom." "The words 'wise' and 'wisdom' are used fifty-three times throughout Ecclesiastes and seventeen times in 1:12–2:26. If you add to those words synonymous or nearly synonymous words—such as 'know' and 'knowledge'—the count for this section rises to twenty-three. This is the highest concentration of wisdom words in the Bible! Undoubtedly this is a section about wisdom."[121] The following questions warrant answers:

• What does Koheleth mean by "wisdom"?

---

[121] O'Donnell, 32–33.

- The contrast between wisdom and folly is important throughout Ecclesiastes (and throughout life for that matter). What is the difference between wisdom and folly?
- What difference does the difference make relative to human experience?

Remember what Michael Fox told us about *hokhmah*, the Hebrew word translated as wisdom here? He notes that the word is very broad and that it is "both the knowledge gained by learning and the intellectual powers that can analyze and evaluate that learning."[122] So wisdom is both what we know for certain and the ability to use that knowledge appropriately to gain more and better knowledge.

Perhaps the best person to define what Koheleth means by "wisdom" is Koheleth himself. First, wisdom is the capacity Koheleth possesses to accurately evaluate and analyze the fruitfulness of human living according to terms he himself has set. "I set my mind to study and to probe with wisdom all that happens under the sun." That means his wisdom must also involve the knowledge of moral absolutes and cultural sensitivities since he is setting the parameters of the study, and if he is not knowledgeable enough and wise enough to set the parameters correctly, his experiment will fail.

The limits of wisdom. Koheleth, however, also recognizes some limitations on wisdom. O'Donnell points out two reflections in these verses that Koheleth makes about wisdom—"Wisdom cannot change reality… Wisdom can increase sorrow."[123] The first reflection means that wisdom also includes the capacity to recognize limits, especially the limits on personal purpose set by personal sinfulness. The second means that the pursuit of wisdom, even when enabled by wisdom, is still utterly futile.

Koheleth calls the living of life under the sun "an unhappy business" that "God gave men to be concerned with." Why is life an unhappy business from the hand of God? The answer lies in an event

---

[122] Fox, xx.
[123] Fox, 33.

that affects every human being and that ought not be forgotten or dismissed by any of us. Think of Genesis chapter 3. Adam and Eve are in the garden where they are fulfilling their creation purpose, their life meaning, their lives putting the personal character (and thereby the glory) of the Creator on display in the earth. They reveal Him through their relationship with God, with each other, and with the rest of creation. Then comes the snake in the grass (okay, the serpent in the tree). Adam and Eve submit to deceit and their own selfishness. They sin in their disobedience (keep in mind that actions are born from attitudes), lose their innocence, and become aware of guilt and shame. God then envisions their inner turmoil in an external curse—for man, the ground would no longer produce fruit without hard labor and the risk of failure.

God imposed the curse as a living picture of their internal condition, hopelessness. No matter how hard they might labor, whether in pursuit of wisdom or collard greens, it was always going to be a hard row to hoe with no guarantees and more than a few occasions of utter failure. That's what Koheleth refers to as the unhappy business given by God to man to be concerned with—the curse and the human inability to lift the curse from us by our own efforts. Examining God-cursed lives, Koheleth states his first preliminary finding, "I observed all the happenings beneath the sun, and I found that all is futile and pursuit of wind." In the end, no matter how wise you are, sin's curse will prove unchangeable, "a twisted thing that cannot be made straight, a lack that cannot be made good." Wisdom includes the capacity to acknowledge and embrace its own limits.

This is where many people falter. They become caught up in their own wisdom as having an ability that human wisdom simply does not have to solve every problem, including the problems of sin and evil. No human being can solve a divine dilemma using human tools. Divine dilemmas require divine solutions. The Apostle Paul describes the situation like this, "For the creation was subjected to futility, not willingly, but because of him who subjected it that the creation itself will be set free from its bondage to decay and obtain the freedom of the glory of the children of God."[124] God has subjected creation to futility on account of Adam's sin, and only God can lift the curse of futility, which, praise His name, He has provided for in the life, death, and resurrection of Jesus Christ!

The question I believe that Koheleth implies in this study is: "What is the divine response to the divine dilemma of human life?" The way he states this question is: "What real value is there for a man in all the gains he makes beneath the sun" (Ecclesiastes 1:3, (JPS)?[125]

Do you ask God what His response is to the situations, circumstances, conditions, and challenges you face? Or do you wait until you've tried every other conceivable avenue and, finally, when you've personally demonstrated that everything under the sun is utter futility ask for His intervention? Faith reaches out to God as the first resort, not the last resort. True wisdom recognizes its own limitations!

The burden of wisdom. Koheleth makes these reflections, but he doesn't stop with the pursuit of wisdom. He is on a quest. He is conducting an experiment to answer the question, "What real value does a man have in all the gains he makes under the sun?" Besides searching out wisdom and finding it to be "futile and pursuit of wind," he takes up to discover the difference between wisdom and folly.

That's where he discovers the second facet of wisdom. Wisdom is also the capacity to rightly recognize that the burden of responsibility is directly proportional to the measure of true wisdom. The more you know, the more responsible you are to put what you know to work. Wisdom doesn't get you out of the cycle of cursed work.

> For as wisdom grows, vexation grows; to
> increase learning is to increase heartache.[126]

When I first became a pastor, even though I'd been to Bible college and seminary, there were a ton of things I didn't know. I had not planned to be a local church pastor, so there was some course

---

[124] Romans 8:20–21 (ESV).
[125] Ecclesiastes 1:3 (JPS).
[126] Ecclesiastes 1:18 (JPS).

work that might have been helpful that I elected to skip. Let me tell you, ignorance was not bliss! Not very long into the beginning of my experience, I got a phone call from a church member who informed me my presence might be helpful right that moment at the local emergency room. A family had been visiting a border country lake. In broad daylight, the mother and a twelve-year-old daughter had been struck by lightning. The ambulance was on its way into town. Reports were uncertain if both had survived. The extended family would be coming to the hospital. Wouldn't it be very good to have a pastor on hand to help?

I had not prepared for that pastoral moment. I had prepared to exposit Scripture passages. I had prepared to instruct and teach, but I had not prepared to stand with a young father as he learned the news that his wife had barely survived but his beautiful little girl had not. I had not prepared to sink to the floor with him in tears or to stand a few minutes later and pray over the lifeless green-tinged body of his child who only a few hours before had been running and laughing, full of life and promise along the rocks of the lakeshore. Gaining wisdom that day meant both gaining responsibility and gaining a further insight into what makes life meaningless and what makes life meaningful. That is the burden of wisdom. The more clearly you see into life, the more clearly you see the hopelessness of a creation subjected to futility and sorrow.

Preliminary Findings: Life, Wisdom, Pleasure, and Self-Indulgence All Futile

It is not unusual, as an experiment progresses, for the researcher to posit preliminary findings. Paul Hollywood's book of bread recipes includes one for *pain de campagne* (French country bread). The recipe uses mostly white bread flour but includes a small portion of dark rye flour. Rye flour usually requires more water than wheat flour does, and I knew that. The first time I made the bread, I followed the directions and found the dough to be fairly firm and dry, so the next time I made that bread, I added more water to get a slightly more sticky dough. There was a notable difference in the finished bread.

My hypothesis was that more water would account for the added rye flour and make a better loaf. (My secondary hypothesis was that I, a truly novice baker who read a book and was baking his second loaf of bread, knew better what would work than Paul Hollywood, the master baker.) My preliminary findings were that it is always good to follow a recipe until you are very competent with what you are baking. After many, many more loaves of bread, I am certain that my preliminary findings were accurate and my hypothesis was wrong!

Koheleth's preliminary findings look good for the hypothesis but not so good for hope and the meaning of life. All of life under the sun reeks of futility because no amount of human effort can lift the curse God has assigned to mankind as a result of the Fall. On top of that, increasing wisdom, which should mean becoming better off in the world, only increases heartache under the burden of responsibility and inability that wisdom brings. So far, the hypothesis bears up under scrutiny.

Koheleth reports his pursuit of two more avenues of interest as he lays out his preliminary findings. First, he identifies merriment and mirth as the next objects of his attention, quickly setting them aside as futile. Then Koheleth gives a more detailed description of a grand experiment in self-indulgence, which he also, ultimately, dubs futile.

The word Koheleth uses for "merriment" or "pleasure" is often translated "happiness" or "joy."[127] Imagine being advised to embrace happiness or joy. Of course, you would want to do that. Of course, you would want life to be filled with conditions and situations that bring a perpetual smile to your face and satisfaction to your belly, right? But that's not life, is it? Telling us to grasp happiness and hold it continually in our hearts is not unlike compelling us to chase the wind in order to grasp the zephyr in our hands, isn't it?

Happy occasions fade replaced with seasons of sorrow. In one of the later seasons of *the Great British Baking Show* aired on Netflix, there was a contestant who could have written Ecclesiastes himself. He is leaning, in one episode, against his workstation with his arms

---

[127] Fox, xx.

crossed, his face forlorn, just short of scowling, his eyes downcast, his demeanor defeated. He has done well and then not so well. He's gotten a deserved but harsh evaluation of a baking effort. The camera turns on him, he looks up, and he says into the camera for all the world to hear, "Every success is followed by disaster."

What is the point of merriment and pleasure if they do not last? What is the point of joy and laughter and mirth if they cannot prevent mourning and crying and grief? "Koheleth longs to do something *effective* [sic], to achieve something substantive," yet all he tries fails "to provide a sense of achievement or efficacy."[128] The experience is real but has no "real value."

And let's not leave out excessive self-indulgence! Koheleth describes how, with wisdom and intentionality intact, in fact, with wisdom "standing alongside" him, he pursued a strategy of unlimited self-indulgence. He confesses, "My wisdom remained with me: I withheld from my eyes nothing they asked for, and denied myself no enjoyment."[129]

Koheleth makes no moral evaluation of his conduct generally nor of any behavior or choice specifically. He does, however, make an intriguing confession. Having written of wine and the multiplication of possessions and the amassing of an almost obscene wealth, he says, "I gained more wealth than anyone before me in Jerusalem,"[130] and then he writes, "I got enjoyment out of all my wealth. And that was all I got out of my wealth."[131]

Can you imagine? Wine, houses, vineyards, gardens and groves, irrigation pools and construction projects, slaves and stewards, cattle in herds and flocks, silver and gold and treasure of kings and provinces, male and female singers, as well as the luxuries of commoners filled up, tapped down, and flowing over and all he gets out of all he has is a little enjoyment! He gained no greater sense of worth, for all he was worth. He gained no deeper sense of purpose or meaning for all the deep pockets of his fancy robes. He had everything the rich

---

[128] Fox, 12.
[129] Ecclesiastes 2:10a (JPS).
[130] Ecclesiastes 2:9 (JPS).
[131] Ecclesiastes 2:10b (JPS).

have and everything the poor have as well, and he still wasn't genuinely happy. He acquired for himself everything of value in the world but lacked anything of real value from the world.[132]

And why not? Why does this vault of value not satisfy his heart and usher in lasting contentment? Because he cannot guarantee that the next owner of all his stuff will appreciate and enjoy the labor it took to collect. For all that he has, there is yet something he cannot have—life long enough to enjoy it fully or a guarantee that the next man into whose hands the wealth must come will deserve to have it. So he has chased after what he cannot hold. It has all been a pursuit of wind. The question is, what will be the conclusion when the experiment is complete?

Koheleth Offers His Initial Conclusions (2:12b–26)

> *My thoughts also turned to appraising wisdom*
> *and madness and folly.* [13]*I found that*
> *Wisdom is superior to folly*
> *As light is superior to darkness;*
> [14]*A wise man has his eyes in his head,*
> *Whereas a fool walks in darkness.*
> *But I also realized that the same fate awaits*
> *them both.* [15]*So I reflected: "The fate of the fool is*
> *also destined for me; to what advantage, then, have*
> *I been wise?" And I came to the conclusion that that*
> *too was futile,* [16]*because the wise man, just like the*
> *fool, is not remembered forever; for, as the succeeding days roll by, both are forgotten. Alas, the wise*
> *man dies, just like the fool!*

---

[132] Fox, 13. "Though not reflected in this translation [JPS], almost every verb indicating production and acquisition is accompanied by *li*, "for myself" "I built for myself...planted for myself...made for myself," and so on. This emphasis on "myself" exposes a sort of consumerism, an obsessive striving to fill an undefined but gnawing spiritual need by material goods. This attempt is, of course, hopeless (6:7).

¹⁷And so I loathed life. For I was distressed by all that goes on under the sun, because everything is futile and pursuit of wind.

¹⁸So, too, I loathed all the wealth that I was gaining under the sun. For I shall leave it to the man who will succeed me—and who knows whether he will be wise or foolish?—¹⁹and he will control all the wealth that I gained by toil and wisdom under the sun. That too is futile. ²⁰And so I came to view with despair all the gains I had made under the sun. ²¹For sometimes a person whose fortune was made with wisdom, knowledge, and skill must hand it on to be the portion of somebody who did not toil for it. That too is futile, and a grave evil. ²²For what does a man get for all the toiling and worrying he does under the sun? ²³All his days his thoughts are grief and heartache, and even at night his mind has no respite. That too is futile!

²⁴There is nothing worthwhile for a man but to eat and drink and afford himself enjoyment with his means. And even that, I noted, comes from God. ²⁵For who eats and who enjoys but myself? ²⁶To the man, namely, who pleases Him He has given the wisdom and shrewdness to enjoy himself; and to him who displeases, He has given the urge to gather and amass—only for handing on to one who is pleasing to God. That too is futile and pursuit of wind.

The first series of experiments has ended. The tenor of the writing changes from a recitation of actions to a report of responses. Rather than seeing what Koheleth did, we now find him revealing what he thought about what he did. The change comes in 2:15 where Koheleth tells us he has begun to "reflect" on what he has seen and done. The Hebrew reads, literally, "I spoke to my heart." It is an internal, deeply personal consideration.

The results seem to support the hypothesis. All is futile. He offers four different facets of the same conclusion.

The first initial conclusion: Death negates all advantage

Wisdom is superior to folly. Wisdom has real value, as the use of *yitron* (superior) suggests. Yet despite that superiority of wisdom over folly and by extension of the wise over the fool, in the end, they arrive at the same place, dead. There was a time when it was popular to quote a pop culture sage who remarked, "The one who dies with the most toys wins." Koheleth would reply, "Yeah, but the one who dies with the most toys is still dead [and somebody else is playing with their toys!]."

The Teacher has broadly examined natural phenomena, intellectual phenomena, personal practice, and cultural conventional wisdom. He has surveyed the superiority of wisdom over folly and the position of the wise man over the fool. The results are in, the evidence tallied, and the conclusions drawn. "I came to the conclusion that that too was futile because...the wise man dies, just like the fool!"[133] Death negates all advantage. Death deletes distinctions of quality, like wisdom and wealth, that should be respected.[134] Every effort of man under the sun is futility at best since, no matter what they do or don't do, what they have or don't have, what they accomplish or not, in the end, they die. Any profit they might have gained from all their toil under the sun either disappears or passes on to someone else for their temporary benefit.

Death in Koheleth's time seems to have different implications than we find in our own post-Calvary, post-resurrection, post-Pentecost, post-apostolic age. Bartholomew points out that the Old Testament has "no clear doctrine of life after death" such as there is in the New Testament, though there is a strong intimation in the direction of eternal life.[135] For Koheleth, death is the end.[136] Because death is the observable end of life, he raises the question, What is the point of excelling in wisdom (or any other labor under the sun, for that matter)?

---

[133] Ecclesiastes 2:16 (JPS).
[134] Fox, 16.
[135] Bartholomew, 142.
[136] Ibid., 117.

We need to take into account here a presupposition or two that we identified earlier. The first is that Solomon has a personal relationship with the Lord God that has resulted in the bestowment of divine wisdom. Koheleth knows more than he is letting on at the moment. He knows something of God's ways in creation, God's personal character, and God's covenant purpose for His people.

We ought also to acknowledge that we, reading in our time and not Koheleth's, know something not immediately brought to our attention (at least directly) in Ecclesiastes. After all, as Bartholomew rightly states, "Any wisdom worth its weight has to come to grips with death, the great enigma of life."[137] We know from Christ's resurrection and from the Spirit-inspired revelation through New Testament authors that death is not the end. Jesus said,

> Let not your hearts be troubled. Believe in God; believe also in me. In my Father's house are many rooms. If it were not so, would I have told you that I go to prepare a place for you? And if I go and prepare a place for you, I will come again and will take you to myself, that where I am you may be also.[138]

The Apostle Paul assures those whose faith is in Jesus Christ for the forgiveness of sin and the promise of eternal life in Him that to be absent from the body is to be present with the Lord.[139] We are further encouraged by that truly awesome passage in 1 Corinthians 15 where Paul explains what awaits those who die in the Lord,

> I tell you this, brothers: flesh and blood cannot inherit the kingdom of God, nor does the perishable inherit the imperishable. Behold! I tell you a mystery. We shall not all sleep, but we shall

---

[137] Bartholomew, 146.
[138] John 14:1–3 (ESV).
[139] 2 Corinthians 5:8.

all be changed, in a moment, in the twinkling of an eye, at the last trumpet. For the trumpet will sound, and the dead will be raised imperishable, and we shall be changed. For this perishable body must put on the imperishable, and this mortal body must put on immortality. When the perishable puts on the imperishable, and the mortal puts on immortality, then shall come to pass the saying that is written: "Death is swallowed up in victory."

"O death, where is your victory? O death, where is your sting?" The sting of death is sin, and the power of sin is the law.

But thanks be to God, who gives us the victory through our Lord Jesus Christ.[140]

"The effect of sin is that God's image bearers forfeit their right to exist and their reason for existence—Qoheleth's great struggle. But God does not give up on his good creation."[141] We know that God has a plan for His glory, for our eternal joy, for the salvation of nations, and for the advancing of His mission to fill the earth with the knowledge of His glory. This knowledge rises with Koheleth's conclusion and demands to know what isn't being said.

For now, though, we'll just have to wait. Koheleth is not done, not with his inquiries nor with his report. These are initial conclusions and not all the evidence is in. At this point, on the basis of intelligent and reasonable observation of living practice, death negates any realized gain, making human effort futile when it comes to supplying life with real value or genuine meaning.

The second initial conclusion: A futile life is a loathsome life

Initial examination of Koheleth's efforts to find meaning in the myriad practices of life that are supposed to be fulfilling has rendered

---

[140] 1 Corinthians 15:50–57 (ESV).
[141] Bartholomew, 147.

the expected conclusion, "utter futility!" His response to a meaning-less, futile life isn't surprising either. He hates life. At this point in the experiment, it's all a bust. What real value is there in all the efforts we make? The answer is "none." And the response to that meaningless-ness? Hate. Loathing.

The Hebrew word *sane'* is a root word that means to hate, abhor, detest, loathe, be hostile, or have a feeling of open hostility and intense dislike.[142] Just for giggles, I googled the phrase "I hate my life." I expected a reference to a syndicated sitcom or a British comedy or something. I didn't expect thousands of pages of people confessing their loathing for their own situations or attempting to assist others with wisdom from their own struggles.

One page called LifeHacks.com offered thirteen reasons why someone might hate their life and in the same article provided ten steps a person could take to either stay in love or restore their love for life again.

Why I Hate My Life?

- I hate my life for being sad all day and having no desire for anything.
- I hate to always think badly of the people and not to trust anyone.
- I hate my life because it is empty.
- I hate my life for not having friends.
- I hate my life because everyone underestimates me.
- I hate when I don't know how to answer to the people who kill my self-confidence.
- I hate my life when I look in the mirror and not like what I see.
- I hate my life when I see how other people have the life that I want.

---

[142] J. Swanson, *Dictionary of Biblical Languages with Semantic Domains: Hebrew (Old Testament)*, electronic ed. (Oak Harbor: Logos Research Systems, Inc., 1997).

How to Love Your Life

- Do not observe the life with glumness!
- Plan the time the best way possible.
- Do not include in your plans only obligations, but also enjoyment!
- Spend more time with people who inspire you with positive energy.
- Never renounce and at any cost, to do what you love the most in your life.
- Never give up on your dreams!
- Learn that there is not much time for grieving, and grief is nothing but hiding from and fear of a new beginning!
- Instead of listening to the opinions of others listen to your own heart.
- The power lies in your patience and understanding.
- Learn to love the ends because they are nothing but fantastic beginnings.[143]

The substance of both lists, as you probably noticed, is decidedly self-centered and neither accounts for the presence or purpose of God. This is the overwhelmingly common approach in our world to personal issues of undersupported self-esteem, situational stagnation, and malignant disappointment. The Apostle Paul reminds us that the majority of people in our world are spiritually crippled. "The god of this world has blinded the minds of the unbelievers, to keep them from seeing the light of the gospel of the glory of Christ, who is the image of God."[144]

---

[143] https://lifehacks.io/i-hate-my-life/. Accessed November 8, 2018.
[144] 2 Corinthians 4:4 (ESV).

People who cannot (or do not) discern the sovereign hand of God in their personal history struggle to find meaning and purpose in their existence. They wind up relying on more self-effort (which is intrinsically meaningless) to encourage and nurture their sense of self-worth. It is a miserable cycle of meaninglessness. Koheleth announces the same conclusion and the same response most people in the world would reach—in the end, even with all the experiences, all the accomplishments, all the possessions, I still feel empty, and I hate it.

But let us take care as we observe Koheleth's loathing of a futile life. Job knew the feeling.[145] So did Jeremiah.[146] So did Jesus, "My God, my God, why have you forsaken me?"[147] There very likely have been moments for all of us when disappointment or despair at the course of life in that moment overwhelmed the soul. Mine came in the darkest hours of the night on the lonely bank of a river swollen by rain and storm surge. I thought there could not be an instance of good left in life for me and was pulling together the courage to cast myself into the flood and let my pain and emptiness be swept away into darkness. It was that moment when Jesus spoke to the deepest need of my weary, guilty, broken heart. There in the suffocating humidity of a late summer night, Jesus interrupted and saved my life.

"Dale," He said, "don't you know it was for this very hour that I died?"

It is not that these moments (or seasons) occur for us. It is what we do with them. More specifically, it is to Whom we entrust ourselves in them. Koheleth's initial conclusion screams for attention. How can he, wise and rich and having enjoyed a personal relationship with God, leave God out now? Where is the relationship? Where is the dependence and reliance on the power greater than his own? It is absent, and we will see along the way, it is intentionally absent.

---

[145] Job 10:1.
[146] Jeremiah 20:14.
[147] Matthew 27:46.

Be patient. The absence of God in this conclusion will ultimately be revealed as a component of the entire experiment.

The third initial conclusion: A futile wealth is a loathsome wealth

My wife and I are absolutely convinced that our lives and prosperity, whether it be abundant or meager in this world, are entirely in the hands of our loving heavenly Father Who always does what is right,[148] who does all things well,[149] who acts out of love on our behalf in time,[150] and who has promised to supply every need we experience.[151] That doesn't stop my wife from participating in every Publisher's Clearinghouse Sweepstakes she can get her hands on. "By law, they have to give it to someone," she says. "It may as well be us." We dream of paying off the mortgage, adding an addition to the church, building dorms for distressed children at a school we work with in Haiti, replacing the building for a community thrift store in our town, sending Bibles to the entire "persecuted church," and funding missionaries to unreached peoples. Our list is long.

We sometimes get the idea that if God would just give us enough all at once, we could accomplish earth-shattering, life-changing good in the world. But look at our list again. Is there anything on that list that God could not (and probably will not) accomplish over time through dozens, if not hundreds, of faithful believers acting in humble submission and grounded commitment to the kingdom of God with their resources?

If I live another twenty years, my house will be paid for. If God grants a vision to His people to expand the facilities of the church, He will provide the means just as He has every time before. If people with a heart for others, especially children, give a few dollars monthly, the dorms for Haitian children whose families are unable to care for them will be constructed. There is simply nothing for which God

---

[148] Genesis 18:25.
[149] Mark 7:37.
[150] John 16:27.
[151] Philippians 4:19.

needs to dump a cache of cash in my lap in order for His plan to get done. So why so much weight on wealth?

Koheleth amassed a huge reservoir of resources and then loathed them, not because they weren't enough or because they didn't do what they were supposed to do. Koheleth hated his wealth because he couldn't keep it and he couldn't guarantee that his heir would honor the effort or the accomplishment such wealth represented. He owns a thousand tables full of the world's most satisfying delights and he is feasting at the table of despair. His wealth can do almost anything except extend his life and his control over his wealth. "Sometimes a person whose fortune was made with wisdom, knowledge, and skill [all things that deserve respect, honor, and real value] must hand it on to be the portion of somebody who did not toil for it [and therefore does not deserve respect, honor, and real value]."[152] This too is futile.

The fourth initial conclusion: What little joy there is comes from God

Koheleth paints a depressing picture. His wise investigation into the meaning of life, using his own life for research, has supported his hypothesis. All is meaningless, utterly futile. He loathes life. He loathes his wealth. He surrenders himself to despair (2:20). Now he adds a fourth to his initial conclusions, "There is nothing worthwhile for a man but to eat and drink and afford himself enjoyment with his means. And even that, I noted, comes from God."[153]

Let's be clear. Koheleth has just made two very important assertions. One is that even in a life that is ultimately futile, there can be real joy. The second is that when there is real joy, it comes from God.

Take a walk with me, please. We're headed for Eden, the garden of creation glory in Genesis 1 and 2. Besides giving Adam and Eve life in the garden, God extended three other provisions to them, two for sustenance and one for meaning. God, having placed the first pair

---

[152] Ecclesiastes 2:21 (JPS). The bracketed comments are mine and are not original to the text.
[153] Ecclesiastes 2:24 (JPS).

in the garden, released the garden to their benefit. "And God said, Behold, I have given you every plant yielding seeds that is on the face of all the earth, and every tree with seed in its fruit. You shall have them for food."[154]

God provided food. God also provided water.

> When no bush of the field was yet in the land and no small plant of the field had yet sprung up—for the LORD God had not caused it to rain on the land, and there was no man to work the ground, and a mist was going up from the land and was watering the whole face of the ground.[155]

God provided food and water for their sustenance. And He provided work for their purpose.

> And God blessed them. And God said to them, "Be fruitful and multiply and fill the earth and subdue it, and have dominion over the fish of the sea and over the birds of the heavens and over every living thing that moves on the earth."[156]
> The *Lord* God took the man and put him in the garden of Eden to work it and keep it.[157]

Food, drink, and work were the gifts God added into the lives of humanity for their joy at their creation. Koheleth recognizes God as the source of life's simple graces as he asks, "For apart from him [God] who can eat or who can have enjoyment?"[158] Food, water, and work parallel wisdom, knowledge, and joy for Koheleth. They are each and all graces God adds to the lives of those He loves and who

---

[154] Genesis 1:29 (ESV).
[155] Genesis 2:5–6 (ESV).
[156] Genesis 1:28 (ESV).
[157] Genesis 2:15 (ESV).
[158] Ecclesiastes 2:25 (ESV).

love Him in return. That is not to say that God withholds any of these from those who do not love Him, but those who do not love Him are far more likely to experience their efforts as meaningless than those who please God. Those who do not please God are more likely to feel the despair of having their efforts handed over to someone else, far more likely to feel the burden of a wasted life, far more likely to experience the justice of God than the mercy of God, and thus far more likely to draw the conclusion Koheleth reports here, "That too is futile and pursuit of wind."

Koheleth's apparent about-face (from deep distress to tentative joy) begs the question though. How do we find joy in the simple pleasures of common grace (food, drink, work, wisdom, knowledge, and joy)? If what little joy to be had comes from God and can be found in these provisions from His hand, then how do we make the most of them without getting lost in a haze of hedonism that obscures our view of Him?

Detour: Finding Joy from God in Common Graces

Detours can be devastating. We were headed to Duluth and arrived in the last little town in our county along Minnesota's Highway 61. Schroeder has a couple of shops, a post office, a museum, a bridge over the amazingly beautiful Cross River, and a couple of resorts. There is also, just a block up the hill to the north from the highway, on the Cramer Road, the Schroeder Town Hall.

On this particular day, in Minnesota's only other season than winter (Road Construction!), the Highway Department was realigning a turn lane and using the Cramer Road as a detour. The detour was only supposed to be a block long. We were supposed to turn right off the highway, go one block north, turn left at the entrance to the Schroeder Town Hall, and then proceed back to Highway 61. Easy-peasy, right? Wrong.

Somewhere in all the commotion, the left-turn sign at the top of the hill got turned around and was pointing for traffic to continue north and west on the Cramer Road. If y'all are not from around here, you don't know what that means. The Cramer Road passes through forty miles of raw wilderness in the other middle of nowhere. There are no houses, no gas stations, no restrooms, and no turns that lead anywhere other than raw forest. There's nothing—just trees, river, and the occasional moose. And that is exactly where we headed, into the middle of nowhere at all!

What should have been a short two-minute jaunt became a two-hour journey through unfamiliar territory only to finally arrive at a town we'd never heard of, on a road we'd never heard of, and located we didn't know where in relation to the highway, home, or Duluth.

We're going to take a short detour. In order to prevent us getting lost, I want to put the directional signs in place right now. Koheleth has raised the possibility of joy in life at the hands of God. He will present something similar several more times in his report. I want us to give sufficient import to these passages that scholars refer to as the *carpe diem* passages (2:24–26, 3:10–15, 16–22; 5:18–20; 8:10–15; 9:7–10; 11:7–12:7). He is not advocating unrestricted, selfish hedonism.

Koheleth is dropping clues that there is more to this report than what may appear at face value. God is not absent after all. His place and presence are secure, but in light of the research, how do we reach beyond futility and find the joy that He offers? That's our detour question.

Following the detour successfully and not getting lost requires we observe three directions. First, we're going to clearly define what we mean when we call food, water, work, wisdom, knowledge, and joy common graces. Then, we are going to take for granted that Ecclesiastes provides both a rationale and a release to pursue joy in common graces and ask how to do that. Then we'll return to the next experimental series Koheleth embarks on in his quest to answer the question, "What real value is there for a man in all the gains he makes beneath the sun?"

The "is" and the "ain't" of common grace

Remember our brief trip to Eden just now. Can we go back there for a second? God created male and female persons and set them in a garden where their need for sustenance, meaning, and even companionship was more than adequately met. There was one caveat, one law they must not break, "Of the tree of the knowledge of good and evil in the midst of the garden, thou shalt not eat."[159] The species of tree is unimportant. What matters is that God picked a tree and set a divine limit that He purposely imposed on Adam and Eve. God established His will in their lives and set in and upon them the responsibility to attend to this one Law.

You know what comes next—the serpent, the fruit, the bite, the guilt, the voice of God calling in the garden, the blame, the blood, the curse, and the consequences. As a result of their disobedience, their willingness to replace God's will with their own will in their lives (sin), Adam and Eve, and all who come from them after them, are subject to God's justice. Wayne Grudem describes their/our situation like this, "This means that once people sin, God's justice would require only one thing—that they be eternally separated from God, cut off from experiencing any good from him, and that they live forever in hell, receiving only his wrath eternally."[160]

The fact that God continues to give blessings to sinners who deserve only death is what we call common grace. Again, turning to Grudem, we find this definition, "Common grace is the grace of God by which he gives people innumerable blessings that are not part of salvation."[161]

Common grace includes the six gifts Koheleth has listed for us, but thousands of others as well. That we draw breath is a common grace. That we live at all, amassing wealth or not, gaining wisdom or not, advancing in prestige or not, this is a common grace. That food grows from the earth is a common grace, as is the rain that falls on the fields of the just and unjust alike.[162] The aesthetic beauty of the natural world, inspiring to all with senses to engage, is a common grace.

---

[159] Genesis 2:16 (KJV)

[160] Wayne A. Grudem, *Systematic Theology: An Introduction to Biblical Doctrine* (Grand Rapids, MI: Inter-Varsity Press; Zondervan Pub. House, 2004), 657.

[161] Ibid.

[162] Matthew 5:44–45.

Common grace is found not only in what we experience for ourselves but also in some things that we don't experience. "Common grace restrains people from being as evil as they could be."[163] That makes conscience a common grace. The gospel delivered into the world and available to any who will hear it is a common grace, a gift from the hand of God to those who by birth and by choice deserve only death.

Do you see that by "common grace," we mean any good (other than salvation) God grants in the lives of those who deserve only death at his hands?[164] It is the difference between the good we experience and the justice we actually deserve. The ability to find joy in food and drink and work comes from God as a gift, as a grace, because even these simple pleasures in life are inestimably more than we deserve! To find joy in common grace is to start down the path of finding joy in God by being satisfied in and with Him. Koheleth calls us to joy in common grace because he is leading us to a larger message of joy later.

Finding joy in common grace

The question that remains on our detour, before we head back to the research report, is this, What steps can we take to find joy in God's common grace? Piper offers an answer worth considering. He conducted a Desiring God Regional Conference in August of 2005 in Greenville, South Carolina. During that conference, he delivered six messages based on his book *When I Don't Desire God: How to Fight for Joy*. The six messages can be accessed at the Desiring God website at https://www.desiringgod.org/series/2005-regional-conference/messages. The fifth and sixth messages of the conference provide fourteen strategies for the fight for joy.

---

[163] Grudem, 660.

[164] Grudem, 657. Grace that results in salvation is called saving grace. Grudem notes that common grace differs from saving grace in its results, its recipients, and in its source.

Here is a summary of those strategies.

- Meditate on the word of God day and night.
- In all your Bible reading, focus on the centrality of God, especially Christ.
- In all your Bible reading, don't spare yourself the terrible glimpses of God's wrath.
- Pray earnestly and continually for everything you need to be happy in God.
- Resolve to fight every known sin in your life.
- Tell someone about Jesus.
- Spend time with God-saturated people who will help you see God and fight the fight of faith.
- Read biographies of great Christian saints.
- Read the great books about God.
- Get the rest and exercise and proper diet that your body was designed by God to have.
- Make proper use of revelation in nature.
- Do the hard and loving thing for the sake of others.
- Get a global vision for the cause of Christ and pour yourself out for the unreached.[165]

Beating at the heart of all these strategies is this one, get and keep a heart for God! This is the message toward which Koheleth is directing us. He will survey every possible alternative and raise every conceivable option, and when he has done that and proven the futility of all the world has to offer, he will deliver us to one sure, absolutely certain, undeniably guaranteed, unshakeable, eternal, unchanging means for real value and true joy.

Whoa! Got a little excited there and almost gave away the ending! The initial conclusions from the first round of experiments is this, life is utterly futile but there may still be joys to be found in

---

[165] John Piper, https://www.desiringgod.org/series/2005-regional-conference/messages. Accessed November 5, 2018.

common grace from the hand of God. From here, we move on to the next set of experimental strategies and their conclusions.

Study Questions

Koheleth describes his experimental methodology

1. Koheleth offers four distinct strategies (1:13, 17; 2:1, 3) as his experimental methodology. List them. Also, offer a generalized category name for the areas addressed by these strategies.
2. Reflect on the ways in which Koheleth investigated and explored his observations.
   a. Summarize Koheleth's efforts and discovery in your own words.
   b. How do the activities of his life mirror your own?

Initial conclusions

1. What do you make of the idea that "he who dies with the most toys is still dead [and someone else is playing with his toys!]"?
2. Personal expectations play a significant role in personal satisfaction and the experience of "meaning" and "purpose" in life. Koheleth seems to announce, with apparent disappointment, that all he got from all his wealth was enjoyment.
   a. What more might he/we have expected?
   b. How does disappointment affect our sense of purpose?
   c. What is the greatest inherent weakness in wealth that prevents it from offering real meaning for life?
3. What fate awaits all people regardless of their life activities?
4. Why does death seem to negate not only life but also any meaning that might be derived through living?
5. What does Koheleth desire from life that he realizes he cannot have as a result of living?

    a.   Trace the uses of the word "joy," "enjoy," or "enjoyment" through Ecclesiastes.

    b.   How are they used?

    c.   What word do they oppose?

6.   What does Koheleth identify as "good" that may come from work of living? From where does this good come?

7.   How does Paul's understanding of death in 1 Corinthians 15 differ from that of Koheleth? What makes the difference?

8.   The good that a man can gain in life, Koheleth attributes to God.

    a.   How should that conclusion be received, with despair or with gratitude?

    b.   What does this statement of God's involvement in the human experience of "good" reveal about Koheleth and his understanding of God?

    c.   If someone were to observe your life, to whom would they attribute your joy?

CHAPTER 6

EXPERIMENTAL SERIES 2 (3:1–5:11)

Certifying the Conclusions with a Second Series of Tests

Organic chemistry, senior year, 1979, Spencer High School, Columbus, Georgia, Mrs. Lawrence. She had been a research and development chemist for a world-renowned cosmetics company. I was seventeen, going to school, working forty hours a week as the program director at the local Boys' Club, participating in the JROTC Drill Team, and struggling to keep a grade point average high enough to maintain my standing in the National Honor Society. I had already fallen behind in Geometry and was most certainly going to fail trigonometry, which I was taking at the same time. I needed advice.

Mrs. Lawrence was not my favorite teacher. I can't say that I remember her with the fondness associated with Mr. Cole, my tenth-grade biology teacher, or Sgt. Gordon Burke, who was the JROTC instructor for the four years I was in the program. Mrs. Lawrence could be harsh. She could be unnerving. She was formidable. But she was never less than professional. Maybe that's why I went to her that day and asked her what I could do to make the grade in her class.

She was classic. "You, sir, need to take your time and actually do the work required, which, for you, means running your lab experiments twice to make sure your results are actually what are expected." I didn't know until that moment that it is standard practice to run experiments more than once to check for accuracy and consistency

both of practice and outcomes. I later learned that lab strategies sometimes include making controlled changes in the method in order to
measure the hypothesis from more than one critical perspective.

Rather than relegate Koheleth to rambling redundancy at this
point in the book, I think his format illustrates the careful application of Mrs. Lawrence's very good advice. For the sake of credibility,
he is certifying his results by running the experiment once more with
a slightly different variable (measuring the dependent variable against
a slightly different but calculated independent variable). Where, in
the first series of experiments, God was hidden behind the scenes
of natural processes, He is now in the forefront exercising sovereign
control over nature and the lives of men. In the first series of experiments, the effect under study is life lived within the larger context
of natural law. Now we will consider life lived in the context of the
divine Lawgiver.

The previous series wondered, "What real value is there for
a man in all the gains he makes beneath the sun?" That question
remains the focus of this series, though here it is worded slightly differently in 3:9[166] and it comes after the set of contextual observations
rather than before. The effect is the same. Koheleth's follow-up methodology will include reflection, meditations, and advanced observations of human experience in the context of intentional divine action.

Observations, Questions, Hypothesis, and Conclusions: Series 2

Summary contextual observations: Series 2

> [1]*A season is set for everything, a time for every
> experience under heaven:*
> [2]*A time for being born and a time for dying,*
> *A time for planting and a time for uprooting
> the planted;*
> [3]*A time for slaying and a time for healing,*

---

[166] "What value, then, can the man of affairs get from what he earns?" (JPS).

> *A time for tearing down and a time for building up;*
> ⁴*A time for weeping and a time for laughing,*
> *A time for wailing and a time for dancing;*
> ⁵*A time for throwing stones and a time for gathering stones,*
> *A time for embracing and a time for shunning embraces;*
> ⁶*A time for seeking and a time for losing,*
> *A time for keeping and a time for discarding;*
> ⁷*A time for ripping and a time for sewing,*
> *A time for silence and a time for speaking;*
> ⁸*A time for loving and a time for hating;*
> *A time for war and a time for peace.*
> *(Ecclesiastes 3:1–8)*

Where the poem in chapter 1 verses 4 through 9 focused on larger natural themes as the observation base for the hypothesis, this poem embraces the personal activities of human life and existence. I have used portions of this poem in a variety of ministry settings. Once, sitting on the curb outside the hospital emergency room, I explained to a young man that the accidental death of his friend was not his fault, that there is a time for everything including a time for being born and a time to die, and that we don't control that time. I have comforted myself in some conflict situations with the reality that there is a time to tear down and a time to build up. I shared the words of verse 4 in a funeral sermon once, "There is a time for weeping and a time for laughing." One time, at a wedding rehearsal, I quoted the second half of verse 8 as part of my advice for the happy couple, "There is a time for war and a time for peace," adding that the happiest, strongest couples know when it's time for what!

The doublets are inclusive, like two slices of dark rye bread embracing a tasty slice or two of pastrami slathered in stone-ground mustard and topped with sauerkraut. The two opposites indicate the extremes of human experience and include everything that occurs between them. So there is a time to be born and a time to die, and inferred in that image is all the life in between. And all the life in between birth and death is circumscribed by the sovereign will of God who determines the time set for everything and brings everything to pass in its time. Nothing just happens. A time is set for everything.

The research question, the sovereignty of God, and the futility of man (3:9–22)

The sovereignty of God and the futility of man introduced. Why speak of God and His sovereign will when God is not even mentioned in these eight verses? Heading this list of inclusive phrases is a guiding statement that sets them all in perspective.

Verse 1 asserts that "a season is set for everything, a time for every experience under heaven." Have you noticed that some of the most important teachings in the Bible are carried by three-letter words (in English)? "But" is one. "All" is another. "Set" rules in this sentence. "A season is set for everything." Koheleth is not simply making an inclusive list of human concerns that happen randomly. He is making a list of events that he declares happen intentionally, purposefully, implemented by Someone who rules over the schedule of the events and the substance of events. "A season is set."

We might rightly ask, if mankind is not the master of our own fate, then who is it that sets the seasons and the times for everything under heaven? But before we ask and answer that question, we have to ask Koheleth's question, his restatement of the refined research question that drives this entire exploration.

The research question restated (3:9).

⁹ *"What value, then, can the man of affairs get from what he earns?[167]"*

The question assumes the hypothesis based on a not yet but soon-to-be identified unknown. We already know the hypothesis

---

[167] Ecclesiastes 3:9 (JPS).

assumes all human effort at meaning is utterly pointless. This question directs the course of inquiry. If everything happens according to someone else's unalterable time frame, then what benefit is human action? If all the seasons are set and wealth cannot alter them, then what real value exists in human effort to gain wealth? What real value since the effort to gain wealth cannot affect any ultimate change? There's the refined research question repeated with slightly different wording. Now we can go back to that other question Koheleth inferred in his observation that "a season is set for everything." The question is if a season and a time is set for everything, for every experience under heaven, then who sets the schedule? Who is responsible for canceling the cosmic impact of human effort? Koheleth answers the question in verses 3:10–22.

The sovereignty of God and the futility of man expanded.

> [10]*I have observed the business that God gave man to be concerned with:* [11]*He brings everything to pass precisely at its time; He also puts eternity in their mind, but without man ever guessing, from first to last, all the things that God brings to pass.* [12]*Thus I realized that the only worthwhile thing there is for them is to enjoy themselves and do what is good in their lifetime;* [13]*also, that whenever a man does eat and drink and get enjoyment out of all his wealth, it is a gift of God.*
>
> [14]*I realized, too, that whatever God has brought to pass will recur evermore: Nothing can be added to it*
> *And nothing taken from it—*
> *and God has brought to pass that men revere Him.*
> [15]*What is occurring occurred long since,* [16]*And what is to occur occurred long since:*
> *and God seeks the pursued. And, indeed, I have observed under the sun:*

Alongside justice there is wickedness, Alongside righteousness there is wickedness.

[17]*I mused: "God will doom both righteous and wicked, for there is a time for every experience and for every happening."* [18]*So I decided, as regards men, to dissociate them [from] the divine beings and to face the fact that they are beasts.* [19]*For in respect of the fate of man and the fate of beast, they have one and the same fate: as the one dies so dies the other, and both have the same lifebreath; man has no superiority over beast, since both amount to nothing.* [20]*Both go to the same place; both came from dust and both return to dust.* [21]*Who knows if a man's lifebreath does rise upward and if a beast's breath does sink down into the earth?*

[22]*I saw that there is nothing better for man than to enjoy his possessions, since that is his portion. For who can enable him to see what will happen afterward? (3:10–22)*

The answer to the question of who sets the seasons and the times is God. "God brings everything to pass precisely at its time." And the answer to the research question ("What real value is there for a man in all the gains he makes beneath the sun?") at this point is as follows: "None. There is no real value in human effort or gains because of the effect of God's will on all human existence." Welcome to a discussion of God's sovereignty and its relation to the futility of human life where human decisions take a back seat to the divine will in everything.[168]

---

[168] The definition of God's sovereignty from the Westminster Confession of Faith in Modern English. "From all eternity and by the completely wise and holy purpose of his own will, God has freely and unchangeably ordained whatever happens. This ordainment does not mean, however, that God is the author of sin (he is not), that he represses the will of his created beings, or that he takes away the freedom or contingency of secondary causes. Rather, the will of created beings and the freedom and contingency of secondary causes are established by

The sovereignty of God is no small discussion, since God the Creator is no small god with no small authority over all He has created. Shelves are filled around the world with books written on the topic of God's sovereignty and the effect of His sovereignty on human lives and reality.[169] We, however, have little space here to delve more deeply into the subject of the nature of God and His relationship to that which He created than Koheleth does himself.

Koheleth's interest lies primarily in how God's sovereignty circumscribes human life activity. God the Creator sets the time for all things relative to human existence in the world God created (3:1–8). God gives man life and sets him upon the business of living in the world but gives humanity no real control over the timing of life (3:10–11a). God places within the human heart a desire to know things bigger and greater than humanity, but God does not set within mankind an ability to personally or aggregately know and embrace all that is possible in the mind and heart of God (3:11b). God grants to mankind whatever enjoyment and success anyone might achieve (3:13), but instead of allowing humans to exalt their own efforts, God has locked human beings into the need to revere Him as they see His hand controlling the context of their lives (3:14). God is so completely satisfied with His will and the product of His Word in all that He created that He seeks nothing new under the sun from the hand and heart of man (3:15). God sits as Judge over the righteous and the wicked, bringing them both to death and then to judgment, making them little better than the beasts whose lives also are created by God and according to His will end in death (3:18–22).

The impression Koheleth leaves is one of being surrounded. Everywhere one might turn to express personal independence, he runs into God already there before him exercising divine privilege and power

---

him." (https://epc.org/wp-content/uploads/Files/1-Who-We-Are/B-About-The-EPC/WCF-ModernEngli sh.pdf. Accessed December 27, 2018.)

[169] Derek Thomas, "God's Sovereignty and Our Responsibility," originally published in *Tabletalk*, added to https://www.ligonier.org/blog/gods-sovereignty-and-our-responsibility (April 4, 2018). Accessed December 27, 2018. Thomas offers a useful summary of the most important points of discussion regarding the relationship between God's sovereignty and human responsibility.

without regard for human effort. Other biblical writers speak of being hemmed in on every side by God and His will. Jesus Himself, moments before His ascension, denied His disciples the right to know God's sovereign timing beyond what God Himself revealed.[170] Ray Ortlund Jr. envisions God's sovereignty as that freedom that God has that, "from his position of absolute supremacy, God rules over all things in a way which necessarily precludes his being limited by creaturely factors."[171]

There is a necessary place for the discussion of the relationship of God's infinite freedom to accomplish His will to human responsibility as created and assigned by God. Jerry Bridges raises and responds to the question of what difference divine sovereignty makes in daily life in his essay in *Still Sovereign: Contemporary Perspectives on Election, Foreknowledge, and Grace.*[172] The essay is worth reading. Koheleth, however, does not undertake that conversation beyond this, "I realized that the only worthwhile thing there is for them is to enjoy themselves and do what is good in their lifetime; [13]also, that whenever a man does eat and drink and get enjoyment out of all his wealth, it is a gift of God."[173]

God's sovereignty releases human responsibility from the burden of control into the paradise of rest and rejoicing, or what O'Donnell identifies as the twin imperatives of holiness and happiness.[174] The times and seasons of life are beyond human control, but God has permitted and provided for human beings to do good and to enjoy the good He gives them. Ours is not to play god, but to rest

---

[170] "So when they had come together, they asked him, 'Lord, will you at this time restore the kingdom to Israel?' He said to them, 'It is not for you to know the times or seasons that the Father has fixed by his own authority'" (Acts 1:6–7, ESV).

[171] Ray Ortlund Jr., "The Sovereignty of God: Case Studies in the Old Testament," in *Still Sovereign: Contemporary Perspectives on Election, Foreknowledge, and Grace,* eds. Thomas R. Schreiner and Bruce A Ware (Grand Rapids, MI: Baker Books, 2000) 25.

[172] Jerry Bridges, "What Difference Does Divine Sovereignty Make in Daily Life," in *Still Sovereign: Contemporary Perspectives on Election, Foreknowledge, and Grace,* eds. Thomas R Schreiner and Bruce A Ware (Grand Rapids, MI: Baker Books, 2000). 295–306.

[173] Ecclesiastes 3:12–13 (JPS).

[174] O'Donnell, 76–77.

and rejoice in the sovereign grace of God throughout the days of our lives, however enduring or brief they may be.

May I direct your attention to a little scriptural detail I point out to my congregation from time to time? Pay attention as you read your Bible any time God repeats Himself. He may repeat a name. He may utter the same phrase repeatedly in a book. He may take an action more than once.

Usually, if God repeats Himself, His intention is to gain someone's attention. Take Samuel, for instance. God repeatedly called out in the night to get his attention. Or Saul, on the road to Damascus, where Jesus asks, "Saul, Saul, why do you persecute me?"[175] Or here in Ecclesiastes where the inspiring Holy Spirit directs Koheleth to mention contentment as a goal for living, five times at least (2:24; 3:12, 22; 5:17, 18).

Contentment assesses the current condition as adequate and responds with peace. Koheleth proposes that joy and righteousness are reasonable expectations for a lifetime, and if there is joy and the opportunity to have the life essentials, that is a gift from God worthy of contentment. In the New Testament, Paul reminds Timothy that "godliness with contentment is great gain."[176] You have to wonder if Paul was thinking of Ecclesiastes as he shared that piece of biblical wisdom with his protégé. As Paul expresses "contentment" to Timothy, he is not thinking of merely "passive acceptance of the *status quo*, but the positive assurance that God has supplied one's needs, and the consequent release from unnecessary desire."[177]

Five times Koheleth points to contentment with our "portion," or our "lot," as the worthwhile good that we can have in an otherwise futile existence. Five times he repeats himself. Five times. The author of Hebrews chimes in with similar words of truth,

> Keep your life free from love of money, and
> be content with what you have, for he has said, "I

---

[175] Acts 9:4 (ESV).
[176] 1 Timothy 6:6 (ESV).
[177] J. C. Connell, *Contentment. New Bible Dictionary (3rd ed.)*, eds. D. R. W. Wood, I. H. Marshall, et al. (Downers Grove, IL: InterVarsity Press, 1996), 222.

will never leave you nor forsake you." So we can confidently say, "The Lord is my helper; I will not fear; what can man do to me?"[178]

John the Baptist teaches as he baptizes in the Jordan River. Luke records a conversation he has one day with the crowds that are coming from throughout Israel to be baptized. They ask John, in response to his preaching, "What then shall we do?"

> And he answered them, "Whoever has two tunics is to share with him who has none, and whoever has food is to do likewise." Tax collectors also came to be baptized and said to him, "Teacher, what shall we do?" And he said to them, "Collect no more than you are authorized to do." Soldiers also asked him, "And we, what shall we do?" And he said to them, "Do not extort money from anyone by threats or by false accusation, and be content with your wages."[179]

Contentment with one's own life and possessions is the key principle of the tenth commandment, "You shall not covet your neighbor's house; you shall not covet your neighbor's wife, or his male servant, or his female servant, or his ox, or his donkey, or anything that is your neighbor's."[180]

Again and again and again, God's Word points the heart to contentment. Biblical contentment rests on faith in the person and promises of the covenant-making, covenant-keeping God.

Contentment is the spiritual antidote to the venomous poison of covetousness; it matters that contentment is more than a default position relative to God's sovereignty. Contentment, to be truly satis-

---

[178] Hebrew 13:5–6 (ESV).
[179] Luke 3:11–14 (ESV).
[180] Exodus 20:17 (ESV). You can check out Luke 10:25–37 for Jesus's answer to the question, "Who is my neighbor?"

fied with God's will and provision, adds much benefit to the soul, and isn't "real value" (benefit, profit) what we are looking for? Jeremiah Burroughs, a seventeenth-century Puritan preacher and writer, sees seven "excellencies" of genuine contentment:

- By contentment we give God His due worship
- In contentment there is much exercise of the strength and beauty of grace
- By contentment the soul is outfitted to receive mercy
- By contentment the soul is prepared to do service
- Contentment delivers from temptation
- Contentment brings an abundance of comfort
- Contentment brings in what we do not possess (like patience, faith, trust, peace.)[181]

Koheleth goes no further than "contentment" in investigating the implications of divine sovereignty. Take stock, he says. Consider where what you have comes from, be content, and rejoice in the gift of God while you enjoy what He has provided. The Teacher goes no further because he is pursuing one question and one question only, "What real value is there for a man in all the gains he makes beneath the sun?" And he is tracking only one hypothesis, "Utter futility! All is futile!" This second set of observations related to the sovereignty of God provides the background for the second set of intellectual experiments recorded in this section of the report.

According to Koheleth's report, the sovereignty of God accentuates the futility of human effort to gain "real value" other than contentment in life under the sun.

---

[181] Jeremiah Burroughs, *The Rare Jewel of Christian Contentment* (London: W. Bentley, 1651). Accessed from Logos Bible Software, 1:47 p.m., December 27, 2018.

Hypothesis Restated and Methodology
Described for Series 2 (4:1–16)

A note on precision, accuracy, and the structure of Ecclesiastes

Do you know the difference between "precision" and "accuracy"? Precision deals with exactness. Accuracy deals with validity. Truth can be expressed with accuracy but not precision, but if truth is stated with precision, then it must be accurate. For example, if I describe a winter sunset over Lake Superior, I can accurately call the primary color orange. However, if I want to be precise, I will say it is the color of tangerines left hanging three too many days in the sun after peak of ripeness. Both are true. The former is accurate, while the latter precise.

Culturally, we twenty-first-century people prefer precision. Our training in the scientific method, our exposure to courtroom procedure, our failed interactions on social media constantly urge us to think and act and speak and expect precision. The demand for precision is grueling, but it has not always been so. As we work our way through this lab report Koheleth prepared for us, we could wish for more precision. We could wish that section headings and section content for that matter were clearly separated, more precisely presented, but that was simply not a concern for Koheleth. His concern is for an accurate representation of the truths garnered through his research. That he has an observation followed by a conclusion without restating the hypothesis is of little concern because he is driven by the need to give us accurate access to truth. He is not driven by slavery to precision. Failing to be precise is a modern, not an ancient, sin. The lack of precision does not invalidate the truth presented as long as the truth is accurate.

A note on the methodology of observations and conclusions

In this section, Koheleth mixes observations and conclusions. I'm not surprised. He's a teacher, after all. He wants his audience to learn something, and he's making the most of each teachable moment, each occasion when the presentation of factual information collides with the current experience or context for the learner. When a child pulls a dog's ears and the dog turns and snaps at the child, that is a teachable moment. When a senior picks up the TV remote, holds it to their ear, and tries to make a phone call, that is a teachable moment. As Koheleth progresses with his presentation in this second series, he draws conclusions along the way, like a good teacher, making the most of teachable moments.

> ¹*I further observed all the oppression that goes on under the sun: the tears of the oppressed, with none to comfort them; and the power of their oppressors—with none to comfort them.* ²*Then I accounted those who died long since more fortunate than those who are still living;* ³*and happier than either are those who have not yet come into being and have never witnessed the miseries that go on under the sun.*
>
> ⁴*I have also noted that all labor and skillful enterprise come from men's envy of each other— another futility and pursuit of wind!*
>
> ⁵*[True,]*
> *The fool folds his hands together And has to eat his own flesh.*
>
> ⁶*[But no less truly,]*
> *Better is a handful of gratification*
> *Than two fistfuls of labor which is pursuit of wind.*
>
> ⁷*And I have noted this further futility under the sun:* ⁸*the case of the man who is alone, with no companion, who has neither son nor brother; yet he amasses wealth without limit, and his eye is never sated with riches. For whom, now, is he amassing it while denying himself enjoyment?*
>
> *That too is a futility and an unhappy business.*
> *(4:1–8)*

145

Observation as method. See the words of observation in these paragraphs? They indicate data collection. "I observed," "I noted," and "I have noted further"—Koheleth continues to include us in the loop of observations that raise a need for analysis in light of his hypothesis that everything under the sun is utterly futile. The words "I accounted," "futility," "pursuit of wind," and "unhappy business" are words and phrases of analysis. They represent data interpretation and conclusion drawing. Data collection and data interpretation are integral components of scientific inquiry.

The hypothesis restated. Koheleth observes the oppressed and the oppressor and finds that neither realizes the comfort for which their souls long, meaning neither has any real advantage over the other. How much better, he concludes, those dead or not yet living who remain untouched by the miseries of life—the pain, the loneliness, the meaninglessness. He notes that the very best human accomplishments grow from the seeds of envy and jealousy rather than other lofty and noble beginnings, a fertile garden if one's goal is to grow futility!

Futility is the laziness of the fool and the labor of an ungrateful man. It is the man who spends his days amassing untold wealth and, having no one to share it with, takes no time to enjoy it for himself. What is that proverb? "All work and no play make Jack a dull boy!"

Making the most of teachable moments. Interestingly, making the most of a teachable moment, Koheleth directs us to sharing and partnerships as a means of increasing "real value" in our efforts to create gain for ourselves.

> [9] *Two are better off than one, in that they have greater benefit from their earnings.* [10] *For should they fall, one can raise the other; but woe betide him who is alone and falls with no companion to raise him!* [11] *Further, when two lie together they are warm; but how can he who is alone get warm?* [12] *Also, if one attacks, two can stand up to him. A threefold cord is not readily broken.* (4:9–12)

Look in this principle of sharing and relationship for a clue to where Koheleth will eventually lead us. Life for a single person who can call on no assistance is measurably more difficult than for someone with companions. Though the *Tanakh* uses the word "earnings" to translate the Hebrew word *'amal* here, Fox suggests the real issue in the word is the "effort of toil," the work that goes into the gain rather than the gain itself.[182] Two gain greater benefit from shared effort. And if two have greater benefit, imagine three working together at the same task. "Many hands make light work," and greater benefits, apparently!

If it is true, in the natural world, that teamwork or relationships have the potential to lighten the load and increase the benefit, what might be true of finding real meaning in life? Is there a potential relationship that might add meaning where singular, personal effort might not? We might suspect there is, but Koheleth does not take us there yet. We're going to have to wait and see.

> [13]*Better a poor but wise youth than an old but foolish king who no longer has the sense to heed warnings.* [14]*For the former can emerge from a dungeon to become king; while the latter, even if born to kingship, can become a pauper.* [15]*[However,] I reflected about all the living who walk under the sun with that youthful successor who steps into his place.* [16]*Unnumbered are the multitudes of all those who preceded them; and later generations will not acclaim him either. For that too is futile and pursuit of wind.* (4:13–16)

As long as we're talking about work and wealth and relationships, let's talk about old kings and young men and the fact that as generations of leaders come and go, regardless of their fame or infamy in life, regardless of their success or failure, their wisdom or foolishness, their wealth or poverty, they are not the first and won't

---

[182] Fox, xvii.

be the last and no one will remember the next better than the first. All they amount to is nothing in the grand scheme of history. That is the definition of futility and pursuing wind.

None of this is to say that the pursuit of wisdom is worthless in and of itself. It is only that wisdom, or anything else that is temporally limited, is limited and should be sought and embraced as such. The value of wisdom is real but transitory. To treat it otherwise is to multiply foolishness. Work, make friends in the work, put forth effort, but ask no more of your effort than it can realistically provide. This, Koheleth presents, is life lived under the sun. He has made his observations, applied his intellect and wisdom to analysis, and drawn some conclusions that answer the research question and support the hypothesis. Before drawing final conclusions from this series of experiments relative to human existence and divine sovereignty, Koheleth offers some practical applications for daily living.

Applications and Initial Conclusions: Series 2 (4:17–5:11)

"Be practical!" Over and over again, I heard the same request. I would ask random people for their opinion of how I might improve Sunday morning sermons. No one ever mentioned improved exegesis, logic, or exposition. They rarely complained about the illustrations or demanded more stories. In fact, I would often get an apologetic affirmation before the critique I asked for was delivered. "Well, Pastor, you preach good sermons. But I wish they were just a bit more practical."

The collections of proverbs and wise sayings included in Ecclesiastes fulfill a recognized function of wisdom literature. They instruct. The book has dealt consistently with the philosophical and theological conundrums of daily life that look for all intents and purposes to be choreographed futility. Situated between the second and third series of experiments, Koheleth, the collector of wise sayings who teaches the people,[183] pauses to get practical.

---

[183] Ecclesiastes 12:9–10.

Koheleth offers three sets of advice in line with three spheres of influence on a person's life, God, the government, and the goods mankind seeks to gain in the world.

God!

> [17] *Be not overeager to go to the House of God: more acceptable is obedience than the offering of fools, for they know nothing [but] to do wrong.*
> [1] *Keep your mouth from being rash, and let not your throat be quick to bring forth speech before God. For God is in heaven and you are on earth; that is why your words should be few.* [2] *Just as dreams come with much brooding, so does foolish utterance come with much speech.* [3] *When you make a vow to God, do not delay to fulfill it. For He has no pleasure in fools; what you vow, fulfill.* [4] *It is better not to vow at all than to vow and not fulfill.* [5] *Don't let your mouth bring you into disfavor, and don't plead before the messenger that it was an error, but fear God; else God may be angered by your talk and destroy your possessions.* [6] *For much dreaming leads to futility and to superfluous talk. (4:17–5:6)*

I know some folks who would probably rejoice to take Koheleth's admonition out of context and assert that the Bible warns them not to be too eager to go to church. Let me assure you, if this is you, this is not the verse you are looking for. Koheleth does not diminish worship. He warns against heartless, inauthentic, religiosity posing as worship. He warns Pharisees not to be Pharisees. You've no doubt heard of Sunday Christians who become weekday sinners, people whose profession of faith only gets lived out in practical ways one day a week? This is what Koheleth warns against. Authentic faithfulness from a heart genuinely in love with God is preferred over cold repetition of loveless legalism.

It would be the height of futility to go often to the temple worship, make the sacrifices, and proceed posthaste to the same old sins, the same old habits, the same old ways. Better by far is the sacrifice of personal obedience to the Word of God than the pretense of faithfulness in attendance to corporate worship without any real obedience. James wrote, "Faith without works is dead."[184] Koheleth wrote, "More acceptable is obedience than the worship of fools." They mean the same thing.

What are some practical ways a wise person can demonstrate faithfulness and obedience? Keep watch over what we say, especially about God and the things that concern Him. If you make a vow to God, keep it. If you can't keep it, don't make it. This principle came home to roost in my heart a number of years ago. Back in the late 1970s, I attended a youth camp. It was a rare occasion for me, but we were there, my sister and I; and the leaders of the camp made a request for pledges toward the ongoing maintenance of the camp facilities. I pledged $20.

It was the summer between my senior year of high school and the first year of college. I was still working at the Boys' Club, trying to save money for tuition and books and things I knew I would need at school but not have funds to buy once I got there. Twenty dollars soon began to seem like a huge sum that I could not spare. I told myself I was just a kid. God wouldn't mind. I let the pledge slip from my mind as I worked my way through five schools and four degrees.

One day, sitting at my desk in the house provided by my first (and only) congregation for their pastor, I read these words again and followed up with a cross reference to Deuteronomy 23:22–23.

> If you make a vow to the *Lord* your God, you shall not delay fulfilling it, for the *Lord* your God will surely require it of you, and you will be guilty of sin. But if you refrain from vowing, you will not be guilty of sin. You shall be careful to do what has passed your lips, for you have volun-

---

[184] James 2:17.

tarily vowed to the *Lord* your God what you have promised with your mouth.[185]

It had been almost twenty years since I made the pledge, but the day came flooding back to memory like yesterday. And there was no way around the fact that the delay in fulfilling the vow I made to the *Lord* was nothing short of guilt-inducing sin. First, I apologized, confessed my sin, and sought God's forgiveness. Then I wrote a check. For more than $20. Then I mailed it to the best address I could find for the camp.

If you make a vow to God, keep it. If you can't keep it, don't make it. Have you ever, in a crisis, said to God, "Dear God, if You will only do such and so, I promise I will love You forever and do this and that" only to disregard "this and that" when the crisis is resolved? You've made a vow to God. God takes vows seriously. Is there something you've put off that you need to get started with? Now is a very good time.

Don't let your mouth bring you into disfavor, Koheleth writes. Fox translates these words literally as "Don't let your mouth make your flesh sin." The bottom line here is honor God, always. Honor Him with both your intent *and* your actions. Honor Him with your faith and your obedience. Honor Him with your heart and your will. Honor Him with your lips and your life.

Make His honor in the world the practice of your life in the world. If you are reading this as a professing Christian, know this—true Christian faith encompasses both a spiritual life and an ethical life. Faithfulness equals faith plus obedience.

Government.

> [7]*If you see in a province oppression of the poor and suppression of right and justice, don't wonder at the fact; for one high official is protected by a higher one, and both of them by still higher ones.* [8]*Thus the*

---

[185] Deuteronomy 23:21–23 (ESV).

greatest advantage in all the land is his: he controls
a field that is cultivated. (5:7–8)

There's that word *yitron* ("advantage") again. See it in verse 8? Fox says the sentence in Hebrew is obscure and no one has proposed a satisfactory solution for what it means.[186] That's somewhat comforting but doesn't let us off the interpretive hook. Koheleth describes a government bureaucracy where oppression is passed down the line from one authority to another, greater to lesser to least. The greatest advantage goes not to the bureaucrat who lives off the efforts of others in order to appease still others, but the man who rules (farms?) a cultivated field that, presumably, can tend to his family's needs. It looks to me like a paragraph in praise of simple contentment. The one with the greatest advantage is the one who can feed himself. The one who has the greatest advantage is the one who relies on no one else for basic needs, who is not beholden to others for their social position or economic station. The one with the greatest advantage is the one who answers to himself and is just ambitious enough to tend to his own business.

I can see where striving to advance in a bloated bureaucracy would fit the definition of futility and a pursuit of wind, can't you? In the end, no matter how high you reach, there is always someone over you holding your "destiny" in their hands, advancing your cause or orchestrating your downfall. And no matter how hard you fight, or what gains you make, in the end, you die and someone else takes your place. Futility. Makes sense to look for something more, something greater, does it not?

Goods.

> [9]*A lover of money never has his fill of money,*
> *nor a lover of wealth his fill of income. That too is*
> *futile.* [10]*As his substance increases, so do those who*
> *consume it; what, then, does the success of its owner*

---

[186] Fox, 35.

amount to but feasting his eyes? [11]*A worker's sleep is sweet, whether he has much or little to eat; but the rich man's abundance doesn't let him sleep. (5:9–11)*

The stories of unhappy lottery winners who suddenly found greedy people coming out of the woodwork in search of their windfall fill the Internet. Take the story of forty-seven-year-old Abraham Shakespeare, who was a 2006 winner of a $30 million lotto prize. Soon after his win was revealed, he was sued by a former friend who claimed Shakespeare stole the winning ticket from the man's wallet. (The case was dismissed.) But that was not the worst! "Shakespeare was murdered by his romantic partner, a woman named DeeDee Moore. Sadly, before his death, Shakespeare told his few remaining confidants that 'I'd have been better off broke. I thought all these people were my friends, but then I realized all they want is just money.'"[187]

This is only one of hundreds of rags to riches to rags again stories. Often the story of financial and personal woe includes a chapter about those who desired to consume the winner's sudden increase in substance. Great wealth seems to have a habit of becoming a great burden. Those who work hard to deserve and gain it seem to have to work even harder to keep it from those who don't deserve it and have not worked to gain it. It's one unhappy cycle of futility. That's why Koheleth figures the worker's sleep is sweet, because he has only what he has, and though he would keep it, should he lose it, he would simply keep working to provide for himself and his family. Wealth with fear solves fewer problems than integrity and hard work with contentment.

Having made some applications regarding wisdom in the context of futility, Koheleth moves to the third series of observations, experiments, and conclusions included in this report. The repeated phrase "grave evil" and the reintroduction of the keywords of "toil,"

---

[187] Scott O'Reilly, "5 Lessons About Money From Unhappy Lottery Winners," https://www.thealternativedaily.com/unhappy-lottery-winners. Accessed December 13, 2018.

"wind," and "futility" mark this as a new section and a new series of concerns.

Study Questions

These questions follow the flow of the biblical text we've just talked about. These are not easy questions. They are designed for investigation beyond what you've just read. They are designed to spark interest and intrigue regarding themes and implications Koheleth points to but does not develop. Treat them like a treasure map marked with many X's. The question is the X. The answer is the treasure. Reaching the treasure takes effort. That's where you come in. Have fun!

1. What purpose motivates Koheleth's use of this series of observations (3:1–8)? What does he intend to describe?
   a. Consider the underlying hypothesis.
   b. Do these realities support or sabotage the initial hypothesis?
2. Consider divine sovereignty.
   a. What factors related to God's sovereignty diminish human value (and under what circumstances)?
   b. What factors related to divine sovereignty exalt human value (and under what circumstances)?
   c. What impact does God's sovereignty have on the meaninglessness of human existence?
   d. What joy can be found in a world where God sets the time for all things?
   e. If true joy is found in confidence and faith in God's glorious and sovereign design for life, then what is the most meaningful life activity a person can be involved in?
3. Koheleth restates the research question following a second series of observations (3:9) about the way in which the world works. What conclusion does Koheleth offer related to the observations?

4. Koheleth, in noting that God puts eternity in the mind of man but that man never guesses all "that God brings to pass" (3:11), provides a useful clue to his real intent in this study.

    a. What does Koheleth mean that God has put eternity into the minds of men?

    b. What attribute of God is highlighted by the idea that God brings everything to "pass precisely at its time"?

    c. What difference would it make if man could guess, from first to last, "all the things that God brings to pass"? What does this ignorance of God's activity suggest about all the efforts of man "under the sun" that are but a "chasing after wind"?

    d. Why do humans not guess the extent and impact of divine sovereignty?

5. Koheleth posits the modified hypothesis that the "only worthwhile thing there is for them is to enjoy themselves and do...good" (3:12). There is a philosophy that promotes the "eat, drink, and be merry for tomorrow we die" idea.

    a. What is that philosophy?

    b. Do you think Koheleth is promoting this philosophy? Why or why not?

6. Koheleth seems to express that joy and the ability to enjoy anything of this world hinges on the expressed grace of God (3:13). Can you find several verses in the writings of the Apostle Paul that also place human experience in the sovereign hands of God?

7. Setting the subjects of study in a different philosophical context potentially allows a researcher to gain insights that might otherwise remain hidden. Here (3:18–21) Koheleth decides to consider humans not in comparison with animals, but as if they are but animals. This is a common approach in the life science world.

    a. To what kind of conclusions does this contextual consideration lead?

b.   Does the Bible offer a different context as more valid? If so, to what conclusions does the biblical context lead?

c.   What evidence is there that one pursuit may be more beneficial here than the other?

8.   Ecclesiastes 3:22 seems to be proposing a rhetorical question, but, in this context, it might be offering a question intended to lead our thinking to a different answer.

   a.   Who does know the answer to this question?

   b.   Can science answer this question?

   c.   How does faith answer this question?

   d.   What happens to interpretation if this rhetorical question is intended to draw a people of faith who are the guardians of divine revelation to bring what they know to a question of which the surrounding cultures have no answer?

   e.   How do our presuppositions about the author, the audience, and our own understanding of the human experience color our approach to this question?

9.   Koheleth suggests that it is a man's "portion" to enjoy his possessions.

   a.   Can you support the proposition that this is a faith statement and not a "faithless" statement?

   b.   If joy in one's possessions is one's portion, who sets this as our "portion"?

   c.   What indicators are given in the Scripture that suggest God delights in our delight in what He has provided? (Or what evidence is there that joy in our possessions is the "portion" assigned to us and therefore God's will for us?)

      i.   Why would God set joy in possessions as a portion for people and then call greed sin or tell us not to store up treasures on earth?

      ii.   What purpose does the creation and gain of wealth serve in the world?

10. Koheleth, in his conclusion in 4:16, seems to dismiss hope on the basis of social historical amnesia, no one will remember. This phenomenon probably motivates the practice of placing headstones and monuments at graves, to provide some sense or opportunity for permanent memory.
    a. Humans consider enduring remembrance of themselves of great significance. What efforts do we make (and in what efforts do we take comfort that we have succeeded) in our quest for immortality?
    b. Is there any real hope for those who wish to not succumb to the passage of time and simply fade away?

CHAPTER 7

EXPERIMENTAL SERIES 3 (5:12–8:15)

Rapid-Fire Rechecks (5:12–6:12): Series 3

¹²*Here is a grave evil I have observed under the sun: riches hoarded by their owner to his misfortune,* ¹³*in that those riches are lost in some unlucky venture; and if he begets a son, he has nothing in hand.*

¹⁴*Another grave evil is this: He must depart just as he came. As he came out of his mother's womb, so must he depart at last, naked as he came. He can take nothing of his wealth to carry with him.* ¹⁵*So what is the good of his toiling for the wind?* ¹⁶*Besides, all his days he eats in darkness, with much vexation and grief and anger.*

¹⁷*Only this, I have found, is a real good: that one should eat and drink and get pleasure with all the gains he makes under the sun, during the numbered days of life that God has given him; for that is his portion.* ¹⁸*Also, whenever a man is given riches and property by God, and is also permitted by Him to enjoy them and to take his portion and get pleasure for his gains—that is a gift of God.* ¹⁹*For [such a man] will not brood much over the days of his life, because God keeps him busy enjoying himself.*

¹There is an evil I have observed under the sun, and a grave one it is for man: ²that God sometimes grants a man riches, property, and wealth, so that he does not want for anything his appetite may crave, but God does not permit him to enjoy it; instead, a stranger will enjoy it.

That is futility and a grievous ill. ³Even if a man should beget a hundred children and live many years—no matter how many the days of his years may come to, if his gullet is not sated through his wealth, I say: The stillbirth, though it was not even accorded a burial, is more fortunate than he. ⁴Though it comes into futility and departs into darkness, and its very name is covered with darkness, ⁵though it has never seen or experienced the sun, it is better off than he—⁶yes, even if the other lived a thousand years twice over but never had his fill of enjoyment! For are not both of them bound for the same place? ⁷All of man's earning is for the sake of his mouth, yet his gullet is not sated. ⁸What advantage then has the wise man over the fool, what advantage has the pauper who knows how to get on in life? ⁹Is the feasting of the eyes more important than the pursuit of desire? That, too, is futility and pursuit of wind. (5:15–6:9)

The author of the New Testament book of Hebrews urges his readers to advance in spiritual maturity, to grow in faith, to make progress in personal discipleship and holiness on account of the excellency of Jesus and all He has made possible through His life and death. His urging takes on a special intensity in the opening to the sixth chapter. He writes,

> Therefore let us leave the elementary doctrine of Christ and go on to maturity, not laying again a foundation of repentance from dead

works and of faith toward God, and of instruction about washings, the laying on of hands, the
resurrection of the dead, and eternal judgment.[188]

His audience understands and embraces the basics of the
Christian faith and practice. They have no need of repeated instruction in the gospel plan of salvation that results in conversion. These
fundamental truths they heard, believed, accepted by faith, and experienced their spiritual impact. Their current need is not to restate or
rehash the basics but to move on to advanced discipleship.

There is a season for everything. Once a foundation has been
well laid, it is time to build. That is what Koheleth does in this section
of his report. He has already meticulously evaluated life experience in
the natural world and under the sovereignty of God and discovered
the smallness of humanity compared to the vastness of creation and
the surrounding sovereignty of God in all things. He does not need
to make those points again. Instead, in this third series of experimental considerations, he proceeds with a "rapid-fire recheck."

I'm certain that if I heard it once, I heard it hundreds of time
from teachers all the way from grade school to graduate school,
"Check your work!" This is Koheleth's strategy here. He is checking
his work. This passage reflects observations, research question, and
conclusions massed together in rapid succession. Three "grave evils"
are quickly examined and deemed conclusive. Three times they provide negative answers to the question whether there is any real value
in the gains of human effort under the sun. Each grave evil draws the
same conclusion. They are each futile and a pursuit of wind.

*Investigative context: Three "grave evils" and the
futility of wealth (5:12–16, 6:1–9)*

The meaning of "grave evil." Like Frodo wandering through the
margins of Mordor with Samwise, we've been here before. The phrase
"grave evil" is not new to us. Koheleth uses it as part of his initial

---

[188] Hebrews 6:1–2 (ESV).

response in chapter 2. He reasons that all the wealth he worked hard to gain will go to someone else at his death, probably before he has an opportunity to fully enjoy it, and he doesn't know whether his heir will be wise or foolish. This situation leads him to loathe his wealth and to decide that the sum total of all his possessions and the effort to gain them is futility. He looks upon all he gained with despair. He explains his despair like this, "For sometimes a person whose fortune was made with wisdom, knowledge, and skill must hand it on to be the portion of somebody who did not toil for it. That too is futile, and a grave evil."[189] The Hebrew word translated "evil" can refer either to that which is morally wrong or to what is disastrous, harmful, or misery-producing.

Three miserable miseries. Having to hand over the work of a lifetime to an undeserving heir is a "grave evil," a miserable misery. So is losing your lifetime's savings to a foolish choice or spending your life amassing great wealth but never actually enjoying any of it before you die (especially since you can't take a cent of it with you!) or, even more miserable, a man who cannot get enough of wealth, spends his entire life energy on grasping for more, and dies not only never having gained enough but also never having been allowed, because of greed and the will of God, to enjoy what he was permitted to gain. A pauper knows how to live with enough, a greedy fool does not, so what advantage is there for the rich man, Koheleth asks, as he reiterates his research question in a very specific theoretical setting? None. No advantage at all.

In fact, according to Koheleth, a stillborn child is better off than a man who is never satisfied with the wealth he gains. Both wind up in the depths of Sheol, but the stillborn never knew unsatiated hunger for what cannot be kept. While the stillborn is an expression of futility, the child itself has never suffered the pangs of futility.

Initial conclusion: The single good and the value of grace (5:17–19)

The single seemingly positive mercy that counters the miserable miseries is contentment in the gifts of God that He allows those who

---

[189] Ecclesiastes 2:21 (JPS).

possess them to enjoy. Koheleth uses a phrase here to denote the idea that the good he perceives is actual and realized not merely perceived or "hoped for." It is a genuine "good," a real value, when a person finds authentic appreciation for the results of the efforts he makes at life.

Our driveway has a slight hill as you turn off the highway toward the house. Once you make the turn and start the short incline, you can look over our entire house. More than once, as I've made that turn, I have heard my wife in the seat next to me whisper, "Thank you!"

The year we moved to Minnesota, we had been married for about a year. My wife had been teaching third grade in a Christian school for seventeen years. She made $17,000 that year. A first-year teacher in public school, straight out of college, that year, started in the local public school system at $34,000. I was out of work. We were headed to graduate school. She worked while I went to school. I graduated and we accepted God's call to a small church in a town that isn't actually at the end of the world, but you can see it from here. There was little that would suggest that we would ever have a home that could accommodate the needs muscular dystrophy places on families.

But here we are. Linda's "thank-you's" are not for me. They are for our heavenly Father who has more than adequately met our needs. She epitomizes one who has encountered "real good" in life. While she struggles often with the increasing limitations imposed by an irreversible genetic condition, she revels in the real grace God gives to simply enjoy and be grateful for what is at hand. Linda enjoys her house and the things in her house with God's own delight, not rejoicing in things as much as the grace of God those things represent.

Koheleth points to that kind of experience and calls it "real good." We can call it "real grace." I wonder if people know that grace today is "real" and not just theoretical. I wonder if we realize that grace is God's goodness active in the sphere of our badness, changing us and our attitudes from the inside out, so that through faith and the working of God's Holy Spirit, people called to faith in Christ are becoming more and more like the Christ they have come to know and love.[190] I wonder if we realize that the things with which we surround ourselves are not ultimately the result of our own efforts but of God's grace working through, and sometimes in spite of, our efforts. I wonder if we realize that it is a gift of God not only to have what we have but also to enjoy it.

Investigation expanded: Disappointment in an unknown future (6:10–12)

> [10] *Whatever happens, it was designated long ago and it was known that it would happen; as for man, he cannot contend with what is stronger than he.* [11] *Often, much talk means much futility. How does it benefit a man?* [12] *Who can possibly know what is best for a man to do in life—the few days of his fleeting life? For who can tell him what the future holds for him under the sun?*

I sat at the top of the polished oak stairs in the renovated home in Minneapolis's Phillips neighborhood. I had come to this home in this Easter season to present myself to the parents of the woman I desired to make my wife. The whole family was there in her sister's house—the parents, the sister and husband and two children, the brother and the one we would find out by surprise was his fiancé, Linda, and me—in three bedrooms, with one bathroom. Yes, it was like that.

We had been there for several days and I had stayed much in the shadows of family events. We had not expected Linda's brother and girlfriend and their surprise announcement a few minutes after we arrived at the Minneapolis house from the airport. The family was adjusting, adapting to the news. I endeavored to stay out of the discussions. Out of the limelight. Out of danger.

But Linda was getting nervous. The family, and especially her parents, were not getting to know me, to like me, to fall in love with

---

[190] 2 Corinthians 3:18.

me; and for Linda, it was crucial that her parents considered me favorably. She had already made it clear that if Mom didn't approve, the relationship was over without possibility of repair. I was not the first to travel this gauntlet. If Mom didn't genuinely approve, I might not be the last.

I appreciated Linda's anxiety, but how could I know what was right to do? How could I know what the future held? The morning after the brother and fiancé returned home, I heard Linda's mom moving around in the kitchen. It was her routine to rise early, make a cup of coffee, and sit at the tiny two-seat, mostly decorative table in the kitchen and read her Bible. I got up, made myself presentable, and went downstairs. She was sitting at the table with her back to the door I would have to pass through to enter the kitchen. I went through the door, around to the only other chair at the table, and sat down.

She looked at me. I looked at her. I said, "Mrs. Fregeau, you have questions for me. I have questions for you. Let's get started." We talked for three hours. No one. No one entered the kitchen for that entire three hours. To this day, I don't know where they got breakfast, but I do know they didn't come into that kitchen. The next morning, we did the same thing. Three hours. It really was amazing.

My meeting with God at the top of the steps happened after the second meeting with Linda's mom. I sat there alone, feeling that something very important was happening, feeling that something was falling into place in my life that I was not fully in control of and not fully prepared for. I sat there with one question, how do I know, this far into it now, whether I am doing the right thing? How do I know if this is the best thing for me to do with my life? Who can tell me what the future holds?

I cannot speak for anyone but myself but there, on that landing, in that house, a verse from Isaiah came to mind and settled in my heart, "And your ears shall hear a word behind you, saying, 'This is the way, walk in it,' when you turn to the right or when you turn to the left."[191]

---

[191] Isaiah 30:21 (ESV).

I would not know the future, but I would know the One who knows the future and He would be my guide. For now, this was the way and I would walk in it. Linda and I have been walking in that way together for almost thirty years.

Koheleth poses a reasonable and oft pondered question, "Who can possibly know what is best for a man to do in life—the few days of his fleeting life? For who can tell him what the future holds for him under the sun?" Look around at your fellow travelers and you can see the reason for his sense of frustration and futility. They don't know their own future, let alone yours. If they can't tell you your future, how can they tell you what meaning your life has? This is the dilemma Koheleth continues to pursue. Without someone who knows our future, how can we know our purpose? And if we cannot know our purpose, then what real value does a man gain from all the toil at which he toils under the sun?

The next set of proverbs Koheleth includes in this science report are wisdom sayings that attempt to provide an answer to that question. If no one can reveal our future, how can we find meaning in this life under the sun?

Applied Wisdom in Series 3 (7:1–22)

If the very best thing we can do with our lives is enjoy with contentment the grace of God and do good, then what does doing good look like in real life? And if we cannot know the future, then what does the best effort to do the best in life under the sun look like? Under the construct of biblical wisdom, it means making godly choices that keep you aligned with God's covenantal will. One way of describing that lifestyle is through proverbs—short, pithy sayings that illustrate the nature of wisdom and foolishness on a personal level. Koheleth is a master of these!

Remember (as if you could forget!) that the theme of the endeavor in Ecclesiastes is futility. Any interpretation or application of these proverbs has to maintain the integrity of the whole context in which they are found. These are not simply parked here because Koheleth liked them and had nowhere else to use them. Everything in this report serves a purpose. The outlook of Ecclesiastes is markedly horizontal, anthropocentric, human! He is looking around and not up, deriving wisdom from around him to support life as he observes it. This series of seemingly unrelated proverbs illustrate actions and attitudes that make the best of life lived in futility under the sun and according to wisdom.

Pursue what is "more gooder"

> [1] *A good name is better than fragrant oil, and the day of death than the day of birth.*
> [2] *It is better to go to a house of mourning than to a house of feasting; for that is the end of every man, and a living one should take it to heart.*
> [3] *Vexation is better than revelry; for though the face be sad, the heart may be glad.* [4] *Wise men are drawn to a house of mourning, and fools to a house of merrymaking.*
> [5] *It is better to listen to a wise man's reproof than to listen to the praise of fools.* [6] *For the levity of the fool is like the crackling of nettles under a kettle. But that too is illusory;* [7] *for cheating may rob the wise man of reason and destroy the prudence of the cautious.*
> [8] *The end of a matter is better than the beginning of it. Better a patient spirit than a haughty spirit.*
> [9] *Don't let your spirit be quickly vexed, for vexation abides in the breasts of fools.*
> [10] *Don't say, "How has it happened that former times were better than these?" For it is not wise of you to ask that question.*
> [11] *Wisdom is as good as a patrimony, and even better, for those who behold the sun.* [12] *For to be in the shelter of wisdom is to be also in the shelter of money, and the advantage of intelligence is that*

wisdom preserves the life of him who possesses it.
(7:1–12)

The interpretive value of repeated words. Repeated words within a passage often provide logical or thematic markers indicating how much of a passage belongs together. The Hebrew word *tôb* is just such a marker. *Tôb* usually means "good" but it can also mean "merry," "pleasant," or "desirable," as well as "prosperity" or "favor." The use of *tôb* in comparisons between nonequals, where one element is contextually superior to another, yields the translation "better" in the *Tanakh* in these verses. About half the uses in Ecclesiastes are the superlative "better." The word is used frequently throughout Ecclesiastes (forty-five times) and in some form thirteen times in chapter 7 verses 1 through 20.

What is the best you can do with your life in a futile world? Pursue what is "more gooder." "Good" in Ecclesiastes serves as a counterpoint to "futility." "Good" does not cancel out "futile" entirely, so they are not equal opposites, but "good" lightens the burden of a life of futility under the sun. It's sort of like a cold glass of homemade lemonade after cutting grass in the sun of a Georgia summer afternoon. Given that "all is futile," anything good is like an oasis of cool water in a desert of despair. To have something "good" is great, but to have something better is "more gooder!"

Gooder pursuits. A "good name," a favorable reputation presumably gained by wise living in the face of the ongoing futility of life, surpasses a pleasant experience. The day of death, when we are released from futility, is more gooder than the day of birth when we enter futility. It is more gooder to head to the morgue than the amusement park, since everyone is going to end up in the morgue eventually, and knowing that fact may help you seek what is more gooder in life! It is more gooder to have troubles than mirth, because with troubles, you've got nowhere else to go but up. Mirth and merriment never last, and they are great heights from which to fall.

It is more gooder to learn a hard lesson from a wise man than to listen to your friends tell you what you want to hear. You'll like the latter more than the former, but you'll get more gooder if you pay attention to the former. Read the whole book, not just the preface, because if you read it all, you'll have a more gooder understanding of the message. Thus, the end of a matter is more gooder than the beginning. Patience brings a more gooder return than arrogance.

Stop pining for the old days. You don't have the old days. You have today, and you may miss the more gooder of today if you're focused backward, and missing the more gooder of today would not be wise!

Speaking of wise, being wise is more gooder than having a sugar daddy because wise people know more gooder how to take care of themselves no matter what their situation is.

Consider God's doing

> [13] *Consider God's doing! Who can straighten what He has twisted?* [14] *So in a time of good fortune enjoy the good fortune; and in a time of misfortune, reflect: The one no less than the other was God's doing; consequently, man may find no fault with Him.* (7:13–14)

Remember what we said about contentment earlier? Here it is again. And remember what we said about the importance of an idea or concept when God repeats it? Here it is again—God is sovereign over all that concerns us regardless of our perceptions or responses to His handiwork in our lives. Nothing in all creation, secondary cause or not, surpasses the will and the power of God to accomplish His will over all He creates. Good fortune or misfortune, they come equally from the hand of God. So what is the best we can do with a life fraught with futility? Consider God's doing!

This is not a new concept. I read somewhere that the book of Job is the earliest written book of the Bible. In that book, after Job suffers the miserable miseries of futility in full force, losing his possessions, his children, his health, and his wife's support, he speaks these words of truth to his desperate and despairing life partner, "Shall we receive good from God, and shall we not receive evil?"[192] Earlier, before the attack on his health, Job maintained, "The LORD gave, and the LORD has taken away; blessed be the name of the LORD."[193]

This admonition from Koheleth to "consider God's doing" challenges society today as deeply as the words of Job challenge his dear wife's overwhelming grief. How often we hear people assign pain, sorrow, discomfort, trouble, and affliction to the work of Satan! Admittedly, most people I know who do this want to spare God the embarrassment of causing His people unpleasant experiences. Sadly, though their intentions may be honorable, people who do this rob God of His glory. A friend of mine, processing the death of his four-year-old daughter from a brain tumor, penned these thoughts on the subject of pain,

> The idea of the evil of pain enters into the church roughly this way: God is good, so God hates pain, and wants to make it go away. God came to save us from evil (pain) so He is itching to rescue anyone who is suffering pain for any reason. If you are suffering pain, it's probably your fault, not God's, because God doesn't do evil (thus pain). Much of our prayer time is consumed with asking God to make painful things go away. Heal, God!
>
> Fix, God! Safety, God! Money, God!
>
> We've advertised to the world a God who makes all the pain go away, while anyone with eyeballs can see the real God is letting us endure plenty of it; as much and sometimes more than non-Christians. What kind of power over evil does God have if he doesn't keep us from pain? But that's like saying, "Why doesn't God protect us from the smell of blue?" It's a nonsensical question.

[192] Job 2:10 (ESV).
[193] Job 1:21 (ESV).

The night Alice died, Pastor Bob, with all the love and sympathy of a man speaking for God, said to my family and me something like, "If I could make the pain go away, I wouldn't. You need to feel it. To embrace it." Who talks like that? A man who recognizes the value of pain, who knows a God who uses pain. Who knows that pain felt is an expression of the value of a thing lost. Pain is not evil. Pain reminds us that evil exists, and bad things still happen. Pain tells us in vivid but unspoken language that this isn't heaven. Pain sharpens our value systems: what will you suffer to get, and what isn't worth the pain? Pain strengthens our resolve: this is worth the pain. Pain glorifies God: He's worth suffering for. He's worth following even if it ends with me on my own cross. When we come to terms with the value of pain, then maybe we too might see being hauled off to Chinese prison as "abundant grace" and a "prolonged sabbatical." I'd like to get there.[194]

Consider God's doing! Consider that pleasant experiences and sorrow-producing experiences come from the same kind, loving, wise, sovereign hand. Consider that every expression of divine sovereignty over good or evil promotes the understanding and embracing of the divine glory, thereby furthering God's established mission to fill the earth with the knowledge of His glory!

Every genuinely God-called and God-sent prophet and preacher urges his audience to this opportunity—consider God's doing! Consider God's sovereign wisdom and authority. Consider God's omniscience and omnipotence. Consider God's righteousness

---

[194] Joe Reed, "(Almost) Too Hot to Handle, and Another Thing Not as Hot as You Might Think," https://commonslaves.com/2018/12/29/almost-too-hot-to-handle-and-another-thing-not-as-hot-as-you-might-think. Accessed December 29, 2018.

and justice. Consider God's compassion and glory. Consider who God is and consider what God does, given who He is. God does not act in conflict with His person nor in any way that denies or betrays His glory. God does act consistent with His person and in ways that reveal or magnify His glory. Consider God's doings!

A Christianity that extols the death of Jesus on the cross but fails to develop an adequate theology of personal pain and suffering deserves lament. What good is a Christian faith that allows Jesus to suffer on our behalf but denies Him the honor of our suffering on His behalf? That seems to me nothing more than selfish, sinful idolatry. It is as if we stand before God shouting, "Crucify Him! Crucify Him! But don't you dare crucify us!"

Throughout God's Word, through clear revelation and recorded anecdote, we are informed that pain, suffering, and sorrow are woven into the fabric of normal life. Job testifies that "man is born to trouble as surely as sparks fly upward."[195] Jesus encourages His disciples noting that in this world, they will have tribulation but they may take heart for He has overcome the world.[196] Apparently the disciples understood and embraced Jesus's words. Paul motivates the Philippian believers by equating their suffering as a privileged uniting with Christ's suffering for them.[197] Peter, like Koheleth, places at least some suffering directly in the will of God and calls suffering believers to "entrust their souls to a faithful Creator while doing good."[198]

Personal suffering can have several functions in our experience. It can be punitive as it was for Adam and Eve and the serpent in Eden. The author of Hebrews describes suffering as an application of divine discipline that ultimately molds our character and assures us of God's love for us.[199] God sets suffering as a moral and spiritual test, with Job as the test subject, in the opening heavenly dialogues with Satan in Job.[200]

---

[195] Job 5:7 (ESV).
[196] John 16:33.
[197] Philippians 1:29.
[198] 1 Peter 4:19 (ESV).
[199] Hebrews 12:5–11.
[200] Job 2:3, 6.

The leaders of his day threw Jeremiah the prophet in a well and a king threw Daniel in a den of lions, both occasions of suffering God used to reveal to observers something of His nature and purpose. Jesus was whipped mercilessly, beaten, mocked, and nailed to a cross to bleed and die, a living picture that there are times when one person suffers as a substitute for someone else.

Beyond that, church history is replete with stories of Christian men and women and children tortured to death, their deaths a testament to the veracity and grace inherent in the Gospel of Jesus Christ. And a day is coming when suffering will mark the fulfilment of this age of the world and the commencement of Christ's eternal kingdom, symbolized by the pouring out of the bowls of God's wrath described in Revelation 16.[201]

A theology of suffering must embrace all the attributes of God as well as the sovereign plan of God to fill creation with the knowledge of His glory.[202] A theology of suffering must account for the various functions of suffering in human experience as components of God's master plan. A theology of suffering must include an unshakeable faith in the goodness and wisdom of God and the worthiness of His glory. So Koheleth urges, "Consider God's doing!" Consider it. Consider Him. Love Him. Trust Him. Surrender to the wisdom of His plan to demonstrate His glory through your life in relationship with Him. Find no fault with Him. Rather, let your faith in Him magnify to the world the wonder of His glory.

One more word here. Since Ecclesiastes presents the findings of a scientific experiment, it is worth noting that the word "consider" means more than just "look and see." To consider is to scrutinize for accurate understanding. It is not a casual word, but an intentional, intense word appropriate for a science experiment that carefully examines data in order to draw true conclusions. The early church

---

[201] James L. Garrett Jr., *Systematic Theology: Biblical, Historical, and Evangelical*, Fourth edition, vol. 1. (Eugene, OR: Wipf & Stock, 2014), 392. Garrett includes these functions of suffering mentioned here in a lengthy discussion of suffering and the providence of God.

[202] "For the earth will be filled with the knowledge of the glory of the *Lord* as the waters cover the sea" (Habakkuk 2:14, ESV).

used the Latin form of this word as "a term applied to the formal testing of catechumens before their Baptism."[203] To "consider" includes the ideas of gathering all relevant data, examining the data for relevance and accuracy, testing the data, testing conclusions formed from the data, and acting appropriately in response to conclusions consistent with the known data.

In other words, "consider" means to work at understanding until you get it, and in this case, you "get it" when you arrive at God's understanding of Himself and His actions in creation.[204] Careful, planned Bible study, faith-filled prayer, and pursuit and application of divine wisdom to the course of life are all incorporated in the Koheleth's call to "Consider God's doings." This approach to the life of faith results in a much clearer perspective on life under the sun.

Develop a clearer perspective

> [15]*In my own brief span of life, I have seen both these things: sometimes a good man perishes in spite of his goodness, and sometimes a wicked one endures in spite of his wickedness.* [16]*So don't overdo goodness and don't act the wise man to excess, or you may be dumfounded.* [17]*Don't overdo wickedness and don't be a fool, or you may die before your time.* [18]*It is best that you grasp the one without letting go of the other, for one who fears God will do his duty by both.*
>
> [19]*Wisdom is more of a stronghold to a wise man than ten magnates that a city may contain.*
>
> [20]*For there is not one good man on earth who does what is best and doesn't err.*

---

[203] *The Oxford Dictionary of the Christian Church*, 3rd ed. rev., eds. F. L. Cross and E. A. Livingstone (Oxford; New York: Oxford University Press, 2005). 1486.

[204] "Trust in the *Lord* with all your heart, and do not lean on your own understanding. In all your ways acknowledge him, and he will make your paths straight" (Proverbs 3:5–6, ESV).

> [21] *Finally, don't pay attention to everything that is said, so that you may not hear your slave reviling you; for well you remember the many times that you yourself have reviled others. (7:15–22)*

A third idea for making the most of life under the sun and doing good springs from these proverbs. Develop a larger, better perspective. Perspective is a difficult thing to master, at least for me. I've tried my hand a few times at drawing and painting. I'm better when I draw with a pencil and a ruler, with the rules for perspective written out in front of me. I have a sketchbook that has several pages of cityscapes where the central road through the scene stretches to the horizon and the skyscrapers shrink from the front of the page to the back.

I also painted a landscape once, freehand, with my mother-in-law's help. She was an artist. We painted a picture of an adult and child sitting under a tree, fishing in a stream that flowed from the left side top of the painting to the bottom right corner. The painting is clearly amateurish, but the perspective, which was the focus of the exercise, is pretty good, except for one thing. The child is a little boy wearing red shorts and a blue shirt. He looks for all the world like he is sitting on two overblown red balloons. I just could not figure out the perspective of his hips to his shoulders in relation to the size of the adult sitting next to him.

Perspective in art has to do with the relationship between the size of things and the distance between them and the one viewing the work. Perspective in life also deals with the relationship between us, as the reference point, and the rest of the world. Perspective can be a difficult thing to master, as Koheleth points out. But Koheleth's advice here is worthwhile. What is the best way to live if everything is futile? Develop a bigger, better perspective.

What do you do when life doesn't work out the way you think it should? A man does all the right things, goes to all the right schools, gets all the right degrees, works at all the right companies, makes all the right choices, lives in all the right houses in all the right neighborhoods, eats all the right foods, exercises in all the right gyms, believes all the right truths, and acts in all the right ways. Yet a drunk driver smashes into him and kills him as he is on the way to visit his elderly mother. What do you do? What do you think?

What do you do when life doesn't work out the way it should? A man steals and cheats his way to the top becoming a celebrated CEO with fame and fortune, and even though everyone knows the lowlife strategy by which he attained his position, he gets away with it and dies an old man, wealthy, indulgent, never coming to justice. What do you do? What do you think?

Koheleth has seen all this and more and he reports what he has seen as an injustice that supports his hypothesis that all is futile. Doing good has its limits and does not guarantee ultimate success. Acting foolishly may lead you to an early death. Avoid both extremes, he says. Instead, he offers this advice—develop a perspective of life broad enough to encompass the reality of the limits of human wisdom and righteousness.

> [18]*It is best that you grasp the one without letting go of the other, for one who fears God will do his duty by both.* (7:18)

Notice that the conclusion here is that the one who fears God, the one who maintains a covenantal relationship with God marked by faith and obedience, will "do his duty by both" or, more literally, "come out from both." The one who fears God will grab hold of God and adopt God's perspective by placing their unrestricted faith in His Person and thus avoid the dangers represented in the two extremes Koheleth describes. This sage advice is another clue that Koheleth is not a disappointed, despairing old man with an ax to grind, but a man who has discovered that real value in life is possible but is experienced in only one context.

So wisdom (by definition) has greater value for someone than the value of ten good leaders to a city. Wisdom brings life into alignment with the divine will and purpose. And since no one is perfect and gets everything right all the time, wisdom offers the best response to the challenges of life under the sun. Wisdom also aids in the development of a gracious perspective on personal experience. A wise perspective minds its own business knowing that our life experiences are not ultimately different than anyone else's.

Having offered practical advice for doing good and living life under the sun, Koheleth moves to an examination of his methodology.

Methodology Scrutinized: Series 3 (7:23–29)

> [23]*All this I tested with wisdom. I thought I could fathom it, but it eludes me.* [24]*[The secret of] what happens is elusive and deep, deep down; who can discover it?* [25]*I put my mind to studying, exploring, and seeking wisdom and the reason of things, and to studying wickedness, stupidity, madness, and folly.* [26]*Now, I find woman more bitter than death; she is all traps, her hands are fetters and her heart is snares. He who is pleasing to God escapes her, and he who is displeasing is caught by her.* [27]*See, this is what I found, said Koheleth, item by item in my search for the reason of things.* [28]*As for what I sought further but did not find, I found only one human being in a thousand, and the one I found among so many was never a woman.* [29]*But, see, this I did find: God made men plain, but they have engaged in too much reasoning.*

The inclusiveness of the study

Not since the opening section of his report has Koheleth expressly pointed out that he is reporting his use of a very specific methodology in order to test his hypothesis that when life is viewed in its entirety, it amounts to nothing more than utter futility.[205] He intentionally pursued the answer to the research question, "What real value is there for a man in all the gains he makes beneath the

---

[205] "I set my mind to study and to probe with wisdom all that happens under the sun" (Ecclesiastes 1:13, JPS).

sun?" through three series of careful analyses. The first analysis was of intentional self-indulgence within the framework of natural law. The second series was of the effectiveness of life effort within the framework of God's sovereignty. Now, having subjected a third set of life observations to careful consideration and having arrived at the same conclusions regarding futility relative to ultimate outcomes, he reminds us this is an experiment and pauses to allow scrutiny of the inclusiveness of his methodology.

The study includes "all this." "All this" may refer to all that has come before in the three series of experiments or to that which will immediately follow. The ambiguity in this case has little impact on the interpretation of these words. Koheleth probes wisely into the matters of life on earth under the sun. He admits that he may have put more trust in wisdom and his methodology than they could sustain, but he also stresses that his considerations have been extensive as possible, not solely into the life experience of one wealthy, wise, powerful man or of a range of men from various walks of life, but of women as well. And he finds that his methodology holds. Women are as subject to the foibles of futility as men are.

The study includes solid methodology. Koheleth offers his methodology to our inspection. "I put my mind to studying, exploring, and seeking wisdom and the reason of things, and to studying wickedness, stupidity, madness, and folly." That's his methodology. He identifies the tools he used (his mind), the strategy he engaged (studying, exploring, and seeking), the subjects of his interest (wisdom and the reason of things), and the avenues of exploration he pursued (wickedness, stupidity, madness, and folly).

In the next sentence, he describes the extent to which he has pressed his endeavor. He has already illustrated his work in the observation of men of various life stations. Now he turns his attention to women, to another source of meaning and happiness and satisfaction men seek out of life, and here is what he finds—"Now, I find woman more bitter than death; she is all traps, her hands are fetters and her heart is snares. He who is pleasing to God escapes her, and he who is displeasing is caught by her."[206]

The study includes women and men. That is not what we expected to hear from Solomon of the seven hundred wives and three hundred concubines. We expected that when Koheleth turned the spotlight on women, we would find gracious, capable, loving partners and helpers with whom we might find hope and comfort in the short miserable days of our lives under the sun. We thought we might find refuge and purpose and all kinds of good things. But no, women are human too. They are as much the victims and the perpetrators of futility under the sun as men.

Some commentators think Koheleth has a misogynistic ax to grind, but I do not. Fox reads the passage as though Koheleth finds wickedness, stupidity, madness, and folly "concentrated in woman-kind."[207] He also offers that these sentences may be a "wisecrack rather than a solemn statement" and concludes that "we should not treat Koheleth's grousing about the opposite sex as a philosophical proposition. It is clearly hyperbolic."[208] Bartholomew[209] and O'Donnell[210] treat as metaphor the women of whom Koheleth writes. O'Donnell writes, "Following Solomon's proverbs in the book of Proverbs, the ensnaring woman in Ecclesiastes is the personification and embodiment of folly, whether sexual or otherwise." While Longman sees in this section a low view of humanity as a whole, he seems to excuse any misogyny on Koheleth's part to the idea that Koheleth's views "are not the teachings of the book of Ecclesiastes any more than the speeches of the three friends constitute the normative teaching of the book of Job."[211]

I think these approaches underestimate what is happening here. If Koheleth is presenting the results of an experimental process, as we think that he is, then it stands to reason at some point he will have

---

[206] Ecclesiastes 7:26 (JPS).
[207] Fox, 51.
[208] Ibid.
[209] Bartholomew, 266.
[210] O'Donnell, 152.
[211] Longman, 204.

to defend the strategy used within the experiment that yielded the results. One aspect of that defense should include an accounting of the extent and inclusiveness of the experimental method. He must answer the question whether he omitted something from consideration that should have been included and whether it having been omitted has drastically altered the results. His reported method has included the lives of men in a variety of common, recognizable conditions. He must demonstrate that he has included the lives of women as well or he cannot claim to have adequately tested his hypothesis that "all is futile and a pursuit of wind."

Koheleth's words here are not of disgusted condemnation of women, or of men for that matter, but of realistic inclusion in the overall life experience of the human species. After examining everything under the sun, he concludes that "all is futile." That includes women in all their latent sinfulness as much as men whom "God made plain" and who have "engaged in too much reasoning."

Men are no better. What the *Tanakh* translates as "much reasoning" in verse 29, the English Standard Version translates as "schemes." It seems that Koheleth means for us to understand that what he has said about women is also demonstrated in men who were created by God to be straightforward and upright, fit for an eternal relationship of love, trust, and obedience with their Creator. Instead, men have given themselves over too much scheming. It started when Adam bought into the serpent's scheme in the garden. The scheming continued when Cain lured his brother out to the field to kill him. Then all mankind schemed to deny God's command to fill the earth by coalescing at Babel and attempting to build for themselves a stairway to heaven. Abram schemed against Pharaoh with Sara. Jacob schemed against Esau. David schemed against Uriah.

And the scheming continues beyond what Solomon might have recounted. Princes schemed against kings and the nation split. Nations schemed against Israel and God's people went into exile. Religious leaders schemed against Jesus and sought to kill Him. Judas schemed against Jesus and gave them a way to kill Him. The Jews schemed against Paul. And let me tell you, the scheming isn't over yet. God made mankind in His image, both male and female, but they have unitedly given themselves over to scheming against one another and, more importantly, against God their Creator. In the end, their scheming amounts to nothing more than an expression of their futile lives.

You might appreciate what Koheleth does here with the word scheme or reason. At the opening of the paragraph, he reports his efforts to search out, with wisdom, the "reason of things" or the "scheme of things," but he is not able. He repeats that he has searched one thing at a time for the "reason of things" (scheme) and come up with only one human being in a thousand.[212] He then concludes the paragraph reporting that though he went about searching for the scheme of things, all he found was things scheming. He looked for reasons and found only ungodly reasoning. He sought fruitfulness and discovered only futility. So where is meaning to be found? If not in men and women as created by God, then "what real value is there for a man in all he gains under the sun?"

The specific findings (7:23–29)

The limits of human wisdom. On December 30th, I set out on my computer at home to upgrade a financial tracking software package I have used for almost two decades. The company offered 40% off the price of a two-year subscription. I knew from my history with the software that this was a good deal. I went online and loaded the purchase page and entered all the relevant information, clicked on "submit," and waited for the process to provide a download code.

I got an error message. I don't know why. Something went wrong. The error message sent me to the software's FAQ page to find an answer. FAQ means Frequently Asked Questions. I was looking for the answer to a *why* question. I wanted to know why I could not

---

[212] The point here is that Koheleth's search among human beings for one who would know or exemplify the "scheme of things" produced such meager results. The weight of discovery is not that there is one good one but that there are 999 who don't measure up. So not among men or women is there to be found a statistically significant number of people whose life experiences under the sun are different than futility.

successfully purchase the product they offered. I read, literally, every question and answer on the FAQ page. Utter futility! I never found the answer to my why question. I'll have to be content with continuing with the software as I currently have it.

If God had an FAQ page, I think the single most frequently asked question would be, why? And, I think, it would be the one question for which most people, most of the time, would find no answer. Koheleth sought out the answer to not only what happens under the sun but also *why*. He searches for "the secret of what happens" (JPS), "the scheme of things" (ESV), "an explanation" (NIV). Longman translates the word here (*hesbon*) as "the sum of things" and notes that this is the first time it is used in Ecclesiastes (though it is now used three times in this paragraph). "It denotes the explanation that stands behind the world."[213]

Koheleth asked, but he didn't get the answer he was looking for. He did, however, find answers. He found that human wisdom has limits.

> All this I tested with wisdom. I thought I
> could fathom it, but it eludes me. [The secret of]
> what happens is elusive and deep, deep down;
> who can discover it?[214]

He brought his A game to the quest but still could not grasp the depths of the mind and heart of God, who alone is the explanation that stands behind the world. The Psalmist declares that "the earth is the *Lord's* and the fullness thereof, the world and all that dwell therein"[215] The apostle Paul places all of creation, everything, in the hands of and for the purpose of God's Son, Jesus Christ.

> He is the image of the invisible God, the
> firstborn of all creation. For by him all things

---

[213] Longman, 203.
[214] Ecclesiastes 7:23–24 (JPS).
[215] Psalm 24:1 (ESV).

were created, in heaven and on earth, visible and invisible, whether thrones or dominions or rulers or authorities—all things were created through him and for him.[216]

Human wisdom cannot fathom the enormity of the "reason for things," because God Himself is the reason for all things and all things exist for His reasons and His reasons alone. Only God, in His infinite, glorious, eternal Self, can know the sum of all things as He knows it. To know the sum of all things is to be God and human beings, for all that they are, created in the image of God, are not God. Only Jesus, Who is fully human and fully God and for Whom all things were created, can fully understand "the secret of what happens."

That's where my counsel comes from when people ask *why* relative to God's intent in their personal crises. I know how limited human wisdom is. I have a whole list of my own why's. Instead of trying to tackle the unfathomable why, I direct us to the truly knowable "who." I follow that up with what I hope will prove a practical "how." "Who does God declare Himself to be in moments like this?" and "How can I experience the real, personal Presence of God in this moment?" While God seems to choose most often to respond to our why questions with holy silence, He never fails to reveal "who" and "how" to the heart that genuinely seeks Him.[217]

The extent of human futility. We've already noted above that futility knows no gender. Futility is genuinely inclusive. We are all born into futility and we all live striving in one form or another against futility. No one gets a pass. Not men. Not women. No one.

The universality of human sin. We mentioned earlier that futility is the fruit of sin.[218] Futility is the condition of lives lived outside the purpose for which God created them. It is most especially true that God created human beings to extend the personal, experien-

---

[216] Colossians 1:15–16 (ESV).

[217] Deuteronomy 4:2, Proverbs 8:17, Jeremiah 29:13, and Matthew 7:7.

[218] "The wages of sin is death but the fruit of sin is futility" (chapter 2, 38).

tial knowledge of His glory throughout the whole earth. God created mankind to fill the inhabitable world with people who live in right relation with Him and therefore demonstrate by their personal and public lives the worthiness of God to be loved, worshiped, and served. Every thought, attitude, affection, and action that does not serve God's glory, but is selfish and self-serving, is essentially sin. James defines sin as knowing what is right to do and not doing it.[219] If we know (and we do know by divine revelation in God's Word, the Bible) that we are created to love and serve God and His glory and that loving and serving Him is the right thing to do, the things humanity was created and we were each born to do, then in every way we fail to serve that purpose, it is sin to us.

The point of attempting to clarify a definition of sin is because Koheleth announces here his experimental discovery that sin is the universal condition shared by every member of mankind. He searches everywhere under the sun to identify expressions of wickedness, stupidity, madness, and folly. Sin. And he finds it. Everywhere. In women. In men. In everyone.

The apostle Paul makes the same assertion in the New Testament letter to the Romans. He writes, "All have sinned and fall short of the glory of God."[220] He also offers this quote from Psalm 14, "None is righteous, no, not one; no one understands; no one seeks for God,"[221] and from Psalm 53, "All have turned aside; together they have become worthless; no one does good, not even one."[222] David said it. Solomon heard it. Paul repeated it. All people are sinners. As a result, all is futile. Woman is more bitter than death and man has engaged too many schemes. These are moral equivalents. Sin is the universal experience that drives futility. If sin is the universal human condition (and thus futility the universal result), then what real value is there for a man in all the gains he makes beneath the sun? There

---

[219] "So whoever knows the right thing to do and fails to do it, for him it is sin" (James 4:17, ESV).
[220] Romans 3:23 (ESV).
[221] Romans 3:10–11 (ESV).
[222] Romans 3:12 (ESV).

is an answer to this question other than what we've seen before, but Koheleth is not ready. He insists we wait.

Three findings, one implied conclusion—"Utter futility! All is futile!" Koheleth has examined life under the sun in several contexts. He has revealed his methods and allowed them to be closely scrutinized for inclusivity. He has shared his findings and initial conclusions along with each set of experiments. After a final set of supporting observations, he restates his initial conclusion and moves on to a final summary and conclusion.

Advanced Observations: Series 3 (8:1–14)

[1]*Who is like the wise man, and who knows the meaning of the adage: "A man's wisdom lights up his face,*

So that his deep discontent is dissembled"?

[2]*I do! "Obey the king's orders—and don't rush into uttering an oath by God."* [3]*Leave his presence; do not tarry in a dangerous situation, for he can do anything he pleases;* [4]*inasmuch as a king's command is authoritative, and none can say to him, "What are you doing?"* [5]*One who obeys orders will not suffer from the dangerous situation.*

A wise man, however, will bear in mind that there is a time of doom. [6]*For there is a time for every experience, including the doom; for a man's calamity overwhelms him.* [7]*Indeed, he does not know what is to happen; even when it is on the point of happening, who can tell him?* [8]*No man has authority over the lifebreath—to hold back the lifebreath; there is no authority over the day of death. There is no mustering out from that war; wickedness is powerless to save its owner.*

[9]*All these things I observed; I noted all that went on under the sun, while men still had authority over men to treat them unjustly.* [10]*And then I*

saw scoundrels coming from the Holy Site and being brought to burial, while such as had acted righteously were forgotten in the city.

And here is another frustration: [11]*the fact that the sentence imposed for evil deeds is not executed swiftly, which is why men are emboldened to do evil—*[12]*the fact that a sinner may do evil a hundred times and his [punishment] still be delayed. For although I am aware that "It will be well with those who revere God since they revere Him,* [13]*and it will not be well with the scoundrel, and he will not live long, because he does not revere God"—*[14]*here is a frustration that occurs in the world: sometimes an upright man is requited according to the conduct of the scoundrel; and sometimes the scoundrel is requited according to the conduct of the upright. I say all that is frustration.*

Along with submitting his methodology to scrutiny for inclusiveness, Koheleth provides a range of advanced observations that also testify to the inclusiveness of his research. These are all observations he has made personally, real stories from the world around him as he experienced it. In that the accounts he records are real events, they mirror events and occasions we might all have observed. This tactic draws us personally deeper into the experiment, the conclusions, and the forthcoming ultimate resolution of the research question. These observations appear to fall into two categories Koheleth has used often in his report—the activities of wise men and the activities of scoundrels.

Observation concerning the wise

Not everyone agrees that the question that opens chapter 8 is the introduction to a new train of thought. Fox and others understand the rhetorical question as concluding the previous section, functioning something like a capstone. Koheleth has discovered that all humans are subject to futility and thus there are none who are like the wise man, "No one who understands the meaning of anything."[223]

Other commentators understand the question to introduce a section on wise behavior in the presence of the king. A wise man knows to keep arrogance and pride off his face in the presence of one whose authority is absolute and whose mood is arbitrary. At the same time, a wise man also knows that at any moment, disaster may strike. No man has control over the future, and it is possible that seeds of disaster are already germinating in the season of joy. And, when the day of death comes, no one can stop it. A wise man knows this and accounts for it in his perspective of life. A wise man knows that trouble will come, even if he doesn't see it coming until it arrives.

Observation concerning scoundrels

From the activities of the wise, Koheleth moves to the activities of scoundrels that frustrate the wise. The ESV calls these perpetrators of injustice the "wicked." The word is also used of criminals. The picture Koheleth paints is of brazen hypocrites who attended to religious matters religiously, gaining much public praise, but deserving not a word of it. And all the while truly righteous people are overlooked by the same community.

Guess what is the Hebrew word translated "frustration" in the *Tanakh* text? That's right—*hebel!* The word translated throughout Ecclesiastes as futility! Futility frustrates! *Merriam-Webster's Collegiate Dictionary* offers that frustration is "a deep chronic sense or state of insecurity and dissatisfaction arising from unresolved problems or unfulfilled needs."[224] Does that not sound like the world Koheleth observes and reports? A deep and chronic state of dissatisfaction? Unresolved problems and unfulfilled needs? Surely frustration is a good symptomatic definition of futility.

---

[223] Fox, 53–54.

[224] Merriam-Webster, I. *Merriam-Webster's Collegiate Dictionary*, Eleventh edition (Springfield, MA: Merriam-Webster, Inc., 2003).

And here's another frustrating example of futility—delayed justice! More than that even, inverted justice. In the former, guilty parties don't get what's coming to them. In the latter, innocent parties get served what the guilty deserve or the guilty get the acquittal the innocent deserve. It's hard to argue with the observations. We've seen it ourselves. Often. Far too often.

We are left with the choice of response. Koheleth reports his response, within the context of his ongoing experiment. The question persists, though. Is this the final, best, or only conclusion?

Initial Conclusion for Series 3 Restated (8:15)

> [15]*I therefore praised enjoyment. For the only good a man can have under the sun is to eat and drink and enjoy himself. That much can accompany him, in exchange for his wealth, through the days of life that God has granted him under the sun.*

If we cannot control the times or the seasons or the weather or the practices and outcomes of justice or the integrity of heirs or the moment of our death, then by golly, what can we do? We can choose those activities more likely than others to result in pleasurable experience as an offset to the inevitable experience of futility and frustration. Activities that may lead to personal, sensory joy are all that we can exchange for our toil. They are the only "real value," the truly "meaningful meaning," we can attain all the days of our lives that God gives us under the sun.

This is not a principle Koheleth is teaching. This is a conclusion he draws based on a limited but inclusive set of intentional observations designed to test a hypothesis. Natural law, God's sovereignty, and even the day-to-day practices of life among humanity all provide limits to the achievement of ultimate meaning and purpose in life lived under the sun, true. But the message of Ecclesiastes is in the whole, not necessarily in any given part. And Koheleth is not done. Not yet.

Study Questions

Once again, these questions unapologetically offer an opportunity for you to think more deeply about what you've encountered in Ecclesiastes in this portion of Koheleth's report. If you are familiar with the inductive Bible study method, the questions intentionally avoid the observation category, also known as "what" questions. They focus more on interpretive analysis and personal application, the "so what?" and "now what?" questions. Enjoy!

Rapid-fire recheck (5:12–6:12)

1. As Koheleth rechecks his methodology, he mentions three "grave evils."
    a. What is another way of saying "grave evils"?
    b. What is the nature of the three miseries mentioned?
    c. Can you think of modern-day proverbs that fit each of these situations?
2. Look carefully at the wording of the sentences in 5:17–19.
    a. What "good" do people have to enjoy?
    b. Who is responsible for the good people enjoy?
    c. Why is it okay to enjoy and find fulfilment in the things God gives us?
3. Taking the opposite approach in 6:1–9
    a. Why is joylessness in what God has given a "grave evil" and a "grievous ill"?
    b. How does this perspective influence the value we place on the things God has placed in our lives for our joy?
    c. What reason can you think of for why God might give someone great gifts of wealth but not let them enjoy it?
    d. Why does Koheleth think a stillborn child is better off than a wealthy man who cannot be satisfied with his wealth?
    e. Why might Koheleth minimize the benefit of feasting the eyes against the pursuit of desire? What is he really saying?

    f.   Think about the idea of "settling for something" rather "striving for what you really want."

        i.   How does this idea play out in the spiritual life?

        ii.   What substantial goal does the Christian strive for (and how do they strive) that Koheleth might be alluding to?

4.   The disappointment of an unknown future (6:10–12)

    a.   Koheleth posits the idea that man cannot contend with what is stronger than him. What could he be referring to with which man cannot contend?

    b.   Koheleth's question ("Who can possibly know what is best for a man to do in life?") begs an answer. Provide one.

    c.   Just before this passage, Koheleth mentions that the only good in life comes from God. Viktor Frankl, in the book *Man's Search for Meaning*, maintains that having a sense of future reward nurtures the human ability to find meaning in even the most difficult circumstances.

        i.   How is the future a major concern for Christianity?

        ii.   What certainties do Christians have regarding both the immediate and the ultimate future?

        iii.   Do you find God's promises for the future adequate provisions for the present? Why or why not?

Applied wisdom (7:1–22)

1.   A series of proverbs sets this section apart as another movement in the research report. How do you think these proverbs and maxims function within the body of this work?

2.   What contemporary expressions of the conventional wisdom can you come up with that mirror the sentiments in this list?

3.   Overall, this series of proverbs present a series of comparisons/contrasts. What impression does the entire passage make on you?

4. Pick one of these proverbs and explain how it is relevant to either your current way of thinking or to your current life practice.
5. If you were going to develop a biblical theology of suffering, what principles would it include?

Methodology Scrutinized (7:23–29)

1. Accepting the initial conclusion at face value, Koheleth has not found what he is looking for. How does he describe the truth he seeks?
2. Koheleth is looking for "the secret of what happens." Give an explanation of what you think Koheleth is looking for?
3. Keeping in mind that we are reading a report of an experiment that follows the scientific method, what is the interpretive significance of stating at this point that he has not found what he is looking for?

Advanced observations (8:1–14)

1. What situation does Koheleth use to illustrate wisdom in this passage?
2. What emotional response emerges in you as you read that man has no control over the timing of his death?
3. Koheleth reminds his readers of a principle he established in chapter 3 especially. He writes, "There is a time for every experience."
   a. What does this "time for every experience" address in a theological sense?
   b. What difference does this theological truth make in your experience?
4. In these advanced observations, Koheleth restates the principal problem, life is "unfair, out of our control, and basically futile." What response do these observations call for?

Initial conclusion

1. Koheleth praises "enjoyment" as the only enduring grace that can accompany a man throughout his life despite his circumstances.
   a. What do you think he means by "enjoyment"?
   b. Can you think of other words synonymous with "enjoyment"?
2. Where does lasting joy come from?
   a. What condition raises genuine contentment?
   b. How have you experienced genuine, lasting joy and contentment in your life?
   c. What, if anything, hinders your experience of lasting joy and contentment?
   d. What plan do you have for removing the obstacles to lasting joy and contentment in your life?

CHAPTER 8

SUMMARY OF METHODOLOGY AND FINAL CONCLUSIONS (8:16–12:8)

Summary of Experimental Methodology (8:16–17)

16For I have set my mind to learn wisdom and to observe the business that goes on in the world—even to the extent of going without sleep day and night—17and I have observed all that God brings to pass. Indeed, man cannot guess the events that occur under the sun. For man tries strenuously, but fails to guess them; and even if a sage should think to discover them he would not be able to guess them.

"The end of a matter," Koheleth writes, "is better than the beginning." He is reaching the end of his report. He now summarizes the methodology he has used, putting everything we have read so far into context. Then he lays out final conclusions based on the observations he has recorded.

Along with the four conclusion statements, he reviews a bit more supporting data. After this bit of housekeeping is done, Koheleth shares with us his own personal conclusion to all he has seen and reported.

The intent, extent, and content of the experimental study

One of the characteristics quickly noted about the book of Ecclesiastes is the redundancy of statements and ideas. The declaration of intent, extent, and content in verse 16 and even the conclusion in verse 17 mirrors what Koheleth set out in chapter 1, "I set my mind to study and to probe with wisdom all that happens under the sun—An unhappy business, that, which God gave men to be concerned with!"[225]

Where the declaration in chapter 1 provides the context for interpreting what follows, the point here is to emphasize the limit of human wisdom to accomplish the goal of the study, to answer the question, "What real value is there for a man in all the gains he makes beneath the sun?" Despite convincing his heart and setting his sights on an answer, Koheleth must admit that, even with wisdom and relentless pursuit, there are some things, important things known to God, that Koheleth still does not know. These are things that even the wisest among us don't know either.

The intent of the study. Koheleth set out to learn and to observe. He directed his effort at identifying and understanding the work of God in the world. He set out to observe events and try to understand them and their impact on human experience, within the context of God's creation and God's Person. He worked at observation and analysis vain day and sleepless night, never giving up, never resigning his quest for wisdom. Intensely, purposefully, relentlessly, he peers into the mystery of meaning to the point that his cogitations keep him awake at night, and the closest he can come to real answers is that all the work of man is, in reality, the work of God.

Many people around us, and maybe even we ourselves, have little heart these days for process. More often than not, as I teach through this study or just talk about Ecclesiastes, people respond to the content of Ecclesiastes with impatience. Why does Koheleth take so long to make a simple point? Why can't we just skip to the good

---

[225] Ecclesiastes 1:13 (JPS).

part? Why are we spending so much time on the first three verses when there are so many more interesting, applicable thoughts to explore? If I were much of a hunting kind of guy, I would say, when it comes to Bible study in general and Ecclesiastes in particular, most people disdain the pursuit and prefer the kill. They don't really like hunting. They just want to get to the barbeque at the end.

Koheleth painstakingly works through the questions and comparisons necessary to thoroughly evaluate the validity (or not) of his hypothesis. Along the way, he becomes wiser, mellower, and more thoughtful. The journey is as personally productive for him as the destination. Sure, it required some unrelenting effort and some restless nights. Sure there were disappointments and moments when the personal vulnerability revealed uncomfortable weaknesses and deficiencies, but having identified his intent, he did not withdraw from the pursuit of the goal.

"I have set my mind to learn," writes Koheleth as he confesses his intent in this study. Marelisa Fabrega, a Panamanian lawyer turned self-help guru, would say that is the first step to remaining determined when tempted to resign. "Not giving up is a mindset," she notes.[226] It is a mind-set she suggests can be sustained by positive, reinforcing self-talk such as:

- I persist when things get tough.
- I will either find a way or make one.
- Every problem has a solution, and I have the perfect ability to find it.
- Every day I gain more knowledge and insight about what works and what doesn't, which means I'm getting stronger and wiser.

---

[226] Marelisa Fabrega, "How to Not Give Up: 8 Strategies for Not Quitting," *Daring to Live Life Fully*, https://daringtolivefully.com/how-to-not-give-up. Accessed February 4, 2019. Fabrega provides eight strategies for not giving up, including adopting an "I won't quit" mind-set, watching someone else persevere, calling someone for support, going back to your "why," finding a different "how," succeeding at something else, using failure as a stepping stone, and keeping chipping away.

- Setbacks are temporary.
- I will find a way through this.
- Think! What's the best thing to do now?

We do not know the exact strategies Koheleth used to keep himself on point, but we do know, by his own admission, something of the nature of his determination, pursuing his intent to the point of "day and night" reflection. He committed himself 24/7/365 to the investigation of the question whether there was real value in the gains a man makes under the sun or whether all is futile, utterly futile.

Remain committed to the fact that the message of Ecclesiastes is contained in the whole, but don't resign from the process of carefully examining the parts. Eternity may be in the cosmic whole, but there is life in the earthly details and no pressing need to miss out on either one! Join Koheleth in the patient, enduring sifting through the evidence at hand to find the truth that gives life meaning. If you lack stamina and find yourself overcome with impatience, take heart and take your cue from this ancient teacher of the people. Set your mind to learn.

You might also keep in mind a promise God makes concerning His Word. In the fifty-fifth chapter of Isaiah, as God exhorts His people to seek Him and find Him, He provides them with a promise regarding His Word designed to encourage their repentance and faith. God says,

> For as the rain and the snow come down from heaven and do not return there but water the earth, making it bring forth and sprout, giving seed to the sower and bread to the eater, so shall my word be that goes out from my mouth; it shall not return to me empty, but it shall accomplish that which I purpose, and shall succeed in the thing for which I sent it.[227]

If you are reading this book and studying Ecclesiastes, it is not by chance. Rather, your encounter with this portion of God's Word

---

[227] Isaiah 55:10–11 (ESV).

comes under the providence of God. He has sent His Word to your attention, and it comes to you accompanied by the certainty that this word will "succeed in the thing for which [the Lord] sent it." So God has something for you in the journey. Set your mind to learn.

The extent of the study. Koheleth set out to observe and analyze "the business that goes on in the world." These are the day-to-day activities of life in which humans engage and from which they draw whatever personal meaning there is to be had. These are the activities that he terms "all that God brings to pass." Once again, he establishes the inclusive nature of his observational practice. He is doing broad spectrum analysis. He is looking for that one event, that one occurrence, that one condition, that will disprove the hypothesis that life under the sun is utterly futile.

The content of the study. Koheleth identifies the content of his study—all that God brings to pass, the events that occur under the sun. They are one and the same set of conditions from a single source, God. There are not those things man is in charge of or responsible for and those things God is in charge of or responsible for. There is only all that happens under the sun that God brings to pass. And what God intends with all that He does, or even all that God will do in a man's life or in the world, remains ultimately inaccessible to any human wisdom.

There is irony in these verses that should not be missed. Bartholomew indicates that "theologically, verse 17a is most important for the interpretation of Ecclesiastes"[228] because Koheleth presents himself as being able to observe all God does, when in fact he can never take into account God's works of creation or redemption, and the idea that Koheleth can remain wiser than most in his audience, experience more of life than most in his audience, and yet achieve no greater benefit from life than any in his audience who are yet mired in futility and bound for death. Koheleth may have had a first-class cabin rather than steerage, but when it comes to the ultimate reality, we're all sailing on the Titanic of life.

This confession of irony fits the function of Ecclesiastes as a formal report more than just a defeatist autobiography. Koheleth

---

[228] Isaiah 55:10–11 (ESV).

presents findings consistent with his observations. He establishes and verifies, repeatedly, the limits of the tools to accomplish the goal of the study, to disprove the hypothesis of utter futility. But while he hints at something more than what he has presented, Koheleth has still not revealed his final personal conclusion.

The conclusion of the study. That God wills and works in creation can be easily observed. But what cannot be fathomed is God's motive and plan in what He wills and works. God's mind relative to human experience is immensely more elusive than merely observing what He does. Often His thoughts in the moment, and certainly for the future, cannot be guessed at all, not even by the wise, not even by the wisest of the wise. So even Koheleth loses sleep at night trying to figure out why God does what He does in the world.

The idea that God is responsible for all that happens in creation ("under the sun") is an idea much debated. People seem to either love the sovereignty of God or dispute it. Those who dispute the idea of absolute sovereignty often prefer to assert some degree of human independence as a countermeasure to God's absolute control over creation. The inclination to be our own god runs deep in us. Like abandoned baby ducks that mistakenly imprint on the family dog, we have imprinted on the serpent in the garden, and there is little that convinces us of our error or changes our mind—little, that is, except grace direct from the hand and heart of God.

A personal connection with the study. In my little corner of the world, we live with the advancing effects of facioscapulohumeral muscular dystrophy. Day after day, we encounter the inevitable effects as my wife loses range of motion in muscles throughout her body, a genetic condition for which there is no cure. Simple tasks taken for granted become simply impossible for her. Day after day, I have the privilege of taking on more and more of the everyday chores couples usually tackle together. Our experience of Koheleth's dilemma, of not knowing the mind of God in the course of life, revolves around divine healing. We note the presentation in the New Testament gospels that Jesus came to reveal the Father. We also note the apparently inclusive and extensive statements that indicate that, as part of revealing the Father to His people, Jesus healed all who came to Him, thus putting God's mercy and power on display. Matthew and Luke give us examples of Jesus's healing ministry and Matthew even fills in the extent of His ministry.

> When evening came, many who were demon-possessed were brought to him, and he drove out the spirits with a word and healed all the sick.[229]
>
> He went down with them and stood on a level place. A large crowd of his disciples was there and a great number of people from all over Judea, from Jerusalem, and from the coastal region around Tyre and Sidon, who had come to hear him and to be healed of their diseases. Those troubled by impure spirits were cured, and the people all tried to touch him, because power was coming from him and healing them all.[230]
>
> Great crowds came to him, bringing the lame, the blind, the crippled, the mute and many others, and laid them at his feet; and he healed them.[231]

We wonder what happened. Suddenly, for millennia afterward, people come to Jesus for healing and are not healed. Some minimize the dilemma by asserting a lack on the part of the petitioner. Perhaps the one seeking healing lacks faith, or they lack being filled with the Holy Spirit, or they lack some other key component that would otherwise make them worthy of divine mercy. But the gospel narratives repeatedly describe the healing by Jesus of people who expressed neither personal faith nor the indwelling Holy Spirit and yet are healed, often on account of the faith of others and sometimes out of the sheer mercy of God.

---

[229] Matthew 8:16 (NIV).
[230] Luke 6:17–19 (NIV).
[231] Matthew 15:30 (NIV).

Consider the centurion's servant.[232] The man never left the centurion's house, never made a personal request, never presented his own need to Jesus as an act of faith. The centurion had faith. Jesus said so. But of the servant, we know only his sickness and his healing. Think also of the Gadarene demoniac, a man possessed by demons who lived among the tombs at the local cemetery, who could break chains used to bind him, and who beat and terrorized the people he encountered.[233] He confronted Jesus. He did not ask to be healed. The legion of demons within him mostly wanted Jesus to just leave them alone. But Jesus healed the man, though no faith on his part is mentioned until after he is healed.

And what of the woman whose story is told in Luke 13. For eighteen years, she suffered the effect of a disabling spirit. Luke records that "she was bent over and could not fully straighten herself." That sounds like a severe case of osteoporosis, but Luke sees the spiritual nature of the physical affliction as he retells her encounter with Jesus. She did not come to Jesus either. Jesus saw her first and called her to come to him. She asked nothing of Him, but He gave everything to her as an expression of glorious compassion. He said to her, "Woman, you are freed from your disability." Then He laid His hands on her and she was made straight.[234]

The faith that healed was sometimes attributed to the sufferer, as in the case of the woman with the issue of blood that touched the hem of Christ's garment and was healed. Jesus said to her that her faith had made her well.[235] Just as often though, it was not the faith of the healed, but the faith of the Healer that brought transformation. It was Jesus acting in His faith in the Father's mercy and power that brought about changed lives.

Other people suggest that divine healing was a one-time thing meant to power launch the church and its testimonial mission in the world. They argue that once the Holy Spirit had come and the canon of God's Word was completed, containing as it does the true and suf-

---

[232] Matthew 8:5–13.
[233] Mark 5:1–13.
[234] Luke 13:11–13.
[235] Matthew 9:20–22.

ficient account of Jesus's death and resurrection, like a moon rocket dropping its initial booster, signs and wonders, including healing, simply ceased. They were no longer necessary.

The problem this presents is this—while it resolves the emotional dilemma of unmet needs, it undermines the adequacy of Christ's revelation of the Father. To embrace this approach means that it took not only the witness of Jesus but also the work of subsequent history to fully reveal the Father's heart, at least in terms of the application of healing mercy. Christ revealed by His life what God could do, but history and human experience reveal what God will do. That means that Jesus Christ, identified by the author of Hebrews as "the radiance of God's glory and the exact imprint of God's nature,"[236] proves inadequate, insufficient, and incomplete in providing an incarnate witness to the Person of God! And that is an untenable position.

The argument that God simply no longer heals in any miraculous sense because the expansion of the gospel witness no longer requires it fails to answer the question why Jesus ever healed at all. If the point of Christ's life was to prove God is merciful, but not to most and not for long, then why did Jesus heal all who came to him, rather than only a select few and only for certain reasons? From a purely empirical standpoint, that selective course of action would have been a more accurate presentation of Who the Father really is given these parameters. (Do you see the "under the sun" type reasoning here?)

The ongoing discussion in our house accepts the revelation of our merciful Father who not only heals, as Jesus showed us, but also accepts that as we observe the world around us, not all who come to Jesus in faith and in the power of the Holy Spirit in our time find the physical healing at the divine hand that they seek. And our truest determination for the reason reflects Koheleth's—we don't know. We are unwilling to diminish the testimony of the Scripture and equally unwilling to dismiss the testimony of believers whose hearts are broken at God's silence. We cannot guess the events that occur under the

---

[236] Hebrews 1:3 (ESV).

sun, events subject to the sovereign plan and will of God, though we strenuously try to understand.

Where does such imposed ignorance leave us? Koheleth supplies an answer to this question at the end of his report. Our answer is here—not knowing all God knows in any given situation leaves us with a choice. We must choose faith in the goodness and glory of God or we must choose self-serving resentment and faithlessness at God's silent response to our plea. Like Israel of old, having crossed the Jordan and begun to inhabit the land of God's promise, we must choose this day whom we will serve.[237]

God reveals that His ultimate purpose for all He created is that it should be touched and filled, to the extent He determines, with the experiential knowledge of His essence, His glory, the magnificence of the sum of all His perfections. God does all that He does in all creation for the sake of His glory, that all that exists that is other than Himself might know the glory of His glory as He does. He does this because nothing exists that is more worthy of being known and experienced and loved than God in all His glory.

So when Koheleth exclaims that God brings everything to pass and man cannot know all that is in the mind of God relative to a particular event, we can know this—all God does in creation and in the lives of those He created in His image, He does so that they may gain personal experiential knowledge of His personal glory, that which is more valuable and desirable than anything else that exists. He makes our lives a living testimony to the glory of His glory as per His plan for all creation. In this certainty, the people of faith take refuge whether in the day of rejoicing or the season of tears.

> And if it is evil in your eyes to serve the *Lord*, choose this day whom you will serve, whether the gods your fathers served in the region beyond the River, or the gods of the Amorites in whose land you dwell. But as for me and my house, we will serve the *Lord*.

---

[237] Joshua 24:15 (ESV).

The natural limit of human wisdom sets a boundary that we cannot cross. God is the Creator and we are the created. God is God and we are not God. Some of the purposes of God are hidden with Him and remain unrevealed, included in His plan to fill the earth with the knowledge of His glory but not spelled out for any of us. We must trust His character, His heart for us (as fully demonstrated in the life and death and resurrection of Jesus), when He acts of His own accord and not of ours. This is not only our conclusion. We will see that it is Koheleth's ultimate conclusion as well.

Final Conclusions and Applications
(9:1–18 and 11:7–12:8)

Conclusion/application set 1 (9:1–10)

Conclusion.

> [1]*For all this I noted, and I ascertained all this: that the actions of even the righteous and the wise are determined by God. Even love! Even hate! Man knows none of these in advance*[2]*—none! For the same fate is in store for all: for the righteous, and for the wicked; for the good and pure, and for the impure; for him who sacrifices, and for him who does not; for him who is pleasing, and for him who is displeasing; and for him who swears, and for him who shuns oaths.* [3]*That is the sad thing about all that goes on under the sun: that the same fate is in store for all. (Not only that, but men's hearts are full of sadness, and their minds of madness, while they live; and then—to the dead!)* [4]*For he who is reckoned among the living has something to look forward to—even a live dog is better than a dead lion—*[5]*since the living know they will die. But the dead know nothing; they have no more recompense, for even the memory of them has died.*

*⁶Their loves, their hates, their jealousies have long
since perished; and they have no more share till the
end of time in all that goes on under the sun. (9:1–6)*

The United States federal government began the year 2019
without an agreed upon budget. That meant that about 800,000
federal employees had jobs but no paychecks. Many were sent home
to wait for Congress and the president to arrive at a compromise and
call them back to work. A few essential personnel were required to
work, but without pay.

The stalemate in Washington dragged on. Desperation crept in.
Tempers flared. Hatreds erupted. Angst and anxiety fueled discontent and dissent. No one knew these things were coming when they
left work for Christmas vacation in December 2018, but there they
were. They did not know in advance that external conditions would
foment these internal responses. Some were angry with the president
and with anyone who supported him. Others were angry at members
of Congress and any who supported them. Anger began to overflow
into communities and gatherings of people as protesters clashed in
various venues. Even children were sucked into the outrage and fear.
Tensions ran high and trouble crouched at the door.

We humans are often so shortsighted. We live out our days in
a world of our own construction that barely extends beyond the end
of our noses. We engage our emotional energy in rage and rhetoric
and revenge, but a day advances on each of us when all our loves and
hates and jealousies will have long since perished. Our momentary
distress will mean not one little eternal thing. We waste our moments
on today with no thought for ever. How sad! For no matter the extent
of our immediate indignation, whether for evil or for good, in the
end, we all wind up dead.

What can we do?

Application.

*⁷Go, eat your bread in gladness, and drink your
wine in joy; for your action was long ago approved*

*by God. ⁸Let your clothes always be freshly washed,
and your head never lack ointment. ⁹Enjoy happiness with a woman you love all the fleeting days of
life that have been granted to you under the sun—
all your fleeting days. For that alone is what you
can get out of life and out of the means you acquire
under the sun. ¹⁰Whatever it is in your power to do,
do with all your might. For there is no action, no
reasoning, no learning, no wisdom in Sheol, where
you are going. (9:7–10)*

Koheleth offers no vision of heaven. He offers no promise of eternal hope. It may be that those ideas are not yet developed within the theological context in which Koheleth lives and teaches. On the other hand, the absence of an ending for life, other than Sheol (the place of the dead), may be intentional. It certainly conforms to the parameters set for Koheleth's social experiment. If he is intentionally omitting certain concepts in order to keep the scope of his observations and experimental strategy "under the sun," then it makes sense he does not offer heaven or resurrection or eternal life as a resolution to the tension raised in his report, whether he knows of these concepts or not.

Throughout this report, God has been the fence that bounds the limits of human effort and wisdom. God sets the seasons. God gifts the possessions and the joys. God determines the conditions and responses. God appoints natural law and guides the course of human history. God gets His way whether man get his way or not. Human beings may run into God or run from God, but no matter their effort, they cannot run past God.

Within the framework Koheleth sets, what is left for a wise person (one who makes godly choices for successful living) to do? Be grateful in the moment. Be confident in the day. Be satisfied in your life. Eat your food (which we've already been informed is a gift from God) with gladness. Present yourself with confidence as one who is not in mourning. Love your spouse and enjoy the fruit of true love throughout the days of your life. Do life heartily because under the sun, that's all you really have. Those really, really good, awesome, powerful experiences exist only in this world. Don't waste them now, because you can't take them with you, where you have no choice but to go.

You should be asking at this point whether Koheleth is being prescriptive or descriptive. Is he talking about the way things are, which would be descriptive, or is he writing about the way things should be, which would be prescriptive? The interpretive task requires an answer. Since he is making a formal report of experimental methodologies (conducted within clearly defined philosophical limits) and has not delivered his final conclusion, his presentation here fits a descriptive rather than prescriptive model. If you only consider life within the scope of the physical creation, and God is Himself the limit to every effort at success, then this activity describes the only avenue open to the most emotional satisfaction one can achieve in life on earth. Focus on the things in your life that foster contentment.

We expect this type of conclusion and application given the content and parameters Koheleth set for this experiment. It does not surprise us to find that as he applies the same parameters to other components of the same content that he arrives at the same types of conclusions and applications. These have been his findings in each of the experimental series he described. His point has been to demonstrate the one-sidedness of life lived destitute of a covenant relationship between created and Creator, between man and God. He is describing now. He will prescribe in his final conclusion.

Conclusion/application set 2 (9:11–12)

> [11]*I have further observed under the sun that*
> *The race is not won by the swift,*
> *Nor the battle by the valiant;*
> *Nor is bread won by the wise,*
> *Nor wealth by the intelligent,*
> *Nor favor by the learned.*
> *For the time of mischance comes to all.* [12]*And*
> *a man cannot even know his time. As fishes are*

enmeshed in a fatal net, and as birds are trapped in
a snare, so men are caught at the time of calamity,
when it comes upon them without warning.

Donald Trump won the presidency of the United States of America, and apparently, no one saw it coming. I confess little passion for politics, but even I was struck at the public reaction on election night 2016. Hillary Clinton was the expected winner throughout the night, but when the final count was tallied and the light of dawn rose on a weary nation, Donald Trump was president. The election did not go as expected.

I tried a new bread recipe. I put in the flour and water and salt and yeast, as expected. The dough rose in the pans in the proofer, as expected. The pans went into the hot oven, as expected.

Twenty minutes later, I checked on the two loaves, expecting them to be about ten minutes from "done." I opened the oven door and a cloud of smoke cascaded in my face. Not expected. I swished away the acrid fumes and spied two loaves of bread, their centers sunk to their bottom crust and their surrounding skin the color of blackstrap molasses. Not expected.

Sometimes, despite your best efforts and best intentions, life just doesn't act as expected. Sometimes the race is not won by the fast rabbit, but by the slow turtle. Sometimes the bad guys win the battle, get the girl, make all the money, and get all the praise. Sometimes we must swallow the most bitter pill of all and own up to the fact that control is an illusion. Stuff happens.

Longman reminds us that "human ability is prey to the ravages of chance."[238] James, the brother of Jesus and leader of the church in Jerusalem, makes this very same principle practical in his advice to his readers,

> [13]Come now, you who say, "Today or
> tomorrow we will go into such and such a town
> and spend a year there and trade and make a

---

[238] Longman, 232.

profit"—[14]yet you do not know what tomorrow will bring. What is your life? For you are a mist that appears for a little time and then vanishes. [15]Instead you ought to say, "If the Lord wills, we will live and do this or that."[239]

We have no idea what unexpected occurrence will turn our world topsy-turvy in the next moments. A family arrives at a state park for a weeklong vacation. As parents unpack the car and begin to set up camp, a son wanders off to the riverbank. A few minutes later, the sounds of panic pierce through the trees, but the parents feel no alarm until the ranger appears out of breath at the opening in the trees. In an instant, the unexpected changes the entire course of a family's life. A father rushed to save a son being swept out to the cold depths of the world's largest freshwater lake. The son was saved. The father died in the effort. The wife became a widow. The boys became fatherless. None of it was planned. None of it expected.

Like fish swimming in a stream caught unaware in a net, like birds pursuing life in a seed, the bait in a trap, death springs suddenly. Unexpectedly. Finally. We've seen it. Felt it. Lived it. So why point this out to us? What does Koheleth hope to accomplish?

First, he is reminding us of what he proposed all along, "All is futile." He is also goading us. He drives us to ask for ourselves, "What real value is there in all the gains a man makes under the sun?" He maneuvers us into the philosophical corner where we have to take his experiments and conclusions personally. We can no longer be a mere audience, a congregation of spectators. No longer is this his story, or their story. These observations and questions morph into our story. No longer the impartial judges, we readers become the distraught subjects of Koheleth's inquiries. We too are subject to what Fox calls "a more fundamental inequity, the lack of a dependable connection between efforts and results, or between what one deserves and what one gets."[240]

---

[239] James 4:13–15 (ESV).
[240] James 4:13–15 (ESV).

Readers can maintain an emotional distance to a report of someone else's experiments, but what do we do when the experiment becomes about us and we see ourselves in the conclusions being drawn? Koheleth continues to make connections with his readers that will draw them personally to the reality he will offer in his final conclusion. He engages us in an unspoken inquiry, "If all this is true, then what can we do?"

Conclusion/application set 3 (9:13–18)

> [13] *This thing too I observed under the sun about wisdom, and it affected me profoundly.* [14] *There was a little city, with few men in it; and to it came a great king, who invested it and built mighty siege works against it.* [15] *Present in the city was a poor wise man who might have saved it with his wisdom, but nobody thought of that poor man.* [16] *So I observed: Wisdom is better than valor; but*
> *A poor man's wisdom is scorned,*
> *And his words are not heeded.*
> [17] *Words spoken softly by wise men are heeded sooner than those shouted by a lord in folly.*
> [18] *Wisdom is more valuable than weapons of war, but a single error destroys much of value.*

Fox offers a different reading of these verses that makes better sense. The anecdote of the city retains no historical support. It may very well be parabolic. Fox reads verse 15 as, "And he [the king] found in it a man who was poor but wise, and it was he who saved the city by his wisdom."[241] This reading supports Koheleth's conclusion in verse 16 that "wisdom is better than valor," a sentiment that would not be true if the city were not saved by the poor man's wisdom. According to Fox's interpretation, the couplet in verse 16 does

---

[241] Fox, 66.

not reflect on the previous anecdote about the city but foreshadows the assertions about wisdom in verses 17 and 18.

Because Ecclesiastes falls under the category of biblical wisdom literature, we expect wisdom to be the final hero in life, the means by which even the poor may attain wealth, the outcast favor, and the sinner righteousness. Once again, however, Koheleth puts forth the limits of wisdom. Wise words may be heeded sooner, even if spoken softly and greeted with disdain, than the shouts of royalty among a court of fools, but a single foolish error can undo all the good wisdom gains. If there is something that will rescue human beings from futility, it will not be human effort and it will not be human wisdom.

So what will rescue humanity from futility? A review of supporting data and a fourth conclusion are presented before Koheleth reveals his final conclusion to this study report.

Review of supporting data (10:1–11:6)

> ¹*Dead flies turn the perfumer's ointment fetid and putrid; so a little folly outweighs massive wisdom.*
>
> ²*A wise man's mind tends toward the right hand, a fool's toward the left.* ³*A fool's mind is also wanting when he travels, and he lets everybody know he is a fool.*
>
> ⁴*If the wrath of a lord flares up against you, don't give up your post; for when wrath abates, grave offenses are pardoned.*
>
> ⁵*Here is an evil I have seen under the sun as great as an error committed by a ruler:* ⁶*Folly was placed on lofty heights, while rich men sat in low estate.* ⁷*I have seen slaves on horseback, and nobles walking on the ground like slaves.*
>
> ⁸*He who digs a pit will fall into it; he who breaches a stone fence will be bitten by a snake.* ⁹*He who quarries stones will be hurt by them; he who splits wood will be harmed by it.* ¹⁰*If the ax has*

become dull and he has not whetted the edge, he must exert more strength. Thus the advantage of a skill [depends on the exercise of] prudence. [11]*If the snake bites because no spell was uttered, no advantage is gained by the trained charmer.*

[12]*A wise man's talk brings him favor, but a fool's lips are his undoing.* [13]*His talk begins as silliness and ends as disastrous madness.* [14]*Yet the fool talks and talks!*

A man cannot know what will happen; who can tell him what the future holds?

[15]*A fool's exertions tire him out, for he doesn't know how to get to a town.*

[16]*Alas for you, O land whose king is a lackey and whose ministers dine in the morning!* [17]*Happy are you, O land whose king is a master and whose ministers dine at the proper time—with restraint, not with guzzling!*

[18]*Through slothfulness the ceiling sags,*
Through lazy hands the house caves in.

[19]*They make a banquet for revelry; wine makes life merry, and money answers every need.*

[20]*Don't revile a king even among your intimates.*
Don't revile a rich man even in your bedchamber;
For a bird of the air may carry the utterance,
And a winged creature may report the word.

[1]*Send your bread forth upon the waters; for after many days you will find it.*

[2]*Distribute portions to seven or even to eight, for you cannot know what misfortune may occur on earth.*

[3]*If the clouds are filled, they will pour down rain on the earth; and if a tree falls to the south or to the north, the tree will stay where it falls.* [4]*If one watches the wind, he will never sow; and if one observes the clouds, he will never reap.* [5]*Just as you*

do not know how the lifebreath passes into the limbs within the womb of the pregnant woman, so you cannot foresee the actions of God, who causes all things to happen. [6]Sow your seed in the morning, and don't hold back your hand in the evening, since you don't know which is going to succeed, the one or the other, or if both are equally good.

Common examples of futility at work. Koheleth expands on his theme of inequities, injustices, and unexpected outcomes with a series of proverbs and wisdom sayings that convey the same general message. Life often hands you results contrary to expectation. This is yet another case of utter futility played out in human experience.

Perfumed ointment should be beautiful and aesthetically pleasing to the senses. In Koheleth's days, ointments had more organic ingredients than we have today. Lanolin from sheep might have been a possible base. Imagine opening a bottle of expensive, aromatic perfume only to find it full of feeding maggots and dying flies. One might expect wisdom to flourish, but it is easily neutralized by just a little folly. This is futility.

Futility abounds as well where fools don't know how to keep their mouths shut. Whether traveling mindlessly down the road not paying attention or taking offense at authority, fools fail to do the right thing. They lack wisdom. They are the epitome of futility.

Koheleth understands a certain social priority principle. Rich men are rich for a reason in his world. Koheleth's assumption is that rich men are rich because they apply wisdom to the affairs and concerns of life. Being wise, they are rich, and being rich, they are wise and worthy to be counted on for leadership in society. Yet Koheleth has seen instances when the wise (rich) are passed over and fools are exalted to rule. This makes no sense to him. Admittedly, there are occasions on the American sociopolitical scene where the very same paradox plays out and makes just as little sense. This is futility.

Futility, however, is not restricted to the category of "wisdom versus folly," nor of exalted social positions. Ordinary people engaged in ordinary activities may encounter extraordinary examples of futility. A person who digs a pit may forget its location and fall in. A person taking down a stone wall may uncover a serpent lair and be bitten. Rocks may fall on the one who quarries them. A dull ax requires more strength to accomplish the work, but I know from personal experience that a sharp ax mishandled will do more damage to fingers than to a stick of wood.

Koheleth opines that "the advantage of a skill [depends on the exercise of] prudence." And so it does, but these examples make clear that even prudence, a form of wisdom, will not guarantee a pleasant experience or expected outcome. There is more at work in the world than any expression of human effort, even prudence, can account for. This is futility.

Advice for life. Preparation for the inevitable unexpected makes good sense to Koheleth. Since futility cannot be avoided and wisdom dictates we ought to expect the unexpected, prepare! You can sit around pondering the mysteries of the universe or lamenting the course of life, or you can do what you can to adapt to the realities that embrace you. Koheleth offers two pieces of advice to those who heed the call to prepare—put your resources to work and cover your bases.

The two sagacious offerings hinge on spending resources with a mind to gaining resources. "Send your bread" and "distribute portions" speak to sharing resources with others so that when the expected unexpected arrives, there will be those who, having benefitted from you, will return the favor and be of benefit in your time of need. An investment in others, advises Koheleth, is an investment in your own security against that misfortune you cannot predict.

That basic bit of wisdom, however, needs a bit of clarification in light of Jesus and the cross. Giving cannot simply be motivated by a quest for self-benefit. Giving on those terms lacks love, and the Apostle Paul makes it clear that even if we give away all that we have, to the point of giving up our lives to death, our bodies to be burned, and have not love, we are nothing.[242] Giving without love is futility. Giving merely to receive is futile.

---

[242] 1 Corinthians 13:3 (ESV).

Love's primary focus is always someone else's benefit. Love caused Jesus to leave the eternal glory He shared with the Father, become a man, and die on the cross as an atoning sacrifice for sinful men. Paul expresses Christ's active love like this, [9]"For you know the grace of our Lord Jesus Christ, that though he was rich, yet for your sake he became poor, so that you by his poverty might become rich."[243]

Again, Paul calls believers and followers of Jesus, disciples, to [5]"have this mind among yourselves, which is yours in Christ Jesus, [6]who, though he was in the form of God, did not count equality with God a thing to be grasped, [7]but emptied himself, by taking the form of a servant, being born in the likeness of men. [8]And being found in human form, he humbled himself by becoming obedient to the point of death, even death on a cross."[244]

Jesus's activity among His disciples, by His own testimony, was to impart to them the same love He received from the Father. He desired the Father's love might be in them, presumably moving them to love as He loved.[245] He made His commitment to love a requirement for His disciples when he commanded them to love on the basis, for the reason, and in the ways He had loved them, [34]"A new commandment I give to you, that you love one another: just as I have loved you, you also are to love one another."[246]

Dr. Les Parrot, blogging about his book *Love Like That*, offers five steps to loving the way Jesus loves, "If you want to love like Jesus, you've got to…become more mindful—less detached, become more approachable—less exclusive, become more graceful-less judgmental, become more bold-less fearful, become more self-giving-less self-absorbed."[247]

---

[243] 2 Corinthians 8:9 (ESV).

[244] Philippians 2:5–8 (ESV).

[245] John 17:26 (ESV).

[246] John 13:34 (ESV).

[247] Les Parrot, "How to Love Like Jesus in Five Steps," https://annvoskamp. com/2018/09/how-to-love-like-jesus-in-5-steps (September 12, 2018). Accessed January 29, 2019.

In other words, you've got to "send forth your bread" and "distribute portions."

Putting together the wisdom of preparation with the commitment to love guarantees that when the day of adversity descends (the timing of which no one can predict but for which we can prepare), God's grace abounds.

The first piece of advice was put your resources to work, benefit others for the sake of future benefit. It is a strategy that works best when motivated by genuine love rather than fear or selfishness. The second piece of life advice Koheleth offers can be simply stated as "cover all your bases."

Some outcomes are known, certain. Rain will fall to the earth. Trees will lay unmoved where they fall. If you spend all your time waiting for perfect conditions, nothing will get done.

Some outcomes are unknown, mysteries hidden in the mind and heart and power of God. How does a baby come to life in a mother's womb? God is in charge of that process. David reminds us that it is God who has knit us together in our mother's womb and that we are "fearfully and wonderfully made."[248] Koheleth restates the truth that we "cannot foresee the actions of God, who causes all things to happen." He makes this point—whether you have knowledge or not, do what is practical and best. Cover your bases. Sow your seed in the morning and sow your seed in the evening. You don't know which will succeed, but you do know that if you do not sow seed, you will not reap a harvest.

The unexpected comes. You have no control over the timing or extent of circumstances, but you can use what you know to prepare, and if you prepare with love, you will be exceedingly better off when the day of trouble arrives.

Conclusion/application set 4 (11:7–12:8)

Conclusion.

> [7]*"How sweet is the light, what a delight for the*
> *eyes to behold the sun!* [8]*Even if a man lives many*

---

[248] Psalm 139:13–14a (ESV).

years, let him enjoy himself in all of them, remem-
bering how many the days of darkness are going to
be. The only future is nothingness!" (11:7–8)

He's talking about death. While you live, live. While you can see the light, delight! No matter how many days or years you live, eternity will be infinitely longer. Don't waste your days, as if they were numberless, for they are not. That's why Moses writes of God,

> You return man to dust and say, "Return, O children of man!"
> For a thousand years in your sight are but as yesterday when it is past, or as a watch in the night.
> You sweep them away as with a flood; they are like a dream, like grass that is renewed in the morning: in the morning it flourishes and is renewed; in the evening it fades and withers.
> For we are brought to an end by your anger; by your wrath we are dismayed. You have set our iniquities before you, our secret sins in the light of your presence.
> For all our days pass away under your wrath; we bring our years to an end like a sigh.
> The years of our life are seventy, or even by reason of strength eighty; yet their span is but toil and trouble; they are soon gone, and we fly away.
> Who considers the power of your anger, and your wrath according to the fear of you?
> So teach us to number our days that we may get a heart of wisdom.[249]

Since our days are not numberless, we ought to learn to count them carefully, to honor them eagerly, to use them wisely. Koheleth

---

[249] Psalm 90:3–12 (ESV).

advises youth on how to do just that, to live wisely while they have the time (which could end at any moment without warning!)

Application.

⁹*O youth, enjoy yourself while you are young! Let your heart lead you to enjoyment in the days of your youth. Follow the desires of your heart and the glances of your eyes—but know well that God will call you to account for all such things—*¹⁰*and banish care from your mind, and pluck sorrow out of your flesh! For youth and black hair are fleeting.*

¹*So appreciate your vigor in the days of your youth, before those days of sorrow come and those years arrive of which you will say, "I have no pleasure in them";* ²*before sun and light and moon and stars grow dark, and the clouds come back again after the rain:*

³*When the guards of the house become shaky, And the men of valor are bent, And the maids that grind, grown few, are idle, And the ladies that peer through the windows grow dim,* ⁴*And the doors to the street are shut With the noise of the hand mill growing fainter, And the song of the bird growing feebler, And all the strains of music dying down;* ⁵*When one is afraid of heights And there is terror on the road. For the almond tree may blossom, The grasshopper be burdened, And the caper bush may bud again; But man sets out for his eternal abode, With mourners all around in the street.* ⁶*Before the silver cord snaps And the golden bowl crashes,*

The jar is shattered at the spring,
And the jug is smashed at the cistern.
[7]*And the dust returns to the ground*
As it was,
And the lifebreath returns to God
Who bestowed it.
[8]*Utter futility—said Koheleth—*
All is futile! (11:9–12:8)

Fox points out that this section of Ecclesiastes is the most difficult in the book. He observes that the "Hebrew is difficult, sometimes obscure, and its imagery is enigmatic." He goes on to note that interpreters have read this section "through three primary lenses: allegorical, literal, and eschatological." The allegorical approach, which I will use here because it seems the most obvious, sees in the poem the deterioration of the human body as it ages.[250] The literal approach assumes each component of the poem is described exactly as that thing is, not intending it to represent something else. The eschatological approach sees in the poem a parallel between the death of a person and the coming "Day of the Lord." Fox comments, describing the eschatological approach, "The imagery that pictures the death and funeral of an individual is also suggestive of a day of vast calamity or even the destruction of the world."[251]

From an interpretive standpoint, unless the entire book has been somehow a code for the final judgment of God upon Israel and the world, it seems a stretch to assign this poem an eschatological function. Also, to be considered is the fact that this section is a poem and poems often use familiar imagery to point to a different reality. Finally, Koheleth's declaration that youth and black hair are fleeting in 11:10 suggests an allegorical context for interpretation. "Black hair" is idiomatic for "youth," just as "gray hair" is idiomatic for elders. If Koheleth employs metaphorical imagery in his intro-

---

[250] It is fair to note, with Fox, that there is no established standard for decoding the imagery of the poem. This is a weakness of using an allegorical approach.
[251] Fox, 76.

duction, it seems reasonable to use the same interpretive filter on what follows.[252]

Koheleth's message is simple. Old age advances and faster than we usually imagine (until we start to get there). Death always arrives too soon. So, Koheleth implores us, make the most of youth while we have it. He does not advise throwing life away, as one might judge him to have done, but of fulfilling joy, keeping in mind the fear of God. Live, he says, but be mindful God will judge the life you live. The caveat of accountability is a call to wise living. It is a reminder that one can find pleasure and wisdom at the same time. He does not suggest we shrink away from personal fulfilment, but he does warn us against selfishness, which would be akin to foolishness and futility.

As we have seen throughout the report, there are limits to be considered. Youth and black hair are fleeting. They are short-lived, so appreciate them while you can.[253] The poem recounts the conditions of chronological superiority. The hands become shaky. The spine bends. The teeth wear away. The eyes grow dim. Speech and hearing fade, one to whispers, the other to silence. Fear takes precedence over courage. Strength succumbs to weakness. Feebleness claims the throne and then death comes. The silver cord snaps, the golden bowl crashes, the jar is shattered at the spring and the jug is smashed at the cistern, the dust returns to the earth from which it came, the breath of life returns to God who gave it in the first place, and all we have done and been and hoped passes away in utter futility. Utter futility, said Koheleth, all is futile.

We are back where we started. Koheleth's exclamation of futility lands like a heavy sigh at the end of his formal report. Bartholomew

---

[252] The use of *hevel* in 11:10, translated as "fleeting," provides an additional contextual clue. What follows that line about youth and black hair should further enhance the imagery of futility, of which aging and death are the ultimate examples.

[253] Fox, 77. The commentator points out that JPS translates as "appreciate your vigor," a Hebrew phrase that more literally means "remember your Creator." Commentators are not agreed on which is best. "Remember your Creator" certainly gives spiritual grounding to the life Koheleth presses youth to pursue in 11:9–10.

identifies verse 8 as an *inclusio* to the book that reintroduces the narrator.[254] He suggests that the *inclusio* offers "the title to the book… indicating the journey of exploration on which Qohelet takes the reader, but without assuming that this is his conclusion."[255] If only he had used the word "hypothesis" instead of "title," we'd be on the same page!

The placement of this restatement of the hypothesis could signal a final conclusion on Koheleth's part, or it could signal the conclusion derived only from the evidence thus far presented, which is how I take it. Careful consideration of all the toil at which humans toil under the sun, to the days of their old age and death, reveals that all is futile. No effort, no human wisdom, nothing under the sun averts the weakness and failings of age or the eventual, inevitable arrival of death. On the basis of the evidence examined in light of established criteria, the hypothesis is not disproven. It seems it's all over. Koheleth has spoken, the report appears ended, and now the narrator returns. Time to turn out the lights and go home. But if we do that, we'll miss the actual ending, the one that comes after the credits roll.

Study Questions

Summary of experimental methodology (8:16–17)

1. How does Koheleth describe his overall methodology in this research report?
2. To whom does Koheleth ascribe direct involvement in the activities he has studied?
3. In what realm does Koheleth firmly seat the events that transpire "under the sun"?
4. What conclusion does Koheleth offer regarding the adequacy of human effort to ascertain meaning from observation of earthbound events and experience?

---

[254] Bartholomew, 360.
[255] Ibid., 362.

Conclusion/application set 1 (9:1–10)

1. What is the first conclusion Koheleth reports relative to his observations?
2. What does the statement that "the actions of even the righteous and the wise are determined by God" tell us about God, the world, and human experience?
3. What might this statement tell us about Koheleth's reason for conducting this research experiment?
4. Verses 7–10 may be an application, or a reporting of a prevailing worldview, or a prescription based in the conclusion arrived at on verse 1. Which do you think this is? Why?

Conclusion/application set 2 (9:11–12)

1. What does Koheleth mean in these apparent contradictions?
2. What does Koheleth report as the final cause behind all causes? Is it "mischance" or the one who orders time (as we've seen since chapter 3)?
3. Each of these apparent contradictions exists because of either random chance or divine plan. Which do you think Koheleth subscribes to? Why?

Conclusion/application set 3 (9:13–18)

1. Koheleth points to wisdom as a foundational value that is often overlooked, to the detriment of those who may have benefitted, had their prejudice not gotten in the way.
   a. How might this very principle apply to interpreting Ecclesiastes?
   b. Has Koheleth given us another interpretive clue?
2. How has Koheleth's application of wisdom in this book impacted your way of thinking?

Review of supporting data (10:1–11:6)

1. Having just extolled the virtue and value of wisdom, Koheleth offers a small feast of general wisdom in these proverbs.
    a. Once again, examine them closely and comment on any that seem particularly relevant to your current life situation.
    b. How does this wisdom apply and how might you put this wisdom to work for you?

Conclusion/application set 4 (11:7–12:8)

1. Joy is the final conclusion. What do you understand Koheleth to mean by "enjoyment"?
2. Given your "filters" having come this far in the study, how do you interact with the application here?
3. What is Koheleth describing in the poem in 12:1–8?
4. What point is the Teacher making?
5. What makes his point valid? What makes it invalid (or at least in need of a different spin)?

CHAPTER 9

THE END OF THE MATTER (12:9–14)

Final Summary Statements

One presenter: check.

One hypothesis: check.

One refined research question: check.

Sufficient, credible supporting observations: plenty of checks.

Experimental methodology to test hypothesis, three series: check, check, and check.

Preliminary findings, including initial conclusions and suggested applications: oh my, yes, check.

What's left in our consideration of this formal report of research conducted, summarized, and presented by one Koheleth, son of David, king in Jerusalem? Four items are left for us—a brief consideration of the nature of the epilogue; a final statement regarding the community function and credibility of the presenter; a final, personal statement to either a student in the target audience or the target audience in general, typical of biblical wisdom literature; and the final conclusion that brings closure to the entire proceedings.

Notes on the epilogue

The return of the narrator at this point in Ecclesiastes signals the start of the epilogue. This sudden and dramatic change of voices gives rise to no small mass of interpretive comments. Traditionally, those who have held to Solomon as the author of the entire book have held to Solomon's authorship of these closing verses as well. They cite the change in voice as a change in perspective, perhaps an older, wiser Solomon mellowing the ramblings of a younger, more philosophically rambunctious Solomon.

Others, not willing to die on the hill of Solomonic authorship, offer that the epilogue was added by a later editor, one who "supposedly considered Koheleth's words too unorthodox and sought to counteract them with pious assurances and precepts."[256] Still others propose that the narrator of 1:1–10 and these verses in chapter 12 is the narrator of the entire book, who has been telling a third-person story in the first person for the sake of dramatic effect.

Whatever the case, Fox is correct when he notes in regard to the narrator's speech, that person's "viewpoint is final and decisive."[257] The viewpoint of the narrator in the epilogue is that of the author of the book, whether that author is Solomon or someone using Solomon's name in order to guide our understanding and interpretation of the content of the book.

I love how commentator Douglas Sean O'Donnell introduces his chapter on the epilogue. He posts the opening words of Augustine's *Confessions* and then parallels those words with Koheleth's words here, writing,

> Like Augustine, Pastor Solomon through-
> out Ecclesiastes has confessed his failings as
> well as his findings. Now in the final verses he
> announces his ultimate discovery.[258]

O'Donnell also notes two errors to avoid as we seek to understand, interpret, and ultimately apply the message of the epilogue in connection with the whole of Ecclesiastes. The first mistake we have

---

[256] Fox, 82. Fox is summarizing at this point. He offers his own perspective later.
[257] Fox, 83.
[258] O'Donnell, 211.

already considered and resolved. O'Donnell identifies the mistake as assuming the past tense voice in the epilogue requires that the actual author of these verses be someone other than Solomon. O'Donnell accepts Solomonic authorship of Ecclesiastes and offers several good examples of why Solomon might have switched to third person at this stage of his presentation. He summarizes by stating his conviction "that Pastor Solomon wrote everything in Ecclesiastes, even the ending."[259]

The second mistake O'Donnell would have us avoid is to interpret the epilogue as an "orthodox corrective" to the rest of Ecclesiastes. He is right. He writes, "There is no thematic disconnect between the final verses and the rest of the book."[260] The question of course is, How do the primary contents of Ecclesiastes and the words of the epilogue fit together? O'Donnell calls the epilogue "the rudder that steers the ship" and completes his thought saying, "Without verses 9–14 (esp. vv. 13–14) to guide, we would easily read Ecclesiastes wrongly."[261]

That's it exactly. Without the epilogue and verses 13–14 in particular, we would easily read Ecclesiastes wrongly. How? Because Ecclesiastes 12:13–14 disprove the hypothesis Koheleth offers in 1:2. The epilogue is not a simple add-on module. It is *the* piece of observational evidence that demands the entire experiment be reconsidered with a different set of independent variables. The epilogue is the control set in the experiment. It is the one set of conditions that is unchanged by the independent variables yet, itself, changes everything.

Remember that it is impossible to prove a hypothesis in a science experiment. The effort of the experiment is to discover whether the proposition can be disproven by the conditions defined in the methodology. We cannot prove a hypothesis because we cannot account for every potential contingency in the entire universe. There can always exist something undiscovered that will disprove our hypothe-

---

[259] O'Donnell, 212.
[260] Ibid.
[261] Ibid.

sis, so we devise conditions to intentionally disprove our thesis, and as long as we cannot disprove it, we accept its working, theoretical credibility. However, should we discover even one instance or condition that disproves our thesis, our thesis must be revised or discarded.

Koheleth has successfully demonstrated, by exploring life from every angle under the sun, that because of death and the limits of human wisdom and human efforts, life is ultimately futile and meaningless. The epilogue contains the single piece of evidence that sets the entire hypothesis on its proverbial ear. Before we get to the details of that evidence, however, we should consider the other final summary statements included here.

A final statement regarding the presenter

> ⁹*A further word: Because Koheleth was a sage, he continued to instruct the people. He listened to and tested the soundness of many maxims.* ¹⁰*Koheleth sought to discover useful sayings and recorded genuinely truthful sayings.* ¹¹*The sayings of the wise are like goads, like nails fixed in prodding sticks. They were given by one Shepherd. (12:9–11)*

Take Ecclesiastes seriously. Why? Because of who the author is, because of what motivates the author, because of the nature of what the author offers, and because of the source of what the author offers.

Who is Koheleth? Koheleth is a sage. He is wise. He knows stuff. Good stuff. Life stuff. The Hebrew word *hakham* ("sage") comes from the word meaning "wisdom" and includes "both the knowledge gained by learning and the intellectual powers that can analyze and evaluate that learning."[262] Koheleth is like a doctor who successfully studied anatomy, physiology, pharmacology, bacteriology, surgical methods, and a slew of other "-ologies" relative to disease processes and symptoms and treatments and who, having understood and

---

[262] Fox, xx.

applied that knowledge to real-life cases over the course of a lifetime, now offers to consult on your problem for free. It's like consulting the top specialists at Mayo and Johns Hopkins all at the same time, in the same room, no charge.

Craig Bartholomew notes that "this description of Qoholet [sic] indicates from the narrator's perspective that Qoholet does indeed resolve his struggle and arrive at a position that fits with traditional wisdom."[263] That the epilogue does not assign Koheleth a place among the fools but honors him as "wise" encourages the readers to view Koheleth's words as worthy of thoughtful consideration, as having meaning for them and for their lives.

Koheleth's career penchant for wisdom and understanding make him a teacher whose words should be carefully considered by those exposed to his teaching. He is acknowledged as one whose life focused on gaining and communicating in understandable terms an advanced insight into life and its meaning. Koheleth has already demonstrated his own imperfections. He is not better than us, but he is certainly wiser than most of us. His wisdom makes him worthy of our attention. Bartholomew summarizes that "we have an attractive portrait of Qoholet as a hard-working and creative wise man with a heart for the people of God as a whole."[264]

What motivates Koheleth? Koheleth is a teacher. He works for the benefit of his audience, his people, by gathering useful data and interpreting it for them. His work enables them to access and apply life-changing, life-giving information, particularly information about God, that will assist them to live wise lives, godly lives, lives more likely to experience God's favor than His just and righteous wrath.

Koheleth is motivated by the opportunity to improve the life experience of those around him. He is motivated by their spiritual well-being. His heart is the heart of a shepherd king looking out for the good of his people. He does not shield them from truth, but instead helps them to understand and engage the truth they cannot hope to avoid. Koheleth's good desire for his people supports

---

[263] Bartholomew, 363.
[264] Bartholomew, 363.

the value of his work and his words and substantiates a call to take Ecclesiastes seriously, personally, and prayerfully even.

The nature of Koheleth's offering. Koheleth has gathered information from sources and observations all around him, and he has not merely embraced each one as valid but has tested them, tested their worthiness to be widely accepted. He has weighed them carefully in the balances and found which ones are wanting and which are sufficient. He both recorded and authored useful and truthful sayings. Eaton characterizes Koheleth's teaching "as more than accumulation of facts. It is closely related to discipline, skill and righteousness."[265]

Koheleth offers "words of delight" according to the ESV of verse 10. The *Tanakh* reads "useful sayings." The Hebrew is *dibre-chephets*. *Chephets* is variously translated as pleasure, desire, and delightsome and is defined as "that in which one takes delight." Koheleth sought hard and with integrity to discover wisdom that would please the ears and satisfy the heart, bringing contentment to the spirit and relief to the soul. He has not collected the cheap thrills so often thrust upon the human spirit and intellect by our contemporary entertainment industry. There is no fluff here, no filler. Koheleth's wisdom penetrates the walls of denial and spiritual blindness that imprison the heart.

Koheleth's "words of delight," his "useful sayings," are understood to be both genuinely truthful and offered with integrity. Eaton observes that "his words are not so pleasing that they cease to be upright"[266] and then offers a useful saying of his own in regard to Koheleth's strategy, "To be upright but unpleasant is to be a fool; to be pleasant but not upright is to be a charlatan."[267] Koheleth is neither a fool nor a charlatan. His words bear the character of trustworthy authenticity.

The source of Koheleth's offering. The wisdom produced and recorded by a man like Koheleth, with his credentials, is like the goads a shepherd uses to move the flock along. They can be prickly

---

[265] Eaton, 173–174.

[266] Ibid., 174.

[267] Ibid.

and prodding, but the intent and outcome is personal benefit for the one so shepherded.

Fox notes that the word "shepherd" here is almost universally understood to refer to God and thus is usually capitalized. He adds, however, that "the metaphor of shepherd for God refers to his role protecting and providing for people—a role that is not relevant here."[268] He continues by pointing out that unlike law and prophecy, the words of the wise are nowhere else (in wisdom literature) ever considered to be given by God.[269] Fox simply maintains the more literal, concrete understanding of this imagery. Perhaps, given that the Psalmist, in other places, recognizes the pastoral work of God in his own life and among God's people,[270] it is adequate to assume that even if nothing more is immediately meant by the narrator than a simple shepherd image, such an image can, and often does, apply to God's leadership of His people, sometimes through the words He inspires others to deliver on His behalf.

Contrary to Fox's perspective, Bartholomew observes, "God as the unified source of the diverse words of the wise would explain their value."[271] Understanding God to be the Shepherd of verse 11 also helps us to interpret the meaning of verse 12, which looks like a warning against the words of the wise but in light of how one reads verse 11 could be a warning against ignoring or "going beyond" the words of the wise derived from the "one Shepherd."

The question, of course, is whether the author intended to add a greater measure of authority to the wisdom just reported by connecting it to a Source greater than the reporter. If so, then we ought to take into consideration the implication that "words of wisdom—even unconventional ones like Koheleth's—ultimately derive from God."[272] It should not surprise us that God, who created language and logic, should be adept at using them as He sees fit in communicating with His creation. Jesus uses parable and hyperbole and a variety of other rhetorical devises to further His mission to reveal the

---

[268] Fox, 84.
[269] Ibid.
[270] Psalm 23, for example.
[271] Bartholomew, 368.
[272] Fox, 84.

Father to His people. God inspired Isaiah to walk around naked for three years, a living object lesson of the future captivity for Israel if they did not repent. God had Noah build a boat in the middle of a dry plain. Paul used sarcasm. The Apostle John recounted visions in the language of prophetic imagery. God knows how to creatively and competently convey His thoughts and revelation to His people.

What should cause us to marvel is not so much the techniques the Almighty uses to communicate the knowledge of the glory of the *Lord* to us, but that He sets as His mission to communicate His glory to us at all. Adam took the word of a snake in the grass over the word of the King upon the throne. The serpent kills. The King pursues with love and mercy and compassion and justice and righteousness and holiness and sovereignty and glory in order to bring life, when, truth be told, He has every right to end the existence of every sinner and start over. But His plan is infinite, glorious, eternal self-revelation of His glory, for His glory, with the overflow of joy into the lives of those to whom He reveals Himself. What wondrous love is this!

A final statement to the audience

> [12] *"A further word: Against them, my son, be warned! The making of many books is without limit And much study is a wearying of the flesh." (12:12)*

"My son!" Isaac used the familial exclamation to command Esau's obedience in preparation for a blessing Esau never got.[273] Rebekah used the same endearment when she sent Jacob scurrying to Laban after Esau discovered his brother's deceit.[274] Moses spoke the warning of the *Lord* to Pharaoh, "Israel is my firstborn son, and I say to you, 'Let my son go that he may serve me.'"[275] David's lament at the death of Absalom reverberates with the passion of his loss, "O my

---

[273] Genesis 27:8 (ESV).
[274] Genesis 27:43 (ESV).
[275] Exodus 4:22–23 (ESV).

son Absalom, my son, my son Absalom! Would I had died instead of you, O Absalom, my son, my son!"[276]

The same phrase, "My son," is used twenty-four times in Proverbs, always as an identifier of one receiving direct advice from the parent speaker. "Be wise, my son, and make my heart glad, that I may answer him who reproaches me."[277]

It is possible to interpret the use of "my son" here in several ways. The narrator may be addressing these words to his own son. Koheleth may not be speaking to his own son or even to a particular son but to the gathered audience. It could be rhetorical, nurturing a relationship between an interested congregation and a well-meaning teacher. The intent is personal even if corporate in scope.

Another question arises, besides the identity of the son. What is the antecedent for the third-person plural pronoun "them"? Does it refer to the collected sayings that are given by the one Shepherd? If so, then the sentence means, "Don't seek out wisdom from other sources when the wisdom from the one Shepherd, the wisdom you have just received, is sufficient." According to O'Donnell, "The book of Ecclesiastes is sufficient to instruct us how to walk in wisdom… What is required is not more books for more study, but more obedience to what has already been revealed."[278]

Discern what is happening here. The narrator/author has just informed his target audience that the teachings of Koheleth presented in Ecclesiastes fulfill the mission of wisdom literature and are sufficient in themselves to accomplish within the reader the full purpose for the existence of wisdom literature—a godly life that pleases God. That statement alone offers guidance for the strategies used to interpret the book. Ecclesiastes, like all of Scripture, fits the criteria Paul outlines for Timothy in his second letter,

> The sacred writings, which are able to make
> you wise for salvation through faith in Jesus

---

[276] 2 Samuel 18:33 (ESV).
[277] Proverbs 27:11 (ESV).
[278] O'Donnell, 214.

Christ. All Scripture is breathed out by God and profitable for teaching, for reproof, for correction, and for training in righteousness, that the man of God may be competent, equipped for every good work.[279]

Surely it is of interest that Koheleth asks, "What profit is there?" and Paul declares God's inspired self-revelation, of which Ecclesiastes is a part, "profitable." Adding the components together equals real value found under the sun only in that which comes from heaven, beyond the sun, from God Himself. And that is just where Ecclesiastes takes us!

A final statement of conclusion

> [13] *The sum of the matter, when all is said and done: Revere God and observe His commandments! For this applies to all mankind:* [14]*that God will call every creature to account for everything unknown, be it good or bad. (12:13–14)*

Anticipation answered. On the night he was betrayed, Jesus reclined at the table with His disciples and He said to them, "I have earnestly desired to eat this Passover with you before I suffer."[280] The occasion flows with anticipation and soon-to-be realized obedience, mercy, judgment, and sovereignty. This is the moment He and they have been waiting for, though their waiting has been less defined than His. This is the inaugural meal. This is the covenant signing. This is what they have been waiting for.

From the moment Koheleth uttered the words, "Utter futility!" we have been waiting for the words in verse 13. With every new example supporting the hypothesis that life, with all its joy and sorrows, accomplishments and failures, victories and defeats, remains

---

[279] 2 Timothy 3:15–17 (ESV).
[280] Luke 22:15 (ESV).

ultimately meaningless, we have longed for and desired just one shred of disproving evidence. We have not wanted to believe all is futile, but the argument has, admittedly, been persuasive. Still we have hoped with hope there might be something that offsets all the others and forces us to draw a much different final conclusion. Here is our relief, our rescue, our reward for wading through all the evidence and all the arguments and all the preliminary findings.

> *The sum of the matter; when all is said and done: Revere God and observe His commandments.*

The phrase "sum of the matter" refers to the final conclusion to the exploratory quest we have been invited to observe.[281]

We have seen the sovereign God, the determining God, the limiting God, and the supplying God in the evidence Koheleth provided but we have wondered (and I know we have wondered because my Sunday school class has asked repeatedly), where is the covenant-keeping God? Where is the God unlike all other gods, Who calls a people to Himself and enters into covenant with them and keeps it? Where is the God Who is near at hand yet sits enthroned upon the cherubim, His glory filling the temple? Where is the God Who spoke Torah and gave it to His people, naming as "My People," those who were once not a people at all?

Where is the God, we have wondered, Who spoke and the worlds were created? Where is the God Whose word does not return to Him void, the God Whose plans cannot be thwarted, the God Who promises that no weapon raised against His people will prosper? Where is the God Who spoke with Moses as friend with friend, Who promised Joshua every place the sole of his foot would tread, Who swore David would never lack a man to sit upon the throne?

Where is the God Who is personal? The God Who called Abraham and provided the lamb? The God Who gave Noah the plans for the Ark and Moses the plans for both the tabernacle and the nation? Where is the God Who warns the pharaohs and sends

---

[281] Bartholomew, 370.

plagues and parts seas and brings water out of rocks and bread from dew and quail from the edges of the horizon? This God, the God of Abraham, Isaac, and Jacob, has seemed to be hidden, distant, aloof in the wisdom of Ecclesiastes. We have missed Him, pined for Him, mourned Him, and wondered at His unexplained absence.

Now, finally, He is here, at the end of the report. He is the one piece of evidence that sets aside the hypothesis. He is the one fact that must be accounted for in order to accurately interpret the book of Ecclesiastes. Here He is, the message of the entire book. Add up all Koheleth has unveiled for us about life and human effort, and it is all meaningless and empty, until you add the covenant-making, covenant-keeping God of grace and glory to the equation. He changes everything!

Instruction offered. "Observe His commandments" is covenant language. It is the language of successful relationship, creature with Creator. This is the missing piece, the fulcrum upon which the entire book rests.

Meaning in life comes within a covenant relationship with the covenant-offering, covenant-keeping God of Israel. Revering God and keeping His commandments, not striving for self-exaltation but for relationship with God on His terms, is the "whole duty of mankind." "Thus," Bartholomew concludes, "the first motivation for revering God is positively that in this way we fulfill our humanity."[282] Jesus set the same wisdom before His disciples, "If you love me, keep my commandments."[283]

The nature and purpose of the divine covenant.

The nature of the divine covenant. What is a "covenant" in biblical context? In simplest terms, a covenant is a mutual agreement that defines a relationship. The *Tyndale Bible Dictionary* defines covenant as an "arrangement between two parties involving mutual obligations; especially the arrangement that established the relationship

---

[282] Bartholomew, 371
[283] John 14:15 (ESV).

between God and his people, expressed in grace first with Israel and then with the church."[284] The *Lexham Theological Wordbook* adds that "a covenant is a legally binding agreement between two parties,"[285] emphasizing the authority over the conduct of the parties inherent in the agreement. The *Eerdmans Bible Dictionary* definition highlights the mutual rights and responsibilities to which covenantal partners submit themselves.[286]

Covenants in the ancient Near East were commonly of two types. Parity treaties (or covenants) were agreements between equals. An example of a parity covenant would be a treaty between the kings of two different nations who draw up a document to describe mutually agreed upon terms of relationship between them and their nations.

The other type of covenant seems to provide the background for understanding covenant in the Bible. This type of covenant is called a "suzerain-vassal" covenant, and it refers to an agreement between a superior authority and a less powerful authority or people. For example, a great emperor with vast armies and resources might extend to a prince of a smaller land with fewer resources protection in exchange for sovereignty. The lesser prince would surrender absolute control over his kingdom in order to gain access to the protection and resources of the more powerful emperor. The two would agree on the terms of the arrangement and strike a covenant between them.

Walter Elwell informs us that "the essence of covenant is to be found in a particular kind of relationship between persons. Mutual obligations characterize that kind of relationship. Thus a covenant relationship is not merely a mutual acquaintance but a commitment to responsibility and action."[287]

---

[284] Walter A. Elwell and P. W. Comfort, "Covenant," in *Tyndale Bible Dictionary* (Wheaton, IL: Tyndale House Publishers, 2001), 323.

[285] M. R. Jones, "Covenant," *Lexham Theological Wordbook*, eds. D. Mangum, D. R. Brown, R. Klippenstein, and R. Hurst (Bellingham, WA: Lexham Press, 2014).

[286] A. C. Myers, *The Eerdmans Bible Dictionary* (Grand Rapids, MI: Eerdmans, 1987), 240.

[287] Elwell, 323

While covenants usually include and outline the benefits of the relationship to each party, it is particularly the responsibility to the covenant that exerts itself in the pages of the Scripture. The term widely associated with the ongoing commitment to keeping the terms of covenant is "faithfulness." God is far more often noted for His faithfulness to the covenants He makes than are the humans with whom He makes these covenants.

A quick survey of biblical passages related to God's covenants with human beings reveals at least five characteristics common to each covenant. Each covenant is initiated by God, established by God, expanded by God, ratified or sealed by God, and is faithfully honored by God.

The covenant is initiated by God. God always initiates the covenants He enters. When God created the first man and woman, before they said or did anything, He set down the terms of relationship. He blessed them. He commanded them to be fruitful and multiply and fill the earth. He gave them His law, "Of the tree of the knowledge of good and evil in the midst of the garden you must not eat." And He outlined the consequences of any faithlessness on their part, "For in the day that you eat of it you shall surely die."[288]

We know, of course, that the first pair did act faithlessly and break the first covenant God made. Their decision to eat the fruit changed their internal, spiritual environment. It also changed the essence of their ability to enter and keep covenant with God. Elwell explains,

> The fall substantially influenced the nature of subsequent religious covenants. The separation of humankind from God clarifies the nature of the human predicament. Created for a relationship with the Creator, sinning humans are excluded from that relationship and cannot, on their own accord, reestablish it. From that circumstance emerges a distinctive feature

---

[288] Genesis 2:16–17 (ESV).

of divine-human covenants, namely, that God alone can initiate the relationship of covenant.[289]

Following the expulsion of Adam and Eve from the garden, every instance of covenant between God and humanity recorded in the Scripture is initiated by God. Covenants with Noah, Abram, Moses and the nation of Israel, and King David as well as the New Covenant between Christ and the church are all initiated by God. Even today, in our post-Calvary, post-Pentecost time, God still initiates His covenant with every believer. Jesus said, "You have not chosen me; I have chosen you." Every person who comes to faith in Christ comes as a result of God initiating covenant with them.

The covenant is established by God. It is one thing to initiate a covenant. It is another thing to establish it. Speaking to Noah on the occasion of the first formal covenant with sin-stricken humanity, God exclaims, "I will establish my covenant with you, and you shall come into the ark, you, your sons, your wife, and your sons' wives with you."[290] God uses the same establishment language later, after the flood waters have receded, "I will establish my covenant with you, that never again shall all flesh be cut off by the waters of the flood, and never again shall there be a flood to destroy the earth."[291] To establish the covenant means to put forth guarantees of faithfulness. God makes promises and guarantees them on the basis of Himself, His Person, His nature, and His glory.

God has no reason to say, "I promise on the grave of my ancestors to do such and such." Parties entering covenant with one another often offer valuable collateral to guarantee faithfulness. God offers Himself. God offers His integrity and honesty, His commitment that arises from His perfect, sinless nature. And granted nothing exists that is more valuable or worthy or glorious than Himself, God swears His faithfulness to the covenant on Himself.

The covenant is expanded by God. In each covenant that God makes with individuals, He expands them to include others in the

---

289 Elwell, 324.
290 Genesis 6:18 (ESV).
291 Genesis 9:11 (ESV).

benefits. The covenant with Adam included all who would follow him. The covenant with Noah included Noah, his wife, his sons and daughters-in-law, and "every living creature that is with you, for all future generations."[292]

God made a covenant with a man named Abram. God offered to make Abram the father of a multitude of nations. But then God expanded the benefits of the covenant He offered, "And I will establish my covenant between me and you and your offspring after you throughout their generations for an everlasting covenant, to be God to you and to your offspring after you."[293]

And beyond the blessings of covenant to Abram's personal descendants, God promised blessing through Abram to all the families of the earth!

On the night Jesus was betrayed, He took bread and wine and inaugurated the new covenant with His disciples. But it was already a covenant intended for expansion. The angel proclaimed to the shepherds on the night of Christ's birth, "Fear not, for behold I bring you good news of great joy that will be for all the people. For unto you is born this day in the city of David a Savior, who is Christ the Lord."[294]

Here is a restatement of God's covenant promise to Abram along with its expansion clause. The baby is born to the descendants of Abram, but his birth will be an occasion of joy for all the people.

Jesus expressed the expansionist intent of the covenant when He instructed His disciples to "go therefore and make disciples of all nations, baptizing them in the name of the Father and of the Son and of the Holy Spirit, teaching them to observe all that I have commanded you."[295] With these words, Jesus makes God's offer of covenant relationship to the peoples of the world.

The covenant is sealed by God. Covenants were often sealed in blood. Noah offered a sacrifice after the flood. God sealed the covenant with Abram when He passed among the pieces of animal sacrifice Abram had prepared. The entire Mosaic covenant with the

---

[292] Genesis 9:12 (ESV).
[293] Genesis 17:7 (ESV).
[294] Luke 2:10–11 (ESV).
[295] Matthew 28:19–20 (ESV).

ancient people of Israel balanced on blood offerings made in faith according to God's instructions. Even the new covenant was sealed in blood, the blood of Jesus Christ, the Son of God, who offered His body to death on the cross, a substitutionary sacrifice.

It should be noted that every time God initiates a covenant with human beings, He makes a sacrifice. Each covenant requires God to limit Himself and His prerogatives in some way so that human beings may encounter His grace. With Israel, it meant overlooking the previous sins until a better sacrifice was made. With the church, it meant making that better sacrifice, the sinless Son of God.

The covenant is honored by God. Most of the Bible's Old Testament is the story of God's covenant faithfulness and the call for God's people to repent and return to covenant faithfulness. The Psalms extol God's faithfulness. The prophets lament the faithlessness of the nations, including God's own covenant people.

Human history is the history of God making and keeping covenant with people who make and break covenant with Him.

God is always faithful. He is faithful to His Person. He is faithful to His Word. He keeps His promises. The promise of eternal life, a primary benefit of God to His people under the New Covenant, is sealed in the death of Christ and guaranteed by the indwelling of the Holy Spirit in the church.

The purpose of the divine covenant.

But why does God make covenant with humanity at all? One commentator suggests, "God chooses to bind himself to his people through covenant to demonstrate the depth of his commitment to them and the depth of commitment he expects from them."[296]

Moses, with whom God made His most well-known covenant prior to the coming of Christ, included the answer to the question in

---

[296] M. R. Jones, "Covenant," *Lexham Theological Wordbook*, eds. D. Mangum, D. R. Brown, R. Klippenstein, and R. Hurst (Bellingham, WA: Lexham Press, 2014).

his final sermon to the people God used him to lead from slavery in Egypt. He instructed them, saying,

> [9]Therefore keep the words of this covenant and do them, that you may prosper in all that you do. [10]"You are standing today all of you before the *Lord* your God: the heads of your tribes, your elders, and your officers, all the men of Israel, [11]your little ones, your wives, and the sojourner who is in your camp, from the one who chops your wood to the one who draws your water, [12]so that you may enter into the sworn covenant of the *Lord* your God, which the *Lord* your God is making with you today, [13]that he may establish you today as his people, and that he may be your God, as he promised you, and as he swore to your fathers, to Abraham, to Isaac, and to Jacob."[297]

The key line is verse 13, "That he may establish you today as His people, and that he may be your God." Why does God initiate, establish, expand, seal, and keep covenant? Relationship.

God, though He has no inherent need to do so being fully satisfied with the relationship that exists between the Father, Son, and Spirit, nonetheless chooses to enter into relationship, Creator with creature, in order to fill the earth with the knowledge of the glory of the *Lord*. God wants a covenant relationship with you for His glory and your joy, because this is what you were made for. It is your purpose, the meaning for your life.

> [13]The end of the matter; all has been heard. Fear God and keep his commandments, for this is the whole duty of man. [14]For God will bring

---

[297] Deuteronomy 29:9–13 (ESV).

every deed into judgment, with every secret thing, whether good or evil.[298]

How to enter and keep covenant with God.

One last question remains. If God has created us for covenant relationship, if through covenant relationship with God humanity finds its full potential and true meaning, then how do we enter and keep covenant with God?

The author of the New Testament book of Hebrews seems to have some things in common with the author of Ecclesiastes. The identity of either author can be speculated upon but not definitively decided. Both books are written to Jewish audiences, primarily. Both books seek to assist the readers to understand the nature of their relationship with God who calls them to keep covenant with Him as a matter of life and purpose.

Hebrews offers answers to a practical question implied within Koheleth's final conclusion. If revering God and keeping His commandments are the means to finding true purpose in life, then what advice might you have for functionally revering God? How does a person "revere God"? Five admonitions from Hebrews might prove useful to a person asking that question at a moment in history after the life, death, and resurrection of Jesus Christ.

First, Hebrews declares in no uncertain terms that "without faith it is impossible to please God."[299] Revering God is always a matter and function of faith more than logic. It is a spiritual practice that embraces rational thought but then exceeds it. Koheleth illustrates this with the book of Ecclesiastes. Logic dictates that life is utterly futile, when God is left out. But when God is considered in right position relative to human life and effort, a work of faith, meaningful life abounds.

Since faith is the first requirement, the second must be that faith has the right object. A person desiring to find the meaning of

---

[298] Ecclesiastes 12:13–14 (ESV).
[299] Hebrews 11:6 (ESV).

life inherent in a covenant relationship with God must not just generically "believe in God," but "must believe God exists and rewards those who seek Him." There must be faith not only in the existence of God but also that God is both personal and present.

The letter to the Hebrews further insists that faith be directed to Jesus Christ as the superior expression of God's self-revelation, incarnate. Underlying every assertion of Christ's superiority within the book of Hebrews is the claim of God's action. It is God who makes Christ superior over angels and God who makes Christ superior over Moses and God who makes Christ a superior high priest and God who makes Christ's death on the cross a more superior sacrifice than the blood of bulls and goats. The call to faith in Christ as the superior Savior is reasonable because this is God's work, and revering God means honoring His work. Honoring God's work means honoring God's plan for our lives, which includes faith in Jesus as God-provided Savior.

Along with accepting by faith Jesus as God's provided Savior, a fourth means of revering God embraces accepting Jesus Christ as the ultimate expression of God's personal love for you. The Apostle Paul in another New Testament book, Romans, confirms that God demonstrates the full extent of His love for us by sending His Son, Jesus, to die for us while we were still sinners, before we ever knew or cared that we need a Savior.[300] The Former Covenant, which was once God's ultimate expression of love for a people, has been replaced in Jesus with the New Covenant, which is God's ultimate expression of His personal love for each of His people and *all* His people. An overtly stated condition under the New Covenant is love. God has acted in love to save us. God's actions deserve (and, frankly, require) a response from us, love.

Love, the final admonition to which we look in our desire to revere God and keep His commandments, calls for four specific choices on our part—first, repentance, turning away from our life of self-centered sinning; second, commitment of our lives to knowing, loving, and serving God on His terms, a commitment commonly sig-

---

[300] Romans 5:8 (ESV).

nified through the ordinance of baptism; third, obedience to the will and purposes of God as revealed in God's written word, the Bible, and God's Word incarnate, Jesus; and the fourth contingency is love, including love for God, love for fellow believers, love for others, and love for all that God loves. These last two might call out a fifth, one that Paul highlights in Romans 12,

> I appeal to you therefore, brothers, by the mercies of God, to present your bodies as a living sacrifice, holy and acceptable to God, which is your spiritual worship. Do not be conformed to this world, but be transformed by the renewal of your mind, that by testing you may discern what is the will of God, what is good and acceptable and perfect.[301]

Revering God and keeping His commandments, in our day, means loving God with all our heart, mind, soul, and strength and loving our neighbors as ourselves. This is the kind of love God imparts to us when we put our faith in Jesus Christ and trust Him to be for us the Savior God sent him to be. Revering God and keeping His commandments turn us from a lifelong quest to be pleased with ourselves to a lifelong desire to be satisfied in God and to please God by living with Him on His covenant terms.

Summation

This is Koheleth's message in Ecclesiastes. Without God, life is futile, meaningless, empty. Life lived in covenant with God, revering Him and keeping His commandments, is the singular path to self-fulfillment. "The epilogue in Ecclesiastes affirms the journey Qohelet has gone through before coming to the place of remembering his Creator."[302] The journey has been personal and, because of

---

[301] Romans 12:1–2 (ESV).
[302] Bartholomew, 371.

its intentionality under analysis, professional. Koheleth the scientist, Koheleth the teacher has reviewed life in detail, under specific parameters, for the sake of determining the validity of a specific hypothesis that, though easily demonstrated, cannot, because of God's covenant-extending, covenant-keeping grace, be proven.

Therefore, taking everything else into account, the best action we can take for ourselves to find meaning in the world is to revere God and keep His commandments. Every effort, every struggle, every aspiration and inspiration, every sorrow and every pleasure, every gifted or withheld grace leads to one of two ends, futility or covenant. Revere God and keep His commandments. This is the whole duty of man, the one thing that defeats futility, covenant with God. Ecclesiastes illuminates for us what happens when we attempt to live life without God. Without a covenant relationship with our Creator, we "simply cannot make sense of life and continually end up on the slippery slope of enigma and despair."[303]

Revere God and keep His commandments! For this applies to all mankind.

Study Questions

1. Describe some of the interpretive challenges presented by the epilogue.
2. What dramatic impact does the epilogue have on interpreting Ecclesiastes as a formal research report?
3. Why should the message of Ecclesiastes be taken seriously?
4. What value does the epilogue express regarding the entire book of Ecclesiastes (see verse 12)?
5. What are the common characteristics of biblical covenants?
6. How does someone engage in a "covenant relationship" with God today?

---

[303] Ibid., 372.

APPENDIX A

RESOURCE BIOGRAPHY PROFILES

Bartholomew, Craig G. (2[304])—Craig G. Bartholomew, PhD, University of Bristol, is the H. Evan Runner Professor of Philosophy and Redeemer University College, Ontario, and principal of the Paideia Centre for Public Theology.

Berger, Warren (2)—Warren Berger, innovation expert and questionologist, has studied hundreds of the world's foremost innovators, entrepreneurs, and creative thinkers to learn how they ask questions, generate original ideas, and solve problems. He is the author of eleven books, including the *Book of Beautiful Questions: The Powerful Questions That Will Help You Decide, Create, Connect, and Lead,* the bestseller *A More Beautiful Question: The Power of Inquiry to Spark Breakthrough Ideas,* and the internationally acclaimed *Glimmer,* named one of *Businessweek's* Best Innovation and Design Books of the Year. His writing appears regularly in *Fast Company, Harvard Business Review,* and *the New York Times.* He lives in New York.

Bratcher, Dennis (1)—Dennis Bratcher is a religious educator and holds a Bachelors of Arts (1974) and Master of Arts (1979) degrees from Southern Nazarene University; a Master of Divinity

---

[304] Note that the number inside the parenthesis after the resource author's name indicates the chapter in this study in which they are first cited.

(1980) degree from Nazarene Theological Seminary, Kansas City, Missouri; and a Doctor of Philosophy (1984) degree from Union Theological Seminary, Richmond, Virginia. He was an ordained elder (1989) at the Church of the Nazarene. He is a recipient of a teaching fellowship and went to Union Theological Seminary in Virginia, Richmond, in 1983. He is also a member of the Member Wesleyan Theological Society, Society Biblical Literature, and Biblical Archaeology Society.

Bridges, Jerry (6)—Jerry Bridges (December 4, 1929–March 6, 2016) was an evangelical Christian author, speaker, and staff member of the Navigators. Born in Tyler, Texas, United States, he was the author of more than a dozen books, including *the Pursuit of Holiness*, which has sold more than one million copies. His devotional *Holiness Day By Day* garnered the 2009 ECPA Christian Book Award for the inspiration and gift category, and *the Discipline of Grace* received a similar award in 1995 for the Christian living category.

Bridges earned his undergraduate degree in engineering at the University of Oklahoma before serving as an officer in the US Navy during the Korean War. He joined the Christian discipleship organization the Navigators in 1955, where he served as administrative assistant to the Europe director, office manager for the headquarters office, secretary/treasurer of the organization, and as vice president for Corporate Affairs before moving to a staff development position with the Collegiate Mission.

Bridges died on March 6, 2016, in Colorado Springs, Colorado, at the age of eighty-six (Wikipedia).

Burroughs, Jeremiah (6)—Jeremiah Burroughs combined harmoniously in his own person what might be considered incompatible qualities, a fervent zeal for purity of doctrine and worship and a peaceable spirit, which longed and labored for Christian unity.

The life and ministry of Burroughs, though comparatively short, exemplify many of the best features of the era to which he belonged. Born in 1599, he was educated at Emmanuel College, Cambridge. Founded in 1584 on the site of an old Dominican college, Emmanuel became the greatest seminary of Puritan preachers. Through it passed Thomas Hooker, John Cotton, Thomas Shepard (all of them founding fathers in New England), and Stephen Marshall, William Bridge, Anthony Burgess, Thomas Brooks, and Thomas Watson. It is recorded that while still at Cambridge, Burroughs was a nonconformist, and eventually he was forced to leave the university for this reason.

The substance of Burroughs' preaching is revealed in his published works, which are mainly sermons. These writings, most of which were published posthumously, were extremely popular in the seventeenth century, but they have never been collected and issued as a complete set. His grasp of doctrine, discernment into the very recesses of the human heart, comprehensive and profound knowledge of the Scripture and ability to apply it, and superb gift of illustration are all exemplified in them. Burroughs died in 1646, two weeks after a fall from his horse.

Cherry, Kendra (1)—Kendra Cherry is an author and educator with over a decade of experience helping students make sense of psychology. She is the author of the *Everything Psychology Book (2nd edition)* and she has published thousands of articles on diverse topics in psychology including personality, social behavior, child therapy, research methods, and much more.

As a psychosocial rehabilitation specialist, Cherry utilized behavioral, cognitive, and socialization strategies to help her young clients cope with family relationships, peer interactions, aggression, social skills, and academic difficulties. Her work has been referenced by numerous media outlets and publications including the *New York Times*, CNN, *Psychology Today*, the *Telegraph*, the *Huffington Post*, *Business Insider*, and the *Guardian*.

Cherry has a Master of Science in education from Boise State University with a primary research interest in educational psychology. She also holds a Bachelor of Science degree in psychology from Idaho State University with additional coursework in chemical addictions and case management.

Christian, C. W. (10)—A native Texan, C. W. Christian holds BA and MA degrees from Baylor, a BD from Southwestern Seminary, and a PhD from Vanderbilt. He taught theology for over forty years at Baylor University. He is married and has four children and two grandchildren.

Comfort, Ray (2)—Ray Comfort is the founder and CEO of Living Waters and the bestselling author of more than eighty books, including *God Has a Wonderful Plan for Your Life*, *How to Know God Exists*, and the *Evidence Bible*. He cohosts the award-winning television program *Way of the Master*, airing in almost two hundred countries, and is the executive producer of *180*, *Evolution vs. God*, *Audacity*, and other films. He is married to Sue and has three grown children and hasn't left the house without gospel tracts for decades.

Cone, Christopher (5)—Christopher Cone (ThD, PhD, PhD) serves as president of Calvary University and as research professor of Bible and Theology. He has formerly served in executive and faculty roles at Southern California Seminary as chief academic officer and research professor of Bible and Theology and at Tyndale Theological Seminary as president and professor of Bible and Theology. He has served in several pastoral roles and has also held teaching positions at the University of North Texas, North Central Texas College, and Southern Bible Institute. He is the author and general editor of more than a dozen books, including *Life Beyond the Sun: Worldview and Philosophy Through the Lens of Ecclesiastes, 2nd edition*.

Eaton, Michael A (1)—Michael Eaton was a preacher and writer who grew up in inner-city London but lived for many years in Nairobi, Kenya, and worked with Chrisco Fellowship. He became a Kenyan citizen in 1992, while his wife Jenny was born, raised, and still lives in Kenya.

Eaton earned degrees from the universities of London, Zambia, and South Africa and did Old Testament work at Tyndale House, Cambridge, which was published as his *Tyndale Commentary on Ecclesiastes*. His doctoral research was on the Christian and the Mosaic law (published in *Theology of Encouragement or No Condemnation*, in James, and in 1, 2, and 3 John). He had a long-standing connection with Westminster Chapel in London and wrote scholarly work on the Puritans and on the theology of Dr. Martyn Lloyd-Jones. He lectured in the Baptist Theological College of Southern Africa (Old Testament exegesis), in the Nairobi Evangelical School of Theology (Old Testament studies and systematic theology), and in the Nairobi International School of Theology (exegetical methods). However his main work was that of a preacher and he pastored the well-known churches Lusaka Baptist Church and Nairobi Baptist Church, as well as pioneering multiracial ministry in Johannesburg. From 1986, he was one of the leaders of the Chrisco Fellowship of Churches, which began as a prayer meeting in 1978, but now has churches in different parts of Africa, India, and Europe. Michael was copastor with his friend Jeremiah Mugala of Chrisco Central Church in Kibera slum suburb, Nairobi.

Eaton studied under well-known Christian leaders such as J. I. Packer, J. A. Motyer, and Professor Adrio König, the leading evangelical theologian of South Africa, and learned a lot from Dr. Martyn Lloyd-Jones and Dr. R.T. Kendall, both past ministers of Westminster Chapel, London.

Michael Eaton died on June 9, 2017, of a heart attack while attending a conference in Johannesburg, South Africa.

Fabrega, Marelisa (8)—Marelisa Fabrega is a lawyer and entrepreneur. She holds a Bachelor of Science in Business Administration from Georgetown University in Washington DC and a Juris Doctor from the Georgetown University Law Center. Fabrega currently lives in the Republic of Panama, which is where she's originally from. According to her bio page on *daringtolivefully.com*, she writes, "I consider myself to be a modern-day Renaissance woman, meaning I have a broad knowledge base, am skilled in different fields, and I love learning new things. I'm an entrepreneur, a writer and blogger, a runner, a meditator, an art and culture lover, a world traveler, an avid reader, a weightlifter, multilingual, an autodidact, and a learning expert."

Fee, Gordon (1)—Gordon Fee is Professor Emeritus of New Testament at Regent College, where he taught for sixteen years. His teaching experience also includes serving schools in Washington, California, Kentucky, and Wheaton College in Illinois (five years) and Gordon-Conwell Theological Seminary in Massachusetts (twelve years).

Fee is a noted New Testament scholar, having published several books and articles in his field of specialization, New Testament textual criticism. He also published a textbook on New Testament interpretation and coauthored two books for laypeople on biblical interpretation, as well as scholarly popular commentaries on 1 and 2 Timothy and Titus and on Galatians and major commentaries on 1 Corinthians and Philippians. He is also the author of a major work on the Holy Spirit and the Person of Christ in the letters of Paul.

Fee currently serves as the general editor of the *New International Commentary* series and on the NIV revision committee that produced the *TNIV*. Besides his ability as a biblical scholar, he is a noted teacher and conference speaker. He has presented the Staley Distinguished Christian Scholar lectures on fifteen college campuses as well as the annual NT lectures at Southwestern Baptist Seminary, North Park Seminary, the Mennonite Brethren Biblical Seminary, the Canadian Theological Seminary, Duke Divinity School, Golden Gate Baptist, Anderson School of Theology, Asbury Seminary, and Crichton College. An ordained minister with the Assemblies of God, Gordon Fee is well known for his manifest concern for the renewal of the church.

Fox, Michael V (1)—Fox holds a BA (1962) and MA (1963) from the University of Michigan (Near Eastern Studies), Rabbinical ordination (1968) from Hebrew Union College, a PhD (1972) from Hebrew University of Jerusalem (Hebrew Bible and the Ancient Near East). He had a postdoctoral study in Egyptology at Liverpool University (1974–1975) as Leverhulme Fellow. He holds an Honorary Doctorate of Hebrew Letters from Hebrew Union College (1993). He speaks Hebrew (all periods), Greek, Egyptian, Ugaritic,

Aramaic, Syriac, and Canaanite dialects and also German, French, and some Italian.

From 1971 to 1974, he was an instructor and then lecturer in Bible at Haifa University and the University of the Negev. From 1975 to 1977, he was a lecturer in Bible and Egyptology at the Hebrew University. In 1977, he became an assistant professor and then a professor (1984) at UW-Madison. From 1982 to 1987, 1993 to 1999, and 2010, he was the chairman of the Hebrew Department. By January 2010, he became Emeritus Affiliate Professor at the University of Haifa. He was editor of Hebrew Studies from 1986 to 1993, editor of the SBL Dissertation Series from 1994 to 1999, and president of the Society for Biblical Literature, Midwest region, from 1998 to 2000. In 2000, he became president of the National Association of Professors of Hebrew. From 2003 to 2005, he became a Fellow at the American Academy of Jewish Research, and by 2000, he was vice president of the Society for Biblical Literature.

Frankl, Viktor E. (1)—Viktor Emil Frankl (March 26, 1905–September 2, 1997) was an Austrian neurologist and psychiatrist as well as a Holocaust survivor. He survived Theresienstadt, Auschwitz, Kaufering, and Türkheim. Frankl was the founder of logotherapy, which is a form of existential analysis, the Third Viennese School of Psychotherapy. His best-selling book *Man's Search for Meaning* (published under a different title in 1959, *From Death-Camp to Existentialism*, and originally published in 1946 as *Trotzdem Ja Zum Leben Sagen: Ein Psychologe erlebt das Konzentrationslager*, meaning *Nevertheless, Say "Yes" to Life: A Psychologist Experiences the Concentration Camp*) chronicles his experiences as a concentration camp inmate, which led him to discover the importance of finding meaning in all forms of existence, even the most brutal ones, and thus a reason to continue living. Frankl became one of the key figures in existential therapy and a prominent source of inspiration for humanistic psychologists (taken from Wikipedia).

Garrett, James (7)—James Leo Garrett Jr. (born November 25, 1925) holds the position of Distinguished Professor Emeritus of Theology at Southwestern Baptist Theological Seminary in Fort Worth, Texas.

He earned a Bachelor of Arts in English from Baylor University in 1945, a Bachelor of Divinity from Southwestern Baptist Theological Seminary in 1948, a Masters of Theology from Princeton Theological Seminary in 1949, a Doctor of Theology from Southwestern Baptist Theological Seminary in 1954, and a Doctor of Philosophy from Harvard University in 1966. He has done additional studies at the Catholic University of America, in Washington DC, Oxford University, St. John's University, and Trinity Evangelical Divinity School in Deerfield, Illinois (taken from Wikipedia).

Grudem, Wayne A (5)—Wayne Grudem is a research professor of Theology and Biblical Studies at Phoenix Seminary in Arizona. He is a graduate of Harvard (BA), Westminster Seminary-Philadelphia (MDiv, DD), and the University of Cambridge (PhD). He has served as the president of the Evangelical Theological Society (1999) and as a member of the Translation Oversight Committee for the English Standard Version of the Bible and was the general editor for the *ESV Study Bible* (2008). He has written more than twenty books, including *Systematic Theology*, the *Gift of Prophecy in the New Testament and Today*, *Business for the Glory of God*, *Politics According to the Bible*, and (with Barry Asmus) the *Poverty of Nations: A Sustainable Solution*. He also coedited (with John Piper) *Recovering Biblical Manhood and Womanhood*.

Jensen, Irving L. (1)—Irving Jensen (BA, Wagner College; STB, Biblical Seminary; ThD, Northwestern Theological Seminary) was professor and chairman of the Department of Bible at Bryan College, Dayton, Tennessee, and the author of numerous books, including the entire *Bible Self-Study Series*, *Jensen's Survey of the Old Testament*, *Jensen's Survey of the New Testament*, *Jensen's Bible Study Charts*, *Acts: An Inductive Study*, *Independent Bible Study*, and *How to Profit from Bible Reading*.

Kaiser, Walter C. Jr. (2)—Walter C. Kaiser Jr. (born April 11, 1933) is an American evangelical Old Testament scholar, writer, public speaker, and educator. Kaiser was the Colman M. Mockler distinguished professor of Old Testament and former president of Gordon-Conwell Theological Seminary in South Hamilton, Massachusetts; he retired on June 30, 2006. Kaiser currently is President Emeritus and Distinguished Professor of Old Testament and Ethics at Gordon-Conwell Theological Seminary in Hamilton, Massachusetts.

Longman, Tremper III (1)—Dr. Tremper Longman III graduated from Ohio Wesleyan University, earned a Master of Divinity from Westminster Theological Seminary, and completed a doctorate in ancient Near Eastern studies at Yale University. He served as the Robert H. Gundry Professor of Biblical Studies at Westmont from 1998 until he retired in 2017. He continues to serve the college as a Distinguished Scholar of Biblical Studies. He has written or coauthored numerous scholarly articles and more than twenty books, including interdisciplinary works, books with psychologist Dan Allender, works on history and historiography, and textbooks for both seminary students and laypeople. He is one of the main translators of the New Living Translation and has served as a consultant on other popular translations of the Bible including the Message, the New Century Version, and the Holman Standard Bible.

O'Donnell, Douglas Sean (2)—Douglas Sean O'Donnell (MA from Wheaton College and MA from Trinity Evangelical Divinity School) was a senior pastor of New Covenant Church (PCA) in Naperville, Illinois, and an instructor for the Charles Simeon Trust. He is currently a senior lecturer at Queensland Theological College in Brisbane, Australia, while obtaining his doctorate.

Ortland, Ray Jr. (6)—Raymond C. Ortlund Jr. is a pastor at Immanuel Church in Nashville, Tennessee. He also serves as the president of Renewal Ministries, regional director in the Acts 29 Network, and council member of the Gospel Coalition.

Ortlund received his BA from Wheaton College in 1971. He then earned his ThM from Dallas Theological Seminary in 1975. He went on to receive his second master's degree, an MA, at the University of California, Berkeley, in 1978. Lastly, he was awarded a PhD at the University of Aberdeen, Scotland, in 1985.

Parrot, Les (8)—Dr. Les Parrott is a master communicator, having impacted people from all walks of life including executives, international government officials, professional athletes, and college students. His charisma, humor, and practical advice have placed him in high demand as a conference and seminar speaker. Les Parrott has spoken internationally to a variety of groups including corporations such as Johnson & Johnson, Price Waterhouse, the armed services, and associations of professional athletes. His breakneck schedule takes him across North America and around the world.

Dr. Parrott has been a guest on many radio shows and featured on national television including CBS *This Morning*, *Good Morning America*, *NBC Nightly News with Tom Brokaw*, *Oprah*, *the View*, and CNN. His work has been written about in newspapers such as *USA Today* and the *New York Times* and many magazines including *Men's Health*, *Family Circle*, *Redbook*, and *Women's Day*.

Parrott is founder of RealRelationships.com and a professor of Psychology at Seattle Pacific University. He is also cocreator, with his wife Leslie, of eHarmony Marriage.

Parrott is an award-winning author of more than a dozen best-selling books including *High-Maintenance Relationships*, the *Control Freak*, *3 Seconds*, *Becoming Soul Mates*, *Your Time Starved Marriage*, and *Saving Your Marriage Before It Starts* (taken from Dr. Parrott's website).

Piper, John (5)—John Stephen Piper (born January 11, 1946) is an American Reformed Baptist continuationist pastor and author who is the founder and leader of desiringGod.org and is the chancellor of Bethlehem College and Seminary in Minneapolis, Minnesota. Piper served as pastor for Preaching and Vision of Bethlehem Baptist Church in Minneapolis, Minnesota, for thirty-three years. His books include ECPA Christian Book Award winners *Spectacular Sins*, *What Jesus Demands from the World*, *Pierced by the Word*, and *God's Passion for His Glory* and bestsellers *Don't Waste Your Life* and *the Passion of Jesus Christ*. The organization Desiring God is named for his book *Desiring God: Meditations of a Christian Hedonist* (1986) (Wikipedia).

Reiger, Wilf (1)—Wilf Reiger is an Honorary Senior Research Fellow, Avondale College of Higher Education, Cooranbong, New South Wales, Australia.

Stuart, Douglas (1)—Douglas Stuart has a BA from Yale Divinity School and a PhD from Harvard University. He was professor of Old Testament, specializing in Assyrian and Babylonian languages and literature, at Gordon-Conwell Theological Seminary, and a cochair of the Old Testament Colloquium for the Boston Theological Institute. He was also visiting professor, guest lecturer, and speaker at colleges, seminaries, and universities across the United States.

His other career highlights include activities in several organizations, including the Evangelical Theological Society, the International Organization for Septuagint and Cognate Studies, and the Society of Biblical Literature. He also had radio and television broadcasts, including appearances in both *Mysteries of the Bible* and *Christianity: The First Thousand Years*.

He is an ordained minister, pastoring numerous churches in Massachusetts and New Hampshire. He also had ministry work among gypsies in Eastern Europe. He is fluent in several languages and able to navigate through several others, including Arabic, Aramaic, Assyrian, Babylonian, Egyptian, English, French, German, Greek, Hebrew, Italian, Latin, Romanian, Syriac, Targumic Aramaic, and Ugaritic.

He is the author of several books, including *Old Testament Exegesis: A Primer for Students and Pastors* and *Studies in Early Hebrew Meter*, and various Bible commentaries including volumes on Hosea, Ezekiel, Malachi, and Jonah. His most best-selling book, *How to Read the Bible for All Its Worth*, has been translated into more than twenty languages.

He is the author of numerous journal articles for publications such as *Christianity Today*, *Decision Magazine*, the *Journal of Biblical Literature*, and *Hebrew Union College Annual* (take from the ChristianUniversity.org).

Thomas, Derek (6)—Derek W. H. Thomas is a reformed pastor and theologian known for his teaching, writing, and editorial work. He is currently the senior pastor of First Presbyterian Church of Columbia, South Carolina, and Distinguished Visiting Professor of Systematic and Historical Theology at Reformed Theological Seminary in Atlanta, Georgia.

Thomas is originally from Wales. In 1978, he completed his ministerial training from Reformed Theological Seminary before moving on to receive his PhD from the University of Wales, Lampeter, with a thesis on Calvin's preaching on the book of Job. He served as a pastor for seventeen years in Belfast, Northern Ireland, before returning to the United States in 1996 to serve as the Minister of Teaching at First Presbyterian Church in Jackson. In 2011, he accepted a call to serve as associate pastor at First Presbyterian Church in Columbia, South Carolina. He was called to be the senior pastor of First Presbyterian Church, Columbia, South Carolina, on August 11, 2013. He has written and edited fifteen books and has also produced a volume for the *Biblical Commentary* series published by Banner of Truth Trust and Evangelical Press. In 2004, Thomas became editorial director for the Alliance of Confessing Evangelicals and the editor of its e-zine, Reformation 21 (taken from Wikipedia).

APPENDIX B

WEEKLY HOMEWORK ASSIGNMENTS

The following assignments were provided for the Monday afternoon Bible study that originally engaged with Ecclesiastes with me. The group did not have the study guide. They were given these questions a week in advance for discussion the following week.

Ecclesiastes Homework Assignment 1
Assigned:

The Literary Genre of Ecclesiastes:
Biblical Wisdom Literature

1. Provide a definition and description of the general function of wisdom literature.
2. Discuss the unique difference of biblical wisdom literature from other wisdom literature in the ancient Near East.
3. Describe and define the various subgenres of biblical wisdom literature and give examples of each (preferably, when they occur there, from within Ecclesiastes). Where there further categories within each subgenre, note those categories, and provide examples of each.

4. In what circumstances or under what conditions did/does wisdom literature develop and is transferred?

5. Three primary subgenres have been identified within Ecclesiastes. Identify them and describe the impact of the identity on the interpretation of Ecclesiastes.

6. How does the general nature of "biblical wisdom literature" tie in with the teachings of Jesus regarding eternal life in John 17?

7. Given what you've learned about biblical wisdom literature, how do these insights assist in the development of your interpretive outlook as you approach Ecclesiastes for study?

Ecclesiastes Homework Assignment 2
Assigned:

1. What is the "scientific method"?
2. What format does a report consistent with the scientific method use?
    a.
    b.
    c.
    d.
    e.
    f.
    g.
3. Consider one of your favorite activities or hobbies. Develop a lesson for teaching us how to do that activity using the scientific method as the format.

Ecclesiastes Homework Assignment 3
Assigned:

1. Fatalism
    a. What are the basic tenets of fatalism?

b. How does fatalism differ from a Calvinistic view of sovereignty?

c. Give an example of potential fatalism in Ecclesiastes.

d. Thank you.

2. Existential Nihilism

a. What are the basic tenets of nihilism?

b. How is nihilism expressed in existential nihilism?

c. Give an example of potential existential nihilism in Ecclesiastes.

d. Thank you.

3. Empiricism

a. Please define empiricism for us.

b. What argument best defeats understanding Ecclesiastes as an expression of empiricism?

c. Give an example of potential empiricism in Ecclesiastes.

d. Thank you.

4. Absurdism

a. Please define absurdism and identify its most famous proponent.

b. What scripture within Ecclesiastes supports an absurdist interpretation?

c. What scripture within Ecclesiastes refutes an absurdist interpretation?

d. Thank you.

5. Existentialism

a. Please define existentialism and identify its most famous proponent.

b. How does existentialism fall short of being an adequate interpretive framework for Ecclesiastes?

c. Give an example of potential existentialism in Ecclesiastes.

d. Thank you.

Ecclesiastes Homework Assignment 4
Assigned:

1. Define "presuppositions" and provide a personal example.
2. List all the presuppositions you can think of that you bring to the study of Ecclesiastes.

Ecclesiastes Homework Assignment 5
Assigned:

1. Describe an experience in your life that has changed your outlook on life and practice and that would make a reasonable lesson in someone else's life.
2. Go back to the section on Solomon in the introduction and review what you know about this man, Solomon, son of David, king in Jerusalem.
    a. Given what you know, what would you expect to be true of what he writes?
    b. What would you expect to be true of any methodology he proposes or describes?
    c. What would you expect to be true of any conclusions he draws regarding his observations?
3. And as long as you're at it, using a Bible dictionary (or other source), define "Koheleth." How does this word help us understand the purpose and content of Ecclesiastes?
4. How has gathering this background information influence your sense of anticipation not merely in reading and studying this book, but in experiencing life transformation through it?

Ecclesiastes Homework Assignment 6
Assigned:

1. Study the key word "futility."
   a. Using a concordance or a Bible software program, make a list of the occurrences of each word as it appears in Ecclesiastes.
   b. What does their location and usage in the text tell you about the meaning of this word relative to understanding the message of Ecclesiastes?
   c. How does this word contribute to the message?
   d. How does this word connect the message of Ecclesiastes to your life and experience?
2. The word "futile" occurs thirty-eight times in Ecclesiastes. The word "God" or a reference to God is made forty times in the book. Speculate on any interpretive significance for the frequency difference. Give reasons why you think your speculation might be valid?
3. How do Koheleth and the Apostle Paul demonstrate that they share a common view of the current condition of the world?
4. How is futility related to sin? Give examples of how the relationship works.
5. How does identifying the root cause of futility give direction to your approach to Ecclesiastes?
6. What is the significance of interpreting "futility" as a proposition (hypothesis to be researched) rather than an assertion (truth to be embraced)?
7. Trace the use of "under the sun" or "under heaven" in Ecclesiastes. What do the occurrences of the phrase in each case suggest about the context for experimentation?

Ecclesiastes Homework Assignment 7
Assigned:

1. Questions open access to information.
   a. What question would you like ask the author of Ecclesiastes?
   b. What question would you like to pursue until you were certain you had the right answer?
2. Try rewriting Koheleth's research question in your own words.
3. What does your understanding of Koheleth's leading question reveal about your assumptions at this point?
4. Read Genesis 3:17–18. How is the curse God imposed on Adam in the garden after the fall reflected in the words of Koheleth?
5. When will man's labor under the sun again have real value?

Ecclesiastes Homework Assignment 8
Assigned: January 28, 2018

1. Carefully consider the question asked in 1:3. It contains three clues to the focus, scope, and method of Koheleth's study. Can you identify three clues to the focus, scope, and method of Koheleth's study?
2. What can you discover about the Hebrew word *yitron* that is translated "real value" in the *Tanakh* version of Koheleth's question?
3. How have you experienced your efforts at achievement as "toil"?
4. The phrase "under the sun" sets a critical boundary for Koheleth's study. How do you understand that boundary? What does it mean?

Ecclesiastes Homework 9
Assigned:

1. Seven Observations (1:3–11)
   a. What seven observations does Koheleth base his first series of theoretical challenges on?
   b. How would you restate these seven observations if you were writing from your own experience and observations about the world in which you live?
2. What role do observations play in the search for genuine truth?
3. "Historical Social Amnesia"
   a. Provide a tentative definition for "historical social amnesia."
   b. What examples of historical social amnesia does Koheleth identify?
   c. What are some areas of personal and cultural development in your observation that show signs of historical social amnesia?
   d. What is the connection between historical social amnesia and futility?
4. What personal choices arise when the effects of historical social amnesia are identified?

Ecclesiastes Homework 10
Assigned:

1. Koheleth offers four distinct methods (1:13, 17; 2:1, 3) as his experimental procedure. List them. Also, offer a generalized category name for the areas addressed by these strategies.
2. Reflect on the ways in which Koheleth investigated and explored his observations.
   a. Summarize Koheleth's efforts and discovery in your own words.

    b.   How do the activities of his life mirror your own?

3.   Why does Koheleth refer to human life activity as an "unhappy business...which God gave to men"?

4.   What theme does Koheleth introduce by reporting that "God gave" an unhappy business for men to be concerned with? How is this theme illustrated in 1:15?

5.   Any good research experiment will include dependent, independent, and control variables.

    a.   Please provide a definition and an example for each type of experimental variable.

    b.   How might these categories apply to the content of Ecclesiastes?

6.   Choose one of the four primary methodologies Koheleth identifies for himself and trace the use of the action word through the Bible.

    a.   What do you learn about the nature of this activity?

    b.   In what ways is Koheleth's exploration of truth mirrored in your own discipleship strategy?

    c.   What could you learn from Koheleth's approach?

Ecclesiastes Homework 11
Assigned:

Three Proverbs

1.   Consider "A twisted thing that cannot be made straight, A lack that cannot be made good" (1:15, JPS).

    a.   What is the immediate context for this proverb?

b. How does the immediate context help set up your interpretation of this proverb?

c. Given the context, what do you think this proverb refers to?

    i. In the human (anthropological) sense?

    ii. In the divine (theological/spiritual) sense?

2. Consider "For as wisdom grows, vexation grows; To increase learning is to increase heartache" (1:18, JPS).

a. What is the immediate context for this proverb?

b. How does the immediate context help set up your interpretation of this proverb?

c. Given the context, what do you think this proverb refers to?

    i. In the human (anthropological) sense?

    ii. In the divine (theological/spiritual) sense?

3. Consider "Of revelry I said, 'It is mad.' Of merriment, 'What good is that?'" (2:2, JPS).

a. What is the immediate context for this proverb?

b. How does the immediate context help set up your interpretation of this proverb?

c. Given the context, what do you think this proverb refers to?

    i. In the human (anthropological) sense?

    ii. In the divine (theological/spiritual) sense?

4. Consider "I withheld from my eyes nothing they asked for, and denied myself no enjoyment; rather, I got enjoyment out of all my wealth. And that is all I got out of my wealth" (2:10, JPS).

a. What does Koheleth mean by these words?

b. Provide biblical support for the idea that enjoying wealth is morally acceptable for the people of God.

c. Explain why enjoying wealth might be morally acceptable for the people of God.

d. Under what conditions might wealth provide more than enjoyment for the people of God?
e. Under what conditions might wealth provide nothing more than enjoyment for the people of God?
f. What New Testament revelations urge us to get more than enjoyment out of wealth?

Ecclesiastes Homework 12 (1:12–2:12)
Assigned:

1. Koheleth uses three principal words to describe his experimental methodology. Using a concordance and/or a Bible dictionary, do a word study on each.
    a. "Set my mind" (1:13)
    b. "Study" (1:13)
    c. "Probe" (1:13)
2. What does Koheleth mean by "wisdom" (1:13, 16, 17, 18; 2:12, 13)?
3. Give an example of "wisdom" at work in your life.
4. What is the difference between "wisdom" and "folly"?
5. How is the difference between wisdom and folly significant for human experience?
6. What is Koheleth's perspective on pleasure and merriment?

Ecclesiastes Homework 13 (2:12–26)
Assigned:

1. Koheleth expects a wise man to be better off than a foolish man. What negates his expectation?

2. How does Jesus encourage His disciples relative to this negating factor? (Cite verses.)
3. What deficit in thinking imprisons most people in the cycle of futility and leads to self-loathing?
4. Why does Koheleth loathe his wealth and possessions?
5. Give evidence that such loathing remains rampant in our day.
6. Where does real joy come from and what does it look like in real life?

Ecclesiastes Homework 14 (3:1–22)
Assigned:

1. What does the poem in 3:1–8 reveal about the context of Koheleth's next experimental series?
2. Who does Koheleth acknowledge sets the times and season that exist in human experience?
3. What specific theological reality is Koheleth addressing in this section?
4. How do God's sovereignty and human contentment relate functionally to one another?
5. What issues related to God's sovereignty provide the greatest comfort to you? The greatest distress?

Ecclesiastes Homework 15 (4:1–16)
Assigned:

1. Relate a "teachable moment" in which you were the student and then add an occasion in which you were the teacher.
2. How does Koheleth make use of the "teachable moments" in Ecclesiastes?
3. Koheleth asserts that neither the oppressed nor their oppressors have any real advantage in the world. Why not?

4. Consider Koheleth's observation in 4:4 that all human advancement proceeds from envy.
   a. What does he mean?
   b. Why is this futility?
5. State the proverbial observation of 4:5–6.
6. What is the point of amassing a fortune but having no one with which to share it and not using any of it for one's own pleasure?
7. How does the answer to question 6 prepare us for Koheleth's observations in 4:9–12?
8. What human social condition does Koheleth revisit in 4:13–16?

Ecclesiastes Homework 16 (4:17–15:11)
Assigned:

1. Koheleth offers three sets of practical advice relates to three spheres of influence on a person's life. Can you name them? (The labels are not specifically posted by Koheleth.)
2. What is Koheleth's perspective on a practical relationship with God?
3. What advice does Koheleth provide for living with a bloated government bureaucracy?
4. What is the problem with amassing a large number of tangible goods?
5. How might a follower of Jesus apply these three sets of wise advice?

Ecclesiastes Homework 17 (5:12–6:12)
Assigned:

1. What does Koheleth mean by the phrase "grave evil"?
2. What three "grave evils" does Koheleth note?
   a. 5:12

b. 5:14

c. 6:1

3. What condition does Koheleth posit as being better than to have endured a "grave evil"?

4. What potential condition counters the "grave evil" so often experienced?

5. Interact with Koheleth's rhetorical question in 6:12, "Who can possibly know what is best for a man to do in life?"

    a. On what basis does Koheleth offers this as an expression of futility (v. 12b)?

    b. How might a Christian respond to Koheleth's question?

    c. How do you determine what is best for you to do in your life?

    d. Would you offer your personal procedures of discernment as adequate for someone else to adopt? Why or why not?

Ecclesiastes Homework 18 (7:1–22)
Assigned:

1. Koheleth offers a series of applications related to his third set of experimental observations. These applications are presented as comparisons, one thing being superior to another. Make a table with three columns. Label the first column: Superior. Label the second column: Inferior. Label the third column: Reason. Using this method, identify all the comparisons and the point (or reason) represented by each comparison.

2. By presenting a series of comparisons, Koheleth demonstrates how one a course of action can be superior to another. What is the real comparison being offered in 7:13–14?

3. Once again Koheleth presents an attribute of God as a limiting factor in human experience.
   a. What is that attribute?
   b. How does this attribute of God limit human experience in this example?
   c. How might you argue against Koheleth's presentation at this point?
4. What disciplines have you developed for considering God's doings?

Ecclesiastes Homework 19 (7:23–29)
Assigned:

1. What criteria does Koheleth establish in 7:23 for all his studies?
2. What is the result of his careful application of this criterion?
3. How inclusive does Koheleth reveal his study to have been (v. 25)?
4. Propose a reasonable, rational purpose for Koheleth's statements about women in 7:23–26.
5. How does what Koheleth says about men in 7:29 balance what he says about women in the previous verses?

Ecclesiastes Homework 20 (8:1–15)
Assigned:

1. Koheleth makes observations in this passage related to two kinds of people. Who are they?
2. Summarize Koheleth's advice to each.
3. Is Koheleth presenting a principle to be embraced or an observation to be understood in 8:15? Support your answer.

Ecclesiastes Homework 21 (8:16–17)
Assigned:

1. Restate in your own words Koheleth's intent with the study he has reported on. Did he succeed? Why or why not?

2. What motivation does God offer in His Word to those whose pursuit of wisdom seems stymied?

3. What is significant about Koheleth's making "all that happens under the sun" parallel with "all that God brings to pass"?

4. How does this significance impact your understanding of your life experiences?

Ecclesiastes Homework 22 (9:1–12)
Assigned:

1. What is left for a wise person to do when every effort at wisdom and meaning is bounded by the sovereignty of God, according to Koheleth?

2. In what way are Koheleth's admonitions appropriate conduct for the Christian? Support your answer with scripture.

Ecclesiastes Homework 23 (9:13–18)
Assigned:

1. There is considerable difficulty with translating the Hebrew of this passage. Survey the commentators and note which interpretations make the most sense to you. Why?

2. Why do you think Koheleth downplays the ability of wisdom in verse 18?

3. How has "biblical wisdom" supported you? How has it failed you?

Ecclesiastes Homework 24 (10:1–11:6)
Assigned:

1. Identify and provide a possible context for each of the proverbs in this section.
2. How is futility illustrated in these proverbs? How is wisdom illustrated?
3. Restate Koheleth's two pieces of sage advice using your own cultural examples.

Ecclesiastes Homework 25 (11:7–12:8)
Assigned:

1. How does Koheleth describe death and what advice does he provide in light of the reality of death?
2. What advice does Koheleth give the young? How does this advice fit into the context of Ecclesiastes?
3. What three interpretative approaches can you find relative to the passage 12:3–8? Which seems most appropriate to you?
4. What point is Koheleth making and how does it apply to you?

Ecclesiastes Homework 26 (12:9–12)
Assigned:

1. List the components of the epilogue.
2. How does each of the components function in this summary of the report?
3. Are you ready for the "sum of the matter"?

Ecclesiastes Homework 27 (12:13–14)
Assigned:

1. Koheleth offers two statements in conclusion. What are they?

2. How does Jesus call His disciples to the same conclusion Koheleth reaches?
3. What is a "covenant" in the biblical context?
4. How are the covenants Koheleth mentions and the covenant Jesus inaugurates the same?
5. How does someone enter into a covenant with God today?

BIBLIOGRAPHY

Bartholomew, Craig C. "Ecclesiastes." In *Baker Commentary on the Old Testament Wisdom and Psalms*, edited by Tremper Longman III. Grand Rapids: Baker Academic, 2009.

Bratcher, Dennis. *The Character of Wisdom: An Introduction to Old Testament Wisdom Literature* (2016). www.crivoice.org. Accessed October 11, 2018.

Bridges, Jerry. "What Difference Does Divine Sovereignty Make?" In *Still Sovereign: Contemporary Perspectives on Election, Foreknowledge, and Grace*, edited by Thomas R. Schreiner and Bruce A. Ware. Grand Rapids: Baker Books, 2000.

Burroughs, Jeremiah. *The Rare Jewel of Christian Contentment*. London: W. Bentley, 1651. Logos Bible Software. Accessed December 27, 2018.

Cherry, Kendra. "Forming a Good Hypothesis for Scientific Research." *Very Well Mind*. https://www.verywellmind.com/what-is-a-hypthesis-2795239. Accessed December 2, 2018.

Christian, C.W. *Covenant and Commandment: A Study of the Ten Commandments in the Context of Grace*. Macon, GA: Smyth & Helwys, 2004.

Cone, Christopher. *Life Beyond the Sun: An Introduction to Worldview & Philosophy through the Lens of Ecclesiastes*. Ft. Worth, TX: Tyndale Seminary Press, 2009.

Eaton, Michael A. "Ecclesiastes: An Introduction and Commentary." In *Tyndale Old Testament Commentary, vol. 18*, edited by Donald Wiseman, et al. Downer's Grove, IL: InterVarsity Press, 1983.

"Ecclesiastes." *Tanakh: The Holy Scriptures*. New York: The Jewish Publication Society, 1985.

Elwell, Walter A. and P.W. Comfort. "Covenant." In *Tyndale Bible Dictionary*. Wheaton, IL: Tyndale House Publishers, 2001.

Fee, Gordon and Douglas Stuart. *How to Read the Bible for All Its Worth*, 3rd edition. Grand Rapids: Zondervan Publishing House, 2003.

Fox, Michael V. "Ecclesiastes." In *The JPS Bible Commentary*, edited by Michael Fishbane. Philadelphia, PA: The Jewish Publication Society, 2004.

Frankl, Viktor E. *Man's Search for Meaning*. London: Rider, 2004.

Garrett, James L. Jr., *Systematic Theology: Biblical, Historical, and Evangelical*, 4th edition, vol. 1. Eugene, OR: Wipf & Stock, 2014.

Gordley, Mark E. "Solomon, King of Israel, Critical Issues." In *The Lexham Bible Dictionary*, edited by J.D. Barry, et al. Bellingham, WA: Lexham Press, 2016.

Grudem, Wayne A. *Systematic Theology: An Introduction to Biblical Doctrine*. Grand Rapids: Zondervan Publishing House, 2004.

Hasel, Gerhard. *Old Testament Theology: Basic Issues in the Current Debate*, 3rd edition. Grand Rapids, MI: Eerdmans, 1972.

Jensen, Irving L. *Enjoy Your Bible: Making the Most of Your Time in God's Word*. Wheaton, IL: Harold Shaw Publishers, 1992.

Jones, M. R., "Covenant." In *Lexham Theological Wordbook*, edited by D. Mangum, D. R. Brown, R. Klippenstein, and R. Hurst. Bellingham, WA: Lexham Press, 2014.

Kaiser, Walter C. Jr. *Ecclesiastes: Total Life*. Chicago: Moody Press, 1979.

Longman, Tremper III. "The Book of Ecclesiastes." In *The New International Commentary on the Old Testament*, edited by Robert L. Hubbard Jr. Grand Rapids: William B. Eerdmans Publishing Co., 1998.

Miessler, Daniel. "What is the Difference Between Existentialism, Nihilism, and Absurdism?" Posted December 11, 2014. https://danielmiessler.com/blog/difference-existentialism-nihilism-absurdism. Accessed May 2017.

Murphy, Roland E. "Wisdom Literature: Job, Proverbs, Ruth, Canticles, Ecclesiastes, Esther." In *The Forms of the Old Testament*

Literature, vol. XIII, edited by Rolf Knierim and Gene M. Tucker. Grand Rapids: William B. Eerdmans Publishing Co., 1981.

Myers, A.C. "Wisdom Literature." In *The Eerdmans Bible Dictionary*. Grand Rapids: Eerdmans, 1987. Exported from Logos Bible Software. Accessed May 10, 2018.

O'Donnell, Douglas Sean. "Ecclesiastes." In *Reformed Expository Commentary*, edited by Richard D. Phillips and Philip Graham Ryken, et al. Phillipsburg, NJ: P&R Publishing, 2014.

Ortlund, Ray Jr. "The Sovereignty of God: Case Studies in the Old Testament." In *Still Sovereign: Contemporary Perspectives on Election, Foreknowledge, and Grace*, edited by Thomas R. Schreiner and Bruce A. Ware. Grand Rapids: Baker Books, 2000.

Rieger, Wilf. "Ecclesiastes as Research: Autoethnography Through a Rear-vision Mirror." In *TEACH Journal of Christian Education* (Vol. 4, Issue 2, Article 11, 43–50). https://research.avondale.edu.au/teach/vol4/iss2/11.

Swanson, J. *Dictionary of Biblical Languages with Semantic Domains: Hebrew (Old Testament)*. Electronic edition. Oak Harbor: Logos Research Systems, Inc., 1997.

The Holy Bible (English Standard Version). Wheaton, IL: Crossway, 2011.

The Holy Bible (New International Version). Biblica, 2011.

Thomas, Derek. "God's Sovereignty and Our Responsibility." Originally published in *TableTalk*. Added to https://wwwligonier.org/blog/gods-sovereignty-and-our-responsibility (April 4, 2018). Accessed December 27, 2018.

ABOUT THE AUTHOR

Dale McIntire (MDiv, DMin, Bethel Theological Seminary) has followed Jesus for fifty years. He has pastored Cornerstone Community Church in the little Lake Superior town of Grand Marais, Minnesota, for twenty-five years and has been married to Linda for twenty-nine years. He has been pet parent to Lucy the Yorkie for eight years and loves long sentences with lots of semicolons.